POWER
IN WORDS

POWER
IN WORDS

THE STORIES BEHIND
BARACK OBAMA'S SPEECHES,
FROM THE STATE HOUSE
TO THE WHITE HOUSE

MARY FRANCES BERRY
JOSH GOTTHEIMER

FOREWORD BY TED SORENSEN

BEACON PRESS
BOSTON

Beacon Press
25 Beacon Street
Boston, Massachusetts 02108-2892
www.beacon.org

Beacon Press books
are published under the auspices of
the Unitarian Universalist Association of Congregations.

13 12 11 10   8 7 6 5 4 3 2 1

This book is printed on acid-free paper that meets the uncoated paper ANSI/NISO specifications for permanence as revised in 1992.

Design and composition by Wilsted & Taylor Publishing Services

Library of Congress Cataloging-in-Publication Data

Berry, Mary Frances.
  Power in words : the stories behind Barack Obama's speeches, from the state house to the White House / by Mary Frances Berry, Josh Gottheimer ; foreword by Ted Sorensen.
    p. cm.
  ISBN 978-0-8070-0104-2 (hardcover : alk. paper) 1. Obama, Barack—Oratory. 2. United States—Politics and government—2001–2009. 3. Presidents—United States—Election—2008. 4. Speeches, addresses, etc., American. I. Obama, Barack. II. Gottheimer, Josh. III. Title.
  E908.3.B47 2010
  973.932092—DC22   2010004085

To my two girls, Marla and Ellie
—J.G.

To my brother Troy
—M.F.B.

For the power of their words

The new circumstances under which we are all placed
call for new words, new phrases,
and for the transfer of old words to new objects.

—THOMAS JEFFERSON

CONTENTS

FOREWORD

The American presidential election of 2008 was historic for many reasons: it was the first election of an African American president; the second election of a non-WASP (the first was John F. Kennedy, in 1960); and the surprise election of a young, progressive Democrat after Republican domination of the modern presidential electoral process. With the possible exception of Bill Clinton's victory in 1992, the election of Obama was also the first presidential election since Kennedy's narrow triumph over Nixon in 1960 in which the victor's campaign oratory was a principal reason for his success.

Obama embodied change, not only with his skin color, his youth, and his newness to the American national political scene, but also with his fresh approach to politics embodied in the themes of his speeches. He reached out to scholars and intellectuals for the expert advice reflected in his thoughtful speeches. Occasionally, as a consequence, some of his speeches seemed aimed more at members of a university faculty or newspaper editorial board than at typical American voters. He refused to talk down to voters, or to dodge difficult issues, or to revert to the worn slogans and clichés that often define political rhetoric. His principal opponent for the Democratic Party nomination, Hillary Clinton, was a better debater; was better prepared, being ready with five-point programs and proposals to meet any issue; and had a special appeal to female voters and loyal Clinton admirers. But she did not represent change.

Neither did Obama's opponent in the general election, John McCain, who would have been the oldest person elected president had he succeeded. McCain was an honorable man with a long record of service and dedication to this country, but he did not prove to be an effective campaigner, and his faltering, sometimes even bewildering, rhetoric could not compete with the clear and forceful messages emanating from the Obama camp.

Obama is a naturally eloquent man, as he often demonstrated when speaking with no prepared text in front of him and in the inevitable spontaneous situations that arise on the campaign trail and its hundreds of formal and informal press conferences. In addition to his own talents, he could rely on a gifted team of speechwriters, some of whom continue to play an important role in the White House today: Jon Favreau, his chief speechwriter; Ben Rhodes, his foreign policy specialist; Adam Frankel, one of his earliest campaign speechwriters; and, later, draftees from the Hillary Clinton campaign. (Adam Frankel is also a personal friend of mine, having served as my principal research assistant in the preparation of my recent book of memoirs, *Counselor: A Life at the Edge of History.*) Once again, we have a president who speaks on current controversies at home and abroad and on major issues in his legislative program. The world once again depends upon the leadership of the United States and its president, both in strengthening the global and American economies and in restoring law and diplomacy to world affairs.

Obama's campaign speeches, carefully compiled and analyzed in this volume, were the first indication that he would rank with Jefferson, Lincoln, Wilson, Franklin Roosevelt, and Kennedy as a president whose oratory the world would hear and remember. Like those eloquent presidents, Obama is neither the tool nor voice of his gifted speechwriters. By nature a leader, a thoughtful decision-maker, and a listener who knows how to draw the best judgment and recommendations from those whom he invites to his table, he has appointed a superb team of advisers to his cabinet and administration. I predict a historic administration, for which this book will long serve as a reference to be consulted by current politicians and future historians.

—TED SORENSEN

INTRODUCTION

It's fair to say that when it comes to politics, there are few things Americans agree on. That said, there is one thing that's not debatable: Barack Obama can deliver one hell of a campaign speech.

Even those who don't agree with his policies can recall the first time they heard Obama, the candidate, thunder away to a crowd of adoring listeners. For many, the first time they heard Obama was his call for hope and unity at the 2004 Democratic National Convention; for others, it was the first time they heard his now-famous mantra, "Yes, we can"—with its roots in Cesar Chavez's 1972 "*Sí, se puede*" campaign—on the evening of the New Hampshire primary. There are few politicians in American history who have used the stage more effectively.

You may have a different view of Obama the president and of his rhetoric in the White House. You may not agree with his policies, or you may believe, like some, that he has overused the presidential podium— or that his deeds have fallen short of his words. You may believe that his signature promises of change and political unity have given way to traditional stagnation and partisanship.

We will leave it to history, and to another author, to judge his presidency, because one thing is clear: the rules of governing are much different than those of campaigning.

Presidents have different agendas from candidates. Candidates must convince the public to vote for them, and the press to adore them; a candidate's agenda is not to convince the Congress or the special interests to pass legislation. They are firing up a crowd at a rally of screaming supporters, not delivering a sober speech from the Oval Office on an impending war.

Presidents, on the other hand, have to be much more careful with their rhetoric; a single word can impact financial markets and foreign affairs. They have to push their budget policies day in and day out, even if it's tedious and the public is bored stiff. As Peter Baker wrote in the *New York Times,* "Speechmaking as a president often presents a sharper challenge than it does on the campaign trail. The audience is different, the desired goals are different, the platform is different . . . and pushing policies requires more explanation than inspiration."[1]

This book covers a period of time that is already inscribed in the annals of politics: the rise and rhetoric of Barack Obama from state senator to president of the United States. It uses eighteen of Obama's most important political speeches to tell the story of his remarkable ascent and his unprecedented use of the podium to win over a strong majority of the American public. As you will see, it's not just about the words themselves, but the stories behind them—why they were chosen, how they were shaped, and their impact on the race.

The narrative draws on several sources: first-hand accounts from Obama's speechwriters, analysis from journalists and others who covered the presidential campaign, and insights from our own experience in presidential politics, policymaking, and speechwriting.

You will meet the five speechwriters who helped Obama craft and communicate the "change" message he embodied and get a behind-the-scenes view of their fast-paced world of swigging Red Bull and pulling all-nighter writing sessions. What will be clear throughout the book is that Barack Obama and his writers understood the impact his words could have on the race and on his ultimate success.

The title itself, *Power in Words*, comes from Barack Obama's presidential announcement speech in February 2007 in Springfield, Illinois, when he said, "The life of a tall, gangly, self-made Springfield lawyer tells us that a different future is possible. He tells us that there is power in words." Obama uttered those words only a few feet from where his political hero, Abraham Lincoln, a former Illinois state legislator and trial lawyer, declared his aspirations to the highest office in the land.

"Power in words" is not a direct quote from Lincoln. Obama was paraphrasing Lincoln, who understood that words mattered; he was fastidious about the language he used to communicate with the country.

Lincoln understood the power of words like few of his contemporaries—he knew that his rhetoric was one of the most powerful tools of persuasion he possessed. He was not particularly verbose: it was about the quality, not quantity, of his words. There was a purpose, a thoughtfulness behind every word he delivered, and history has judged his rhetoric kindly.

Lincoln's Gettysburg Address was only 278 words, but it is viewed as a singular moment in repairing the disjointed union. We all remember the opening: "Four score and seven years ago our fathers brought forth on this continent, a new nation, conceived in Liberty, and dedicated to the proposition that all men are created equal." His celebrated Emancipation Proclamation was only 696 words; it took less than five minutes to deliver. In fact, the entire speech fits on the wall of the Lincoln Memorial. Could you imagine that happening today?

Lincoln's Second Inaugural Address was only 703 words in length and 505 of those were one-syllable words. In advance of the speech, the Associated Press reported that it would be "brief—not exceeding, probably a column in length." They were about right.

Our sixteenth president spent days writing, rewriting, and fine-tuning with the draft on foolscap, a type of paper that was thirteen by seventeen inches long; according to biographer Ronald White, Lincoln kept it in a drawer near him because "when he knew he was to present an important speech, he toiled far ahead." He usually wrote his speeches "first with pencil on stiff sheets of white pasteboard or box-board. . . . He laid the sheets . . . on his knee. He crossed out words and edited until the text was ready to copy as the final version of the speech to be delivered."[2]

Lincoln weighed carefully every word of his Second Inaugural, which was ultimately delivered on March 4, 1865, with the country still mired down in the Civil War. He understood that it would take a remarkable public campaign to convince the country to continue the bloodiest war in history, against their fellow citizens, to outlaw slavery.

Obama, too, recognized the impact he had on the stump. When he spoke about hope or change, or when he was forced to address himself to the race issue, the American people listened intently. He knew he had to choose his words wisely and that he could persuade, and dissuade, in an instant.

According to White, Lincoln was mocked early in his presidency for his concise texts and simple, monosyllabic words. Calling him a "Simple Susan," his critics didn't understand that Lincoln's simplicity was intentional. Like Obama, "Lincoln wrote primarily to be heard. He crafted his speeches as much for the ear as for the eye" and, as noted, was careful with his diction. According to Lincoln, "In my present position . . . every word is so closely noted that it will not do to make trivial ones. I have kept silent for the reason I supposed it was particularly proper that I should do so." Jeffrey K. Tulis explains in *The Rhetorical Presidency,* "Lincoln indicates that 'silence' will enhance the persuasive power of those speeches that he does deliver."[3]

Obama was not the first presidential candidate to learn from Lincoln. Theodore Roosevelt coined the phrase "bully pulpit" because he believed that he could use the presidential podium and the direct communication with the American public it provided to "bully" Congress into enacting his agenda. Franklin Roosevelt likewise was a master communicator who seized the radio airwaves, then a brand-new medium, to allay the nation's fears during the Great Depression and sell his ambitious New Deal program. John Kennedy used the stump and a new political tool, television, to help win the presidency and the hearts of millions of Americans. Decades later, Ronald Reagan earned the moniker the Great Communicator for his masterful use of the public stage, using it to unify the country behind his agenda. Bill Clinton took a page out of the Reagan playbook as the Great Empathizer; few politicians felt more comfortable, and were more popular, on the world stage.

Thus, compared to his successors, Lincoln hardly ever used the bully pulpit to go over the heads of Congress and address the American people directly. In the eighteenth century, it wasn't customary for presidents to speak directly and with frequency to the American people. Tulis reported that our earliest presidents spent most of their time working behind closed doors with Congress and their cabinets. Partly this was an issue of logistics. Even if presidents had wanted to reach the masses, the tools required to do so didn't exist; there were no twenty-four-hour cable news stations, satellite radio stations, Internet news and gossip Web sites, or armies of citizen-journalist bloggers such as those that patrol the Web today. So instead, politicians targeted their communication to the legislators and to a small, elite population who had regular access to newspapers.

Beyond that, there was a fear that speechifying would lead to dema-goguery. The Founding Fathers believed, writes Carol Gelderman in *All the Presidents' Words*, "that popular oratory might undermine the rational and enlightened debate of the citizens' representatives that their system was designed to foster."[4] Believe it or not, George Washington only de-livered an average of three speeches per year during his presidency; John Adams, only one per year; Jefferson, only five per year; and the man of the people, Andrew Jackson, only an average of one per year. There were a few exceptions: Abraham Lincoln delivered sixteen per year, Andrew Johnson twenty-three, and Rutherford B. Hayes thirty-one. But their re-marks were by no means partisan statements or policy pronouncements. In fact, before the turn of the century, 80 percent of the speeches tracked were "very brief thank-you remarks."

Furthermore, Americans simply didn't expect to hear from their presi-dents on a daily basis—and it certainly wasn't considered appropriate for their chief executive to campaign either for office or for his legislative pri-orities. Washington didn't actually deliver his famed Farewell Address.

On September 19, 1776, an article Washington addressed to the "Peo-ple of the United States" appeared in Philadelphia's major newspaper, the *American Daily Advertiser.* In it, Washington announced, "I should now apprise you of the resolutions I have formed, to decline being considered among the number of those, out of whom a choice is to be made." It was reprinted by every major newspaper over the coming weeks. But even then, because of the high-brow language Washington used, only the most educated Americans could decipher it—after all, most of Americans were illiterate in the eighteenth century.

The practice of direct democracy—targeting the presidential com-munication to the mass American audience—did not become common practice until the early twentieth century. Teddy Roosevelt was partly responsible for breaking the mold by holding speaking tours, which he referred to as "swings around the circle." He toured the country for eighteen months, starting in 1905, to push for the passage of the then-controversial Hepburn Act, which would give the Interstate Commerce Commission the power to set maximum railroad rates (it passed in 1906). Roosevelt believed in a strong executive power "limited only by specific restrictions." Part of his strategy was to loosen Congress's grip on the

White House and policymaking by appealing directly to the American people by means of the power of the presidential megaphone. And he used it energetically. Gelderman writes that one critic of Roosevelt noted, "While he is in the neighborhood, the public can no more look the other way than the small boy can turn his head away from a circus parade followed by a steam calliope."[5]

Similarly, after World War I, Woodrow Wilson toured the country to help sell the idea of the League of Nations and became the first president to deliver a State of the Union address in person to Congress since John Adams did so in 1800. The constitution requires that the president "report to Congress from time to time" about the state of the union, but since Adams, presidents had done so only in writing.

Wilson was ridiculed in the days leading up to the planned speech, and one Congressman called his tactic "a speech from the throne . . . a cheap and tawdry imitation . . . of monarchical countries." But Wilson opened his oration by explaining his in-person appearance: "I shall ask your indulgence if I venture to depart in some degree from the usual custom of setting before you in formal review the many matters which have engaged the attention . . . of the Government." He successfully disarmed his audience and the media by closing with an ode to Congress, rather than any personal accolade, "Surely it is a proper and pertinent part . . . to express my admiration for the diligence, the good temper, and the full comprehension of public duty which has already been manifested by both Houses."[6]

According to Robert Alexander Kraig, in *Woodrow Wilson and the Lost World of the Oratorical Statesman,* Wilson trained himself to be an "oratorical statesman."[7] He believed a leader had a duty to be articulate and persuasive, and that a self-governing republic depended on it. During a 1907 lecture at Columbia University, Wilson made clear that the president "has no means of compelling Congress except through public opinion."[8]

Since then, the use of the most powerful pulpit in the world has grown exponentially. In 1948, according to Michael Waldman in *POTUS Speaks,* President Truman delivered an average of 88 public speeches per year. Ronald Reagan gave a remarkable 320 speeches. Bill Clinton, the first president in the age of cable news and the Internet, delivered on average 550 speeches every year of his presidency.

In his first year as president, Barack Obama delivered 411 speeches.[9]

According to his press secretary Robert Gibbs, Obama's philosophy on using his bully pulpit was "you may not agree with what I'm doing, but you at least will have a better understanding for why if I can explain to you why I'm doing this." Gibbs added: "So in that way I do think he does put value on the words, on the explanation of what the policy is."[10]

In the realm of campaign rhetoric, Franklin D. Roosevelt stands out as one of the great innovators. In 1932, he upended centuries of tradition by traveling to his party's convention, held at the Chicago Stadium, and accepting the nomination in person. Until then it was customary for presidential nominees to be asked to serve, and the more humble they were—the more they resisted before accepting the call to serve—the more respect they earned. To the day he died, Jefferson claimed that he would rather have been spending his twilight years on his farm in Virginia than in the White House. This was a bit apocryphal, but it certainly helped solidify the myth that Jefferson sought to create.

Other candidates over the next century or so kept that tradition alive. In theory, their peers used the convention to select someone whom they would then ask to serve their country. Most politicians didn't overtly campaign and they certainly didn't go out on the road. Benjamin Harrison campaigned from his porch, where he received delegations and made frequent pronouncements.

This helps explain why even today presidential nominees don't arrive at their party convention until the final day, after the ballots have been officially counted. FDR thought that this tradition was foolish, noting in his convention address: "The appearance before a National Convention of its nominee for President . . . is unprecedented and unusual, but these are unprecedented and unusual times. I have started out on the tasks that lie ahead by breaking the absurd traditions that the candidate should remain in professed ignorance of what has happened for weeks until he is formally notified of that event many weeks later. My friends, may this be the symbol of my intention to be honest and to avoid all hypocrisy or sham, to avoid all silly shutting of the eyes to the truth in this campaign. You have nominated me and I know it, and I am here to thank you for the honor."[11]

It was pure genius, and every nominee since, Democratic and Republican, has accepted the nomination in person. Moreover, the nominee's speech, along with the ones leading up to it, has become one of the major spectacles of every presidential campaign. Today's party conventions are mainly theater. Senator John Kennedy was the first nominee to deliver his address in an outdoor stadium to eighty thousand enthusiastic attendees at the Los Angeles Coliseum. In 1964, President Lyndon Johnson descended on his party's convention in Atlantic City, New Jersey, and boldly challenged members to confer a mandate for his Great Society, which he had unveiled only months earlier in Ann Arbor, Michigan, stating: "This nation . . . has man's first chance to build the Great Society—a place where the meaning of man's life matches the marvels of man's labor."[12]

Convention keynote addresses have also taken their place in history. When Hubert Humphrey took on the controversial topic of civil rights for African Americans in his famed speech at the 1948 Democratic National Convention in Philadelphia, a coterie of thirty-five southern Democrats, led by Governor Strom Thurmond of South Carolina, marched out of the hall. The Dixiecrats, as they were called, held their own convention in Birmingham, Alabama, and nominated Thurmond for president; he carried Louisiana, Mississippi, Alabama, and South Carolina in the 1948 election, and the Dixiecrats never returned to the Democratic Party.

Texas governor Ann Richards's keynote address at the Democratic convention in 1988 is well remembered for the line, "Poor George. He can't help it. He was born with a silver foot in his mouth." A little-known Southern governor, Bill Clinton of Arkansas, gave one of the longest nominating speeches in history at the 1988 Democratic convention that nominated Michael Dukakis. After Clinton dragged on for more than twenty-five minutes, his words "in conclusion . . ." received a standing ovation.

New York governor Mario Cuomo was well-known as an effective speaker, and in 1984 his keynote address at the Democratic convention in the Moscone Center in San Francisco was one of the best speeches of his career. Cuomo later said, "You campaign in poetry. You govern in prose." Few politicians better exemplify that adage than Barack Obama, and there have been few presidential candidates in American history whose "poetry" on the stump has had as profound an effect on their electoral success as Obama.

In 2004, Obama was a little-known state senator from Illinois who was running for a seat in the United States Senate. John Kerry, the Democratic

Party's presidential nominee that year, plucked him out of obscurity and gave him the chance of a lifetime: to deliver his party's keynote address at the Democratic National Convention in Boston. Obama more than rose to the occasion. That was the night when the country first met its future president and was first enraptured by his magical rhetorical performance.

The state senator was in his element that summer evening in Boston, Kerry's hometown. His style was built for campaigning: his confident, mellifluous voice; his good looks and natural stage presence; his poise; his young and attractive family; his preacher-like cadences. Add to that his background—the son of a black Kenyan father and a white Kansan mother, who grew up in Honolulu, Hawaii, and Jakarta, Indonesia. The country had never quite seen anything like him, and he was the talk of the country. His autobiography, first published nearly a decade earlier, found its way back into bookstores, and a print run of 75,000 quickly sold out. His face soon adorned the cover of *Newsweek*. Beginning that night, the Illinois state legislator could hardly go anywhere without getting mobbed by adoring crowds and story-hungry journalists. A Democratic star was born.

To fully understand what Obama does with language, you can't just turn to politicians or other gifted orators for comparisons. Obama's rhetoric comes most directly from a specific source, namely, the homiletic, or preaching, traditions of the black Protestant churches, where the best rhetoric combines substance and style.

According to Dale Andrews, "I think Obama understands the nature of rhetorical strategies. He's not called to perfectly replicate a preaching event, because there's a difference between a pulpit and a political platform, although there [is an] exchange between the two." The "preaching moment," says Andrews, comes awfully close to what Obama seems able to achieve with his audiences—that point where the speaker and listener are engaged in a conversation of meaning with each other.[13]

Traditional black preachers who are effective start with a low-key introduction and then rise in tempo to a crescendo. They then ease down slowly and offer a prophetic or reassuring phrase at the end. In homiletics, it's known as the black preacher's dictum: "Start low, go slow, rise high, strike fire and sit down."[14]

Beyond his style, Obama's message was immediately appealing, and refreshing, to a broad swath of the country. It wasn't shrill or radical; like the state senator himself, it was perfectly moderate. Early in his state legislative career Obama had leaned more to the left; he introduced legislation on racial profiling, affordable housing, predatory lending, and pro-choice policies. But by the time he ran for Congress in 1999 he had begun to move toward the center. By 2008, he was against the war in Iraq, but not against war itself (he supported U.S. efforts in Afghanistan); he called for health care reform, but not universal coverage; he pushed for tough education reform, but with strong accountability for teachers. He called for a stimulus package, but with careful deficit controls. From day one, he spoke of bipartisanship and the urgency for change in Washington.

In his 2004 keynote address he stated, "There is not a liberal America and a conservative America—there is the United States of America." He also spoke of the importance of core morals and values, that "we are our brother's keeper, that we are our sister's keeper." He urged responsibility. He called for reform in education, for economic investment at home, and—the policy that drew him early praise—an end to the war in Iraq.

The speech launched Obama toward his future run for the presidency. But many have noted its remarkable consistency with the rhetoric of his past, the language and themes that had characterized his speeches since his first state senate campaign nearly a decade earlier. The speech would also become the message frame of his presidential campaign. The themes are familiar: unity, responsibility, change.

In 1995, at the Ramada Inn Lakeshore Hotel in Chicago, during his speech announcing his candidacy for the state legislature, Obama declared, "Politicians are not held in highest esteem these days. . . . I want to inspire a renewal of morality in politics." Several months later he wrote, "From the moment I announced my candidacy for the State Senate, friends and associates have . . . warned me of all the corrupting influences lurking in Springfield: the influence peddling and the political gridlock, the fat cat lobbyist and the narrow partisanship. . . . It's precisely my desire to restore a sense of mission and service to state government that led me to throw my hat into the political ring. . . . It's people power that lifts up issues and frames the debate in new ways. It's people power that puts pressure on every elected official . . . to act responsibly and ensure that the most vulnerable among us have a real opportunity to achieve the American dream."[15]

Two years later, in his announcement for his (ultimately unsuccessful) congressional bid, Obama delivered a similar message about influence peddling in politics and the need to clean politics up—a core element of the change theme he would emphasize for years to come. To a room of about three hundred supporters at the Palmer House Hilton, Obama said, "Nobody sent me. I'm not part of some long-standing political organization. I have no fancy sponsors. I'm not even from Chicago. My name is Obama."

The night he conceded that he had lost his congressional bid he told a reporter from his hometown paper, the *Hyde Park Herald*, "We need a new style of politics to deal with issues that are important to the people."[16] Denny Jacobs, one of Obama's Chicago friends, recounted to the *New York Times* the advice he gave Obama at the time: "Not only the black community but [all] less privileged people are looking to you for that hope. . . . Hope is a pretty inclusive word. I think he is very good at selling that."[17]

This was a theme that dated back to his days as Harvard Law School, where he became the first African American president of the prestigious *Harvard Law Review,* in the spring of 1990. In his closed-door speech to its members, even though he leaned to the left, he appealed to both factions of legal theorists—the liberals and the more conservative or "federalists." Bradford A. Berenson, a classmate and former Bush administration lawyer, noted, "Even though he was clearly a liberal, he didn't appear to the conservatives in the review to be taking sides in the tribal warfare . . . He genuinely cared what conservatives had to say and what they thought. The politics of the *Harvard Law Review* were incredibly petty and incredibly vicious. . . . And Barack tended to treat those disputes with a certain air of detachment. . . . The feeling was almost, come on kids, can't we just behave here?"

Another classmate, Crystal Nix Hines, discussed Obama's approach to a fiery debate at the *Law Review* over their affirmative action policy: "While other students were determined to prove the merits of their beliefs through logic and determination, Obama preferred to listen, seek others' views, and find a middle way."

Thomas J. Perrelli, a classmate and former counsel to Attorney General Janet Reno, added, "He was leading the discussion but he wasn't trying to impose his own perspective on it. He was much more mediating."[18]

Journalist Michael Heilemann summarized Obama's approach to

leadership at Harvard, a clear foreshadowing of years to come: "His wariness toward identity politics was reinforced. And so was his belief that the old ideological divisions and polarities were irrelevant and counterproductive. That progress would require dealing with, not demonizing, conservatives. That conciliation isn't tantamount to mealy-mouthed accommodation—it's the highest of civic virtues. . . . The tendency to seek common ground, to find a win-win, that emerged at Harvard was central to his most dexterous political achievement."[19]

When Obama announced his United States Senate bid, he stuck to his already-developed script. "I don't have personal wealth or a famous name, but I have a fire in my belly for fairness and justice. Four years ago, Peter Fitzgerald [his Republican opponent and the incumbent] bought himself a Senate seat, and he's betrayed Illinois ever since." No one has published this text in its entirety, but the excerpts from the media clips are revealing. He said at an event a few months later, "I am your instrument potentially to create a new kind of politics in this town. So roll up your sleeves and kick off your bedroom slippers, because we are gonna take the U.S. Senate in the state of Illinois."

His remarks on the senate floor in Springfield were consistent, too. In his statement in November 1999 on child welfare reform, he spoke of personal responsibility: "Ultimately, what we want to do is to encourage folks to be more self-sufficient, to keep more of the dollars that they're earning in work. We also want to make sure that noncustodial parents are doing more to support the children who they've born."

A month later, in a clear move to unify opposing interests, something he would do often and campaign on, Obama stated to the Ninety-third General Assembly of the Illinois Senate, "I've devoted much of the early Session on working with law enforcement to try to . . . strike a balance between concerns of the community with respect to racial profiling and the concerns of law enforcement in making sure that they can carry out their functions."

Obama was equally consistent during his tenure in the United States Senate and throughout his presidential campaign. He favored bipartisanship and unity when it served the greater good. For example, he worked with Indiana senator Richard Lugar, a seasoned Republican, on nuclear nonproliferation and with the Republican senator from Oklahoma, Tom

Coburn, on transparency in government. In 2005, in the well of the Senate, Obama stated, "These are challenges we all want to meet and problems we all want to solve, even if we don't all agree how to do it. But if the right of free and open debate is taken away from the minority party and the millions of Americans who asked us to be their voice, I fear that the already partisan atmosphere of Washington will be poisoned to the point where no one will be able to agree on anything. That doesn't serve anyone's best interests, and it certainly isn't what the patriots who founded this democracy had in mind."

When he announced his presidential bid, in Springfield, he called for a new form of politics—as he had done in his Senate race and later as a United States senator—saying: "In the face of despair, you believe there can be hope. In the face of a politics that's shut you out, that's told you to settle, that's divided us for too long, you believe we can be one people, reaching for what's possible, building that more perfect union. . . . I know I haven't spent a lot of time learning the ways of Washington. But I've been there long enough to know that the ways of Washington must change."

He also hammered on the point of personal responsibility, as he had done in the state senate: "Each of us, in our own lives, will have to accept responsibility—for instilling an ethic of achievement in our children, for adapting to a more competitive economy, for strengthening our communities, and sharing some measure of sacrifice."

Similar to his congressional race against an incumbent, Obama acknowledged that he was running against the establishment, against "the cynics, and the lobbyists, and the special interests who've turned our government into a game only they can afford to play. They write the checks and you get stuck with the bills. They get the access while you get to write a letter. They think they own this government, but we're here today to take it back."

The night he was elected president, he touched on similar themes in his speech. He told a brimming crowd in Chicago's Grant Park about the importance of responsibility: "So let us summon a new spirit of patriotism, of service and responsibility, where each of us resolves to pitch in and work harder and look after not only ourselves but each other." He continued, stressing his oft-touched-upon theme of unity, "In this country, we rise or fall as one nation, as one people. Let's resist the temptation to fall back on the same partisanship and pettiness and immaturity that has poisoned our politics for so long."

And then, on the cold January day of his Inaugural Address, Obama exhorted the American people, "What is required of us now is a new era of responsibility—a recognition on the part of every American that we have duties to ourselves, our nation and the world; duties that we do not grudgingly accept, but rather seize gladly, firm in the knowledge that there is nothing so satisfying to the spirit, so defining of our character than giving our all to a difficult task."

He continued, speaking of political unity: "What the cynics fail to understand is that the ground has shifted beneath them, that the stale political arguments that have consumed us for so long no longer apply. . . . On this day, we gather because we have chosen hope over fear, unity of purpose over conflict and discord."

Few modern-day politicians have evidenced this level of thematic consistency over the course of their political careers. Now, this assessment does not account for Obama's words or actions as president. In fact, by January 2010, Obama's ratings in "uniting the country" had dropped 33 percent (from 60 to 40), and "changing business as usual in Washington" had sunk 36 percent (from 47 to 30) from a year earlier.[20]

But as a young politician and as a presidential candidate, no matter what the obstacle or opportunity, Obama stuck to his script. His chief speechwriter, Jon Favreau, reinforced this point in an interview soon after arriving at the White House: "It's funny, every reporter I sit down with asks me how our messages or themes have evolved. They compliment what they believe is a new theme. But it isn't. It's often something he's been saying forever. Whether that's the theme of responsibility, his line about the American dream being 'built brick by brick, calloused hand by calloused hand,' his use of Lincoln or King."

As Favreau suggested, it's possible that part of Obama's consistency comes from what he learned from the words of his political heroes, such as Lincoln and King, who espoused unity and responsibility. In a letter to Horace Greeley, the editor of the *New York Tribune*, Lincoln wrote, "My paramount object in this struggle [the Civil War] is to save the Union, and is not either to save or to destroy slavery. If I could save the Union without freeing any slave I would do it, and if I could save it by freeing all the slaves I would do it." Obama later wrote, "I like to believe that for Lincoln, it was never a matter of abandoning conviction for the sake of expediency. Rather . . . that we must talk and reach for common understandings, precisely because all of us are imperfect and can never act with the certainty that God is on our side." Striking a similar chord as Lincoln had a century earlier, King preached, "We've learned to fly the air as birds, we've learned to swim the seas as fish, yet we haven't learned to walk the earth as brothers and sisters."[21]

It was at the Democratic National Convention in Boston in 2004 that Obama first collaborated with Favreau, a twenty-three-old Holy Cross graduate who would become Senator Obama's speechwriter and later his chief speechwriter for his presidential campaign and in the White House. At the time Favreau was a speechwriter for Kerry, the Democratic nominee, and he was on assignment at the convention to ensure that the speakers delivered the campaign message.

Obama was not accustomed to using a speechwriter. During his time in the state senate, when he actually used a prepared text, which was rare, he wrote his remarks himself, often in longhand on a yellow legal pad or on the back of whatever scraps of paper he could find. He had written his now-famous 2002 speech against the Iraq War resolution in the cramped study of his Chicago home. He wrote most of his convention speech by himself, though he had some help from colleagues in the state senate, from his communications director, Robert Gibbs, and from his media and campaign strategist, David Axelrod. The reality is that Obama has always been a gifted writer. He wrote *Dreams from My Father* shortly after finishing law school, and he later drafted *The Audacity of Hope* by himself, often working late at night after Michelle and his two daughters had gone to sleep. During his presidential campaign, he crafted several of his major speeches in the same fashion. He typed the first draft of his speech on race as well as a majority of his address to the Democratic National Convention. But these writing exercises took precious time that the senator simply no longer had; Obama, a leftie, needed a right hand.

Favreau's lone contribution to Obama's Boston speech was to deliver the news to him that he couldn't use a certain line he had written in his speech because it was too similar to one of the lines in Kerry's speech. Soon after Obama was elected to the U.S. Senate, Gibbs called Favreau and asked him if he'd be interested in a job as a speechwriter for Senator Obama. The young Bostonian was considering other offers, including one from Kerry, but he was taken by his brief encounter with Obama at the convention and, like most people, was impressed with his convention speech. He also trusted Gibbs, who had been boss for a time on the Kerry campaign. Favreau and Gibbs had a long conversation about the opportunity in the cafeteria of the Dirksen Senate Office Building on Obama's first day in office. Favreau questioned the young senator's need for a speechwriter; after all, he had penned the draft of his Boston speech, as well as a best-selling autobiography.

Gibbs, according to Favreau, took the point head on: "If there were 48 hours in a day, we wouldn't need a speechwriter. But he needs to work with someone." Favreau took the job and became that someone. Axelrod later made a similar point: "He is the best speechwriter in the group and he knows what he wants to say and he generally says it better than anybody else would."[22]

Obama found himself in a territory familiar for politicians: he had a clear sense of what he wanted to say, but simply didn't have enough time to write speeches himself. This was nothing new in politics. George Washington's most famous communication, his Farewell Address, was written by James Madison and Alexander Hamilton; Andrew Jackson's Nullification Proclamation was composed by his secretary of state, Edward Livingston; and Andrew Johnson's First Annual Message, in 1865, was written by his secretary of the navy, George Bancroft.

Judson T. Welliver is credited with being the first official White House ghostwriter. He served President Warren Harding in 1921 as a "literary clerk." His lasting contribution was the phrase "Founding Fathers," which was used in Harding's March 4, 1921, Inaugural Address, but otherwise, he was invisible, like most who succeeded him (founders of the only organization of presidential speechwriters named their organization the Judson Welliver Society).

Other presidents employed ghostwriters: Herbert Hoover, for instance, hired French Strother to write for him. But most presidents in the twentieth century, including William McKinley, Theodore Roosevelt, William Howard Taft, and Woodrow Wilson, wrote their own material.

This formula changed with Franklin D. Roosevelt, who tapped one of his closest policy and political aides, Samuel Rosenman, to serve as his speechwriter. Roosevelt understood better than most the value of mass communication in selling his social agenda to the public. It was one of his central tools of persuasion. Another Roosevelt speechwriter, Robert Sherwood, noted, "Roosevelt knew that all those words would constitute the bulk of the estate that he would leave to posterity."[23] Every president thereafter employed staff speechwriters in one form or another, though it wasn't until some thirty years later that Richard Nixon would establish the first official Office of Presidential Speechwriting.

Roosevelt's relationship with Rosenman, Sherwood, and his other writers was deeply personal and collaborative. Harry Truman, Kennedy, and many subsequent twentieth-century presidents had similar bonds with their writers, and many of these relationships dated back to their earlier political campaigns. Rosenman had worked closely with Roosevelt in his 1932 race; Ted Sorensen played an integral part in Kennedy's victory; Ken Khachigian worked for candidate Reagan and then became his first White House chief speechwriter; David Kusnet wrote for Clinton on his 1992 campaign before joining his White House staff; and Michael Gerson served as George W. Bush's wordsmith in his victory over Al Gore and throughout most of his first term in office.

In Favreau's first job interview with Senator Obama, Obama asked him why he had chosen a career in politics. Favreau discussed his work in college defending the legal rights of welfare recipients. According to a *Newsweek* account, he also admitted to Obama that he had no "theory" of speechwriting, "but when I saw you at the convention, you basically told a story about your life from beginning to end, and it was a story that fit with the larger American narrative. People applauded not because you wrote an applause line but because you touched something in the party and the country that people had not touched before. Democrats haven't had that in a long time." Obama responded, "That's exactly what I try to do."[24]

In the years to come, Favreau would become known as Obama's muse; the two developed a symbiotic relationship enjoyed by only a few speechwriters and their bosses. Another famous duo was Ted Sorensen and President Kennedy. Sorensen, a celebrated writer and policy wunderkind, is credited with drafting Kennedy's famous Inaugural Address. Interestingly, Sorensen and Favreau had similar paths—they both joined the offices of young senators as young men themselves. When Senator John Kennedy was elected to office he was thirty-five, and Sorensen was just twenty-four. Obama was forty-three when he was elected and Favreau was twenty-four when he came on board. Both Sorensen and Favreau went on to serve as the chief writers for their bosses in the White House.

But the White House and the development of a speechwriting team were a long way off when Obama and Favreau first met. The 2004 convention was the first time Obama ever had formal, professional speech coaching, and the first time he used a TelePrompter, though it would soon become standard at his campaign events.

According to his speechwriters, the TelePrompter played a critical role in Obama's success. First, it helped ensure consistency of message; with the words scrolling in front of him, there was little chance that he would stray from the rhetoric he and his writers had crafted. Second, and most important, it allowed Obama to focus on the passionate delivery that was critical to his candidacy. He became a master of the political rally; Obama had no problem, as he put it, getting "fired up" and "ready to go."

Although his masterful delivery ultimately became as good as second nature, that hadn't always been the case. There was always a risk that he would slip back into a professorial mode, particularly in smaller settings, such as town halls. In fact, early in his career as a state senator, Obama was often criticized for coming across as too erudite and out of touch; only later did he develop the preacher-like populist style that would become his signature.

It's easy to understand where this earlier tendency originated. For many years, after his time at Harvard Law School, Obama taught constitutional law at the University of Chicago. Like most academics, and most lawyers, he was deliberate in the classroom, carefully selecting each word. He wasn't patronizing, and as his friend George Haywood said, "He doesn't have the handicap that a lot of smart people have, which is that they come across as 'You're not smart enough to talk to me.'"[25]

Still, as Obama's former staffer Dan Shomon, campaign manager for his Senate race, commented, "There was a gradual progression of Barack Obama from thoughtful, earnest policy wonk . . . to Barack Obama the politician, the inspirer, the speaker." Abner Mikva, an early Obama supporter, described the advice he gave Obama soon after he lost his first congressional race, advice he had heard Cardinal Richard Cushing give Senator John Kennedy: "Jack, you have to learn to speak more Irish and less Harvard."[26]

Going back to his time at Occidental College, Obama had enjoyed public speaking, even if he had yet to master it. In his book *Dreams from My Father,* Obama described his transformation into a public speaker and his realization that his words could have an impact. He described one of the first speeches he wrote for an anti-apartheid rally: "When I sat down to prepare a few notes for what I might say, something had happened. In my mind it somehow became more than just a two-minute speech, more than a way to prove my political orthodoxy. . . . With the right words, everything could change—South Africa, the lives of the ghetto kids just a few miles away, my own tenuous place in the word."

Obama then described the event itself: "I knew that I had them, that the connection had been made. I took hold of the mike, ready to plunge on, when I felt someone's hands grab me from behind. . . . They started yanking me off stage. . . . I really wanted to stay up there, to hear my voice bouncing off the crowd and returning to me in applause. I had so much left to say."

In the spring of 1991, at Harvard, the Black Law Students Association asked Obama, instead of the usual professor, to deliver the keynote address at their annual conference. Before hundreds of people, he gave a stirring call to action—what Harvard law professor Randall Kennedy dubbed a "clarion call" to use their law school education "not just to feather our nests" but to "address the many ills that confront our society."[27]

During Obama's early years in politics, his rhetoric was often interrupted with professorial tics—lots of um's and ah's. The TelePrompter helped solve this problem, although his dependency on the device also drew criticism. Some complained that it forced him to target his delivery toward the television audience, not to his actual audience. Others said that it made him look disconnected and out of touch or too much like an actor reading from a script. But on balance it worked for him.

Like Ronald Reagan and Bill Clinton, he was quickly seen by the media and the public as a great communicator. He didn't necessarily ooze empathy like Clinton, who "felt your pain," and wasn't the master of the small setting, or the routine policy address. But few politicians have ever owned a large political rally like Obama. He could grab a crowd of fifty thousand the way Clinton could ensnare a town hall of fifty.

His former campaign manager, Shomon, explained, "I've seen him get going, and he just hits it. He feeds off of the crowd. [In smaller groups,] Obama gets sleepy."[28] In fact, part of the challenge of his early presidency, and a subject of criticism, is that Obama didn't show the appropriate level of empathy—he was too aloof in the face of crushing economic times. The daily drumbeat of policy speeches and smaller events simply hasn't allowed President Obama to hit his sweet spot—the large political rally.

Writer Garrett Graff described Obama's core strengths: "At the heart of 'Obamania' is his personality and presence—part preacher, part professor, part movie star. His charisma seems effortless, his charm an afterthought."[29]

The speechwriting team Obama assembled for his presidential campaign played a critical role in his rhetorical and stylistic transformation. The moment Gibbs told Favreau that Senator Obama had decided to run, Favreau picked up the phone and hired Adam Frankel, a former colleague of his from the Kerry campaign who was finishing a book with Ted Sorensen. The two had remained close since 2004; Favreau trusted the young Princetonian implicitly. Favreau and Frankel packed up and headed to the brand-new office space the campaign had rented in the Windy City.

Within a few months Favreau added another young accomplished writer, Ben Rhodes, who had strong foreign policy credentials. Rhodes, who had studied English and political science at Rice University and earned an MFA in fiction writing from New York University, had recently finished a stint with the 9/11 Commission, where he had worked closely with former Congressman Lee Hamilton and former Governor Tom Kean crafting the commission's report.

The trio of Favreau, Frankel, and Rhodes was later joined by a junior writer and researcher, Cody Keenan, and, after the primaries ended, by Sarah Hurwitz, Hillary Clinton's chief speechwriter and a Harvard Law School graduate. Hurwitz was also a veteran of several presidential and Senate campaigns, and like Frankel, had met Favreau on the Kerry campaign. She and Favreau were archenemies during the primary that pitted Obama against Clinton, but Hurwitz penned Clinton's concession speech and then flew to Chicago.

By the time the campaign for the presidency started in earnest, Favreau and Obama had already found their rhythm. Favreau understood the best way to work with his boss. He knew the books to read (anything about Lincoln); he knew whom to quote (Martin Luther King Jr. and Scripture); he discovered the best resource for good anecdotes and personal stories (*Dreams from My Father*)—all tips Favreau shared with his speechwriting team as part of their indoctrination process.

Before delivering any significant speech in Congress, Obama would sit down with Favreau, usually in his Senate office, and dictate his thoughts. Favreau would often take down the notes on his laptop, pen a first draft (often back home, late at night, fueled by a steady stream of caffeine), and then send it along to his boss for edits. Obama would usually toil on the speech until late into the night. This process continued until they were in the throes of the presidential campaign, when the candidate's travel precluded one-on-one sessions.

At that point, Favreau or one of the other writers would speak to Obama on the phone and then, after seeing edits from Axelrod, Gibbs, and others, e-mail or fax the speech to Obama's assistant, Reggie Love, who was on the road with the candidate. Obama would then send back his comments through Axelrod or Love or simply pick up the phone and call the writer. In some cases Obama would e-mail comments to the speechwriter from his BlackBerry or send a document with tracked changes directly from his laptop. Other times he would grab Love's BlackBerry and send a text to the writer, beginning with "This is Barack." In short, there wasn't a protracted and bureaucratic editing process by committee, which often plagues campaigns and nearly always diminishes the quality of a speech.

No matter how the process changed, however, one thing was consistent right up to the election: Obama worked on his speeches until the last minute. For example, during the writing process for his "More Perfect Union" speech on race, Favreau recalls receiving edited drafts from Senator Obama well after 2:00 a.m. on consecutive nights. The process was equally last-minute in the case of his speech to the 2008 Democratic convention, when Obama put the finishing touches on the draft only minutes before he delivered it.

The magic wasn't just how the speechwriters worked with Obama, but how they worked with each other. They were a team in the office, sharing drafts and ideas, and they were friends who enjoyed each other's company outside the office as well. After a long day, Frankel and Hurwitz often put on their running shoes and hit the Chicago streets for a midnight run and a late-night brainstorming session.

To craft the big speeches, the writers sat together for hours at headquarters, often deep into the evening, drinking Red Bull and writing the text together, one line after another, calling out ideas and language as they sat in front of their own laptops typing out the remarks as they went along. Many of Obama's most famous speeches, such as the one he gave the night of the Iowa caucus and his 2008 address to the Democratic convention, were group efforts, with great lines crafted by all of the speechwriters and, of course, by the candidate himself. There were exceptions to this process, certainly, but this was the usual way candidate Obama worked with his speechwriters and they worked with each other.

This book offers a window into that process and to the decision making behind several of his speeches. Its focus is solely on the speeches delivered before Obama was sworn in as president. This was a deliberate decision on the part of the authors. Cuomo's observation that campaigns are a time for "poetry" resonates with us because, from experience, we realize that this is when candidates are at their best: in "sell" mode, offering new ideas, original themes, and innovative language. It's often the first time the public is meeting a candidate up close and he is hoping to emerge as a fresh national voice. It is a time to inspire, to be free, still, of the real-life ramifications and responsibilities that come with governing, after assuming office.

This was certainly true for Obama. His words and his disposition on the stump embodied the "change" message he preached. He moved crowds with an infectious energy. A *New Yorker* profile noted, "His surface is so smooth, his movements so easy and fluid, his voice so consistent and well-pitched that he can seem like an actor playing a politician, too implausibly effortless to be doing it for real."[30]

Early in the primary process, Obama's ease was in stark contrast particularly to Senator Hillary Clinton's demeanor, and later, in the general election, to John McCain's. In many ways, Obama's speeches were his trademark on the campaign; few other contemporary politicians have possessed his gift for writing and delivery.

During his campaign, Obama's words helped create a movement. Americans hung on his every word. They blogged about his speeches; they tuned in on their televisions and computer screens; they got involved in numbers never before seen in history. He drew not only young people but a cross-section of Americans of all ages and backgrounds from both political parties.

Obama's 2008 race set a high bar for himself and for his successors. The real question is, Will it be possible for him to meet those expectations as president? Only time will tell. But in the meantime, we can enjoy, appreciate, and debate the words and the moments that made the 2008 election, and the rise of Barack Obama, historic.

Speech against the
Iraq War Resolution

October 2, 2002 • *Federal Plaza, Chicago, Illinois*

I don't oppose all wars. . . . What I am opposed to is a dumb war.
What I am opposed to is a rash war.

More than anything else, Barack Obama's position on George Bush's preparations to invade Iraq differentiated him from his chief primary opponent, Hillary Clinton. It also gave him credentials with the far-left, anti-war wing of the Democratic Party—a constituency that never fully embraced Senator Clinton.

When he delivered this speech at a Chicago rally in Federal Plaza in 2002, Obama was just beginning his run for the United States Senate (he wouldn't publicly announce for another four months). He hadn't yet delivered his now-famous speech at the 2004 Democratic National Convention in Boston. In fact, the newspaper stories covering the event didn't even mention Obama. Longtime Chicago leaders such as the Reverend Jesse Jackson and Juan Andrade were the stars of the rally.

At the time, Obama was a relatively unknown state senator from Illinois, a position driven by local politics, not one that required him to take positions on foreign policy. Unlike other Democrats considering a run for the presidency, including Senators Clinton, Edwards, and Kerry, Obama didn't have to vote one way or the other for the war. He could easily have stayed quietly out of the fray.

But Obama was already an astute politician. He didn't take lightly the decision to give President Bush authorization to invade Iraq. He also understood that what he said carried serious risks. He was standing up against what was a largely popular position—in March 2003, just days before the invasion, 58 percent of Americans supported sending troops into Iraq. As the *Washingtonian* magazine put it, "Just as Abraham Lincoln's antislavery speech at New York's Cooper Union in 1860 launched his national career, Obama's Federal Plaza speech might be seen as his launching pad."[1]

Although Obama was fundamentally opposed to invading Iraq, he wasn't a peacenik and he knew that in the long run he couldn't afford to be branded as one. Unlike some on the left, including many at the rally that day, he wasn't against war in all cases, but believed that this was the wrong war at the wrong time. His grandfather had fought in World War II, signing up to serve the day after Pearl Harbor, and Obama had supported the country's move into Afghanistan after 9/11 to root out the Taliban and al Qaeda. As he put it that day, "I don't oppose all wars. . . . What I am opposed to is a dumb war. What I am opposed to is a rash war."

His comments about war that morning were deliberate and careful. According to the *Chicago Tribune* reporter Bill Glauber, who was there that day, many at the rally sang "Give Peace a Chance" and held placards with "War Is Not An Option." They handed out more than one thousand buttons. The crowd was filled with Vietnam War–era protesters and liberal college students. "The rally wasn't a replay of the Days of Rage—it was more like a gentle call to arms for a nascent peace movement desperate to head off a new Gulf War."[2]

In the long run, Obama's stance that day and in the months ahead allowed him to own a piece of political real estate that others—such as John Edwards and Hillary Clinton—couldn't claim six years later. They had both voted for the resolution in 2002 that gave President Bush the authority to use the military "as he determines to be necessary and appropriate in order to . . . defend . . . against the continuing threat posed by Iraq."[3] Clinton called her yes vote "probably the hardest decision I've ever had to make."[4] Obama became an immediate hit on the blogosphere with liberal groups like Moveon.org. He was the antiwar candidate they had been searching for, as they had found in Howard Dean in 2004.

Many critics noted that the resolution gave Bush a blank check in Iraq, and that's precisely what Obama was worried about. As Obama told the Chicago talk show *Public Affairs with Jeff Berkowitz* in November 2002, "[What I'm] concerned about was a carte blanche to the administration for a doctrine of preemptive strikes that I'm not sure sets a good precedent."

By the time Obama announced his run for the presidency, the American people had turned against the war. More than 26,000 soldiers had been killed or injured in battle, and the war seemed to be getting worse by the month. What President Bush had proclaimed to be a "mission accomplished" on May 1, 2003, was now considered a quagmire. Brutal attacks on American soldiers and U.S.-trained Iraqi police were a daily occurrence and translated into daily headlines back in the United States. Bush's job approval rating sank to 32 percent, one of the lowest levels of his presidency.

Obama wasn't the only politician opposed to the resolution in 2002, but he was in a minority comprising mainly those on the far left of the Democratic Party, including Senators Ted Kennedy and Barbara Boxer. Most Democrats, including John Kerry, Harry Reid, and Tom Daschle, had supported the measure. It passed 297 to 133 in the House and 77 to 23 in the Senate on October 11, 2002, about a month after Bush asked the United Nations General Assembly for quick action against Iraq. The *Chicago Tribune* and *Washington Post* had both written editorials supporting it. The *Tribune* titled its September 20, 2002, editorial, "Pass the War Resolution." Although cautious regarding an invasion, there was no doubt on the *Tribune*'s stance in terms of the resolution: "The unassailable truth is that whatever concessions are now being wrung from Hussein have been provoked by one and only one catalyst: the president's frenetic insistence on ousting him."

This sentiment wasn't surprising. The country was still reeling from the 9/11 attacks and the president had made a strong and convincing public case against Saddam Hussein and Iraq. Although the invasion of Iraq was still months away, support for it was growing every day.

Obama wasn't convinced: "Now, let me be clear. I suffer no illusions about Saddam Hussein. He is a brutal man. A ruthless man. . . . But I also know that Saddam poses no imminent and direct threat to the United States, or to his neighbors, that the Iraqi economy is in shambles, that the Iraqi military a fraction of its former strength, and that in concert with the international community he can be contained."

The state senator from Illinois also understood that Iraq would be a sinkhole for American troops and tax dollars, stating prophetically: "I know that even a successful war against Iraq will require a U.S. occupation of undetermined length, at undetermined cost, with undetermined consequences."

Obama also thought President Bush had foolishly taken his eye off enemy number one—Osama bin Laden and the al Qaeda network, believed to be based in northern Afghanistan. "You want a fight, President Bush?" Obama asked in his 2002 speech. "Let's finish the fight with bin Laden and al Qaeda." He went on to present the many steps our country had failed to take. Foremost was sidestepping the UN and disallowing the UN inspectors to "vigorously enforce a nonproliferation treaty." Obama also condemned the administration for failing to safeguard the country's allies in the Middle East, and for failing to wean the United States off Middle East oil.

He reiterated his position two years later in his 2004 Democratic National Convention speech, stating, "When we send our young men and women into harm's way, we have a solemn obligation not to fudge the numbers or shade the truth about why they're going . . . and to never ever go to war without enough troops to win the war, secure the peace, and earn the respect of the world."

It's no surprise that by the time people started floating names for the 2008 presidential run, Obama stood out as the only serious Democratic antiwar candidate, aside from Congressman Dennis Kucinich, who had opposed the war from the beginning. John Edwards had already declared that he had made a mistake with his vote in 2002. Hillary Clinton refused to do so, standing by her vote. Despite calls from the left for her to apologize, she maintained her position throughout the primary race. This issue was the key differentiator between Obama and Clinton; it helped him draw a base of support Clinton had alienated. Day by day during the primary season, Obama's prescient view looked increasingly attractive to a growing number of Democrats.

Interestingly, Obama's stance almost cost him his keynote-speech slot at the convention. Many of Kerry's advisers thought it could bring unnecessary attention to Kerry's own nuanced stance on the war. Kerry's camp decided that the pros outweighed the cons and decided to let Obama speak, but his position didn't go unnoticed in the days leading up to his speech. The late Tim Russert, host of *Meet the Press,* asked Obama about his views on the war the Sunday before he gave his speech in Boston. Russert quoted from Obama's 2002 speech and asked, "The nominee of your party, John Kerry . . . said he [Saddam Hussein] was an imminent threat. . . . How could they [Kerry and Edwards] have been so wrong and you so right?" Obama answered carefully, "I think they have access to information that I did not have."

Russert, not satisfied with the answer, pushed again. "So you disagree with John Kerry and John Edwards?" Obama wiggled his way out, telling Russert, "As I said, I wasn't there and what is absolutely clear as we move forward is that if we don't have a change in tone and a change in administration, I think we're going to have trouble making sure that our troops are secure and that we succeed in Iraq."

This was similar to what Obama told National Public Radio at the time: "I don't consider [voting for the war] to have been an easy decision, and certainly, I wasn't in the position to actually cast a vote on it. I think that there is room for disagreement in the initial decision."[5]

Obama would continue to use similar language in the months leading up to announcing his presidential bid. In October 2006, for instance, he told David Remnick of the *New Yorker*, "I didn't have the benefit of U.S. intelligence. And for those who did, it might have led to a different set of choices."[6]

In his definitive biography, *Obama: From Promise to Power*, David Mendell, a reporter for the *Chicago Tribune*, offers a more pragmatic reason for Obama's decision to attend the antiwar rally in Federal Plaza: Bettylu Saltzman was the lead organizer of the rally, at which about a thousand people were expected.[7] According to Ryan Lizza, a staff writer for the *New Yorker*, Saltzman, a scion of a wealthy Chicago family and a well-known donor to liberal causes, gathered a group of friends at her Chicago home in mid-September and over plates of Chinese food the group decided to organize the protest. Saltzman had met Obama a decade earlier at Bill Clinton's campaign office, after he had graduated from Harvard Law School and moved back to the city to practice civil rights law. She was taken by him back then and was an early supporter of his campaign for the state legislature. It would be hard to turn down such an important figure in Illinois politics. When Bettylu called his home to invite him to speak at the rally, Obama had little choice but to accept her invitation.

Coincidentally, Saltzman was also close to the well-known Chicago media strategist David Axelrod; they regularly spoke on the phone about national and local politics and about their other love, the Chicago Bulls basketball team.[8] According to Mendell, Obama was eager to get Axelrod on his Senate campaign team. Friends told him that this speech might help him seal the deal: if Obama attended the rally organized by Axelrod's good friend Bettylu Saltzman, she would certainly lobby Axelrod. And that's exactly what happened. Although Saltzman's call to Axelrod wasn't the deciding factor—he was close to signing on with Obama anyway—it certainly didn't hurt. A few months later, Axelrod joined the campaign.

Obama didn't have any speechwriters at that point in his career. He wrote this now-famous speech himself, scratching it out longhand in a single evening. That he prepared formal remarks in advance at all was unusual—he was generally more comfortable speaking extemporaneously. But he knew just how important these remarks were and felt that it was too risky to speak off the cuff. Obama's speech was only a few minutes long, but, as he told Mendell, he thought it was his best pre-presidency speech: "I knew that this was going to be an important statement on an important issue and I didn't want it [to be] subject to misinterpretation. . . . The nice thing is, because I thought the politics of [the invasion] were bad, it was liberating—because I said exactly what I truly believed."[9]

At noon on October 2, Obama took the stage to deliver his brief remarks. Police looked on from the perimeter. As noted previously, he was not the headliner that day. Glauber later said, "We didn't quote Barack Obama [in the *Tribune*] at his famous antiwar speech. He was not the main guy."[10] Instead, Obama stayed in the background as the Reverend Jesse Jackson told the crowd, "This is a rally to stop a war from occurring." After urging the crowd to look at the sky, he continued, "I just diverted your attention away from the rally. That's what George Bush is doing. The sky is not falling and we're not threatened by Saddam Hussein." Ironically, within hours of Obama's remarks, Dennis Hastert, then Speaker of the House, introduced the resolution giving the president the authority to invade Iraq.

As far as anyone knows, Obama didn't keep his original written version. Most of the text of Obama's address was later cobbled together by his campaign from the few recordings his staff could recover. They even recreated portions of the speech for a campaign television ad, for which Obama reread the speech.

In an interview with Mendell, months after he was elected to the

Senate, Obama recalled his October speech: "That's the speech I'm most proud of. It was a hard speech to give . . . because I was about to announce for the United States Senate and the politics were hard to read. . . . And it was just, well, a well-constructed speech."[11]

Remarks by State Senator Barack Obama: Speech Against the Iraq War Resolution

Good afternoon. Let me begin by saying that although this has been billed as an antiwar rally, I stand before you as someone who is not opposed to war in all circumstances. The Civil War was one of the bloodiest in history, and yet it was only through the crucible of the sword, the sacrifice of multitudes, that we could begin to perfect this union, and drive the scourge of slavery from our soil. I don't oppose all wars.

My grandfather signed up for a war the day after Pearl Harbor was bombed, fought in Patton's army. He saw the dead and dying across the fields of Europe; he heard the stories of fellow troops who first entered Auschwitz and Treblinka. He fought in the name of a larger freedom, part of that arsenal of democracy that triumphed over evil, and he did not fight in vain. I don't oppose all wars.

After September eleventh, after witnessing the carnage and destruction, the dust and the tears, I supported this administration's pledge to hunt down and root out those who would slaughter innocents in the name of intolerance, and I would willingly take up arms myself to prevent such tragedy from happening again. I don't oppose all wars. And I know that in this crowd today, there is no shortage of patriots, or of patriotism.

What I am opposed to is a dumb war. What I am opposed to is a rash war. What I am opposed to is the cynical attempt by Richard Perle and Paul Wolfowitz and other armchair, weekend warriors in this administration to shove their own ideological agendas down our throats, irrespective of the costs in lives lost and in hardships borne.

What I am opposed to is the attempt by political hacks like Karl Rove to distract us from a rise in the uninsured, a rise in the poverty rate, a drop in the median income—to distract us from corporate scandals and a stock market that has just gone through the worst month since the Great Depression. That's what I'm opposed to. A dumb war. A rash war. A war based not on reason but on passion, not on principle but on politics. Now let me be clear— I suffer no illusions about Saddam Hussein. He is a brutal man. A ruthless man. A man who butchers his own people to secure his own power. He has repeatedly defied UN resolutions, thwarted UN inspection teams, developed chemical and biological weapons, and coveted nuclear capacity. He's a bad guy. The world, and the Iraqi people, would be better off without him.

But I also know that Saddam poses no imminent and direct threat to the United States, or to his neighbors, that the Iraqi economy is in shambles, that the Iraqi military a fraction of its former strength, and that in concert with the international community he can be contained until, in the way of all petty dictators, he falls away into the dustbin of history. I know that even a successful war against Iraq will require a U.S. occupation of undetermined length, at undetermined cost, with undetermined consequences. I know that an invasion of Iraq without a clear rationale and without strong international support will only fan the flames of the Middle East, and encourage the worst, rather than best, impulses of the Arab world, and strengthen the recruitment arm of al Qaeda. I am not opposed to all wars. I'm opposed to dumb wars.

So for those of us who seek a more just and secure world for our children, let us send a clear message to the president today. You want a fight, President Bush? Let's finish the fight with bin Laden and al Qaeda, through effective, coordinated intelligence, and a shutting down of the financial networks that support terrorism, and a homeland security program that involves more than color-coded warnings.

You want a fight, President Bush? Let's fight to make sure that the UN inspectors can do their work, and that we vigorously enforce a nonproliferation treaty, and that former enemies and current allies like Russia safeguard and ultimately eliminate their stores of nuclear material, and that nations like Pakistan and India never use the terrible weapons already in their possession, and that the arms merchants in our own country stop feeding the countless wars that rage across the globe.

You want a fight, President Bush? Let's fight to make sure our so-called allies in the Middle East, the Saudis and the Egyptians, stop oppressing their own people, and suppressing dissent, and tolerating corruption and inequality, and mismanaging their economies so that their youth grow up without education, without prospects, without hope, the ready recruits of terrorist cells.

You want a fight, President Bush? Let's fight to wean ourselves off Middle East oil, through an energy policy that doesn't simply serve the interests of Exxon and Mobil. Those are the battles that we need to fight. Those are the battles that we willingly join. The battles against ignorance and intolerance. Corruption and greed. Poverty and despair.

The consequences of war are dire, the sacrifices immeasurable. We may have occasion in our lifetime to once again rise up in defense of our freedom, and pay the wages of war. But we ought not—we will not—travel down that hellish path blindly. Nor should we allow those who would march off and pay the ultimate sacrifice, who would prove the full measure of devotion with their blood, to make such an awful sacrifice in vain.

KEYNOTE ADDRESS AT THE 2004
DEMOCRATIC NATIONAL CONVENTION

July 27, 2004 • *FleetCenter, Boston, Massachusetts*

*The pundits like to slice and dice our country into
red states and blue states. . . . But I've got news for them, too.
We worship an awesome God in the blue states, and we don't like
federal agents poking around our libraries in the red states.
We coach Little League in the blue states and have
gay friends in the red states. . . . We are one people . . .
all of us defending the United States of America.*

It's fair to say that no one could have expected what resulted from Barack Obama's prime-time speech at the July 2004 Democratic National Convention. Not the Senate candidate himself nor his two key aides and traveling companions, David Axelrod and Robert Gibbs, nor Mary Beth Cahill, the campaign manager for John Kerry, the Democratic nominee for president.

No one could have imagined how that seventeen-minute speech would catapult Obama into stardom and onto the national political stage and eventually into the White House itself. After all, no one had even heard of Barack Obama before he took the podium. On the morning of the speech, the *Philadelphia Inquirer* headlined, "Who the Heck Is This Guy?"

True, Obama had captured the attention of people in his home state and had become the leading candidate for the Illinois seat in the U.S. Senate vacated by Peter Fitzgerald, a Republican. But he had grabbed the lead only after his well-funded Republican opponent Jack Ryan dropped out of the race in the wake of a sex scandal. Having served only in the Illinois State Senate for eight years, Obama was not a national figure by any stretch. In fact, he has since reminded people that in 2000, after his failed bid for Congress, he had trouble even getting a pass onto the floor of the Democratic National Convention in Los Angeles and ended up watching the proceedings on a TV screen near the convention hall. He was so broke that the rental car facility rejected his American Express card.

Obama wrote in his 2006 book, *The Audacity of Hope*, "The process by which I was selected as keynote speaker remains something of a mystery to me."[1] In truth, there wasn't much mystery about it. The Kerry campaign had thought long and hard about whom to pick for the slot. A team of about a dozen convention organizers, including Cahill, the Massachusetts politico Jack Corrigan, and the campaign strategist Robert Shrum, considered their options. The group narrowed their list of appealing Democratic Party politicos to Governors Jennifer Granholm of Michigan, Janet Napolitano of Arizona, Tom Vilsack of Iowa, and Obama.

In the end, the campaign concluded that Obama was the politically wise choice; he would help them attract African American voters, a demographic that had been lagging in the polls. He was eloquent and youthful and delivered the right optimistic message (his campaign speeches for the U.S. Senate included the now familiar "Yes, we can"). Illinois was also a critical Senate seat. It was true that the campaign was concerned about Obama's position on the war in Iraq—Kerry had initially voted to authorize military action. But ultimately, as Cahill put it, "I was convinced he was going to be the best."[2]

Plus, on a personal level, Kerry and Obama had hit it off during a joint campaign swing in spring 2004, first at a vocational center on Chicago's West Side and then at a downtown fund-raiser at the Hyatt Regency Hotel. According to David Mendell, there was a clear rapport between the two: "It's Kerry kind of looking at him and picking up tricks from the rookie."[3]

Obama and his aides had pursued the speaking slot with intensity and purpose. The team composed an eight-minute video that included excerpts from Obama's Illinois Senate primary victory speech and campaign photos set to music from the documentary movie *When We Were Kings*, featuring Muhammad Ali. And Gibbs, a former Kerry campaign staffer, worked the phones to his former colleagues. They knew the promising history of past keynote speakers, including Franklin D. Roosevelt, who delivered rousing nomination speeches for Alfred

E. Smith in 1924 and 1928, and Bill Clinton, who introduced Governor Michael Dukakis in 1988. Even though Hubert Humphrey, Barbara Jordan, and Mario Cuomo didn't ascend to the presidency, their convention speeches have become important historical footnotes: Humphrey delivered a fiery defense of civil rights in 1948; Barbara Jordan was the first black woman to deliver a keynote speech in 1976; Cuomo's 1984 "Tale of Two Cities" speech, about rich and poor in America, received critical acclaim.

Barack Obama began working on his speech in early July, as soon as Cahill delivered the good news that he had been chosen. Without missing a beat, Obama turned to his aides and delivered a clear message: he would write this speech. According to Gibbs, "He wanted to write this speech . . . in a way that was personal." Axelrod later commented, "Almost immediately he said to me, 'I know what I want to do. I want to talk about my story as part of the American story.'"[4]

Obama toiled away on the draft assiduously, at all hours of the day and night, up until a week before the convention, when the convention speechwriting team demanded to see a copy. He wrote one version after another, scribbling lines on scraps of paper, on the corners of envelopes, on yellow legal pads, and on the top of memos from his aides. Obama tested lines from the speech on everyone, from crowds at his campaign events to his state senate colleagues. At one point, after coming up with a new idea, he went and sat on a stool in the bathroom off the Illinois General Assembly floor to write it down. According to one former campaign aide, David Katz, "We'd finish [the senate day] at nine or ten p.m. and he'd write till one or two in the morning."[5]

The Kerry staff gave Obama eight minutes of speaking time. Obama's first draft was twenty-five minutes, so he sent drafts back and forth to his aides; they'd cut out lines and he'd invariably add them back into the text.

The Kerry campaign was a little anxious about what Obama's speech would say; he was still an unknown quantity. Vicky Rideout, the convention's chief speechwriter, had been expecting a draft in mid-July and it was getting late.

But the moment Rideout received and read the draft, she knew they had a hit. At seventeen minutes the speech was longer than they had asked for, but it didn't matter. Rideout asked to take out one line, but otherwise accepted the speech as it was submitted.[6]

Obama arrived in Boston the evening before his first rehearsal at the FleetCenter. Gibbs had scheduled a flurry of interviews, including a one-on-one with Tim Russert for *Meet the Press*—so many, in fact, that Obama started to lose his voice.

Obama had never used a TelePrompter when he went to his first rehearsal. According to Mendell, "Obama was kind of winging it—that is how he was doing things back then."[7] But this was different. Michael Sheehan, a veteran speech coach, offered Obama his standard tips, including how to handle the three competing audiences the night of the speech—the screaming party delegates in the hall, the giant JumboTron screen that would beam his image and words out to the far reaches of the hall, and the millions sitting in front of their television sets.

Obama had three hour-long rehearsals at the practice podium in front of blue velvet curtains in what was normally the Celtics locker room. His initial run-throughs weren't particularly strong; he seemed to be adjusting to his new setting. But he soon found his groove. Jon Favreau, then working as Kerry's speechwriter, who later became Obama's chief speechwriter, remembered watching his future boss and being awestruck by his passion and charisma. He knew immediately that Obama was different from everyone else he had watched rehearse that week.

Unfortunately, Favreau also had to deliver some tough news to the future senator. One of the lines from Obama's text was virtually identical to one in Kerry's acceptance speech. Obama's draft read: "We're not red states and blue states; we're all Americans, standing up together for the red, white, and blue." Kerry's speech included the line, "Maybe some just see us divided into those red states and blue states, but I see us as one America: red, white, and blue."

After Favreau told Obama that he would have to drop the line, Obama replied peevishly, "Are you telling me I have to take this line out?" Favreau remembered stuttering, unsure how to respond. Axelrod could see that Obama was frustrated, so he grabbed Favreau, quickly introduced himself, and asked him to step out into the hallway where they could discuss the line.

The two spent the next few minutes rewriting the sentence, changing it to: "We are one people, all of us pledging allegiance to the stars and stripes, all of us defending the United States of America." Axelrod and Favreau had nipped the problem in the bud before it erupted into a larger issue. At the time, neither knew that it would be the first of many such collaborations between them.

Obama awoke at 6:00 a.m. the day of the speech. After a big breakfast, a rally sponsored by the League of Conservation Voters, and a quick lunch gobbled down between interviews, Obama retired to his room for a breather. The break didn't last long. There was a last-minute crisis. His wife, Michelle, didn't like his tie, so Axelrod grabbed Gibbs's tie literally off his neck.

When Obama finally made it into the car that would ferry him to the FleetCenter, he relaxed the way he knew best. He called his grandmother, Madelyn, in Hawaii, and his two daughters, Sasha and Malia.

With a sea of Democrats cheering him on, and millions more watching on television, Barack Obama walked onto the national stage—literally and figuratively—beaming from ear to ear. From his vantage point in front of the crowd, all he could see was a sea of placards with "Obama" painted on them. For seventeen minutes Obama mesmerized his audience, first with his biography and then with a ringing endorsement of John Kerry—2,297 words in all. He told America the meaning of his African name, Barack: "blessed"; he spoke about the importance of bipartisanship and the need to provide opportunity to all Americans.

His delivery started slowly and was a little stiff. His long-time Chicago friend Valerie Jarrett was so nervous that she "was digging [her] nails into [her] hands." But then, Rideout recalls, a metaphorical light bulb went on. "His shoulders settled down and this wave of support from the crowd looked like it literally washed over him. . . . Something happened to him physically."[8] His polish, poise, and preacher-like cadences drew in the crowd. It was clear that he was comfortable in his own skin, unlike so many other politicians. One of his Harvard Law professors, Christopher Edley, later said, "He was almost freakishly self-possessed and centered. . . . He doesn't strive for an Everyman quality: he is relaxed but never chummy, gracious rather than familiar. His surface is so smooth, his movements so easy and fluid, his voice so consistent and well pitched that he can seem like an actor playing a politician, too implausibly effortless to be doing it for real."[9] Democratic strategist Stephanie Cutter recalled the evening and his energy, saying, "I remember standing behind him and watching his feet move. It was like he was dancing at the podium. His feet were moving to the rhythm of the speech."[10]

Obama was interrupted with applause thirty-three times. The reviews were unanimous: it was a barnburner. People immediately compared his oratorical skills to those of John Kennedy, Ronald Reagan, and Martin Luther King Jr. He was mobbed by crowds, not just that evening, but also every day thereafter. The throngs at his senate campaign events regularly shot up from hundreds to thousands. His political future would be forever changed. As Senator Dick Durbin of Illinois put it, "Without that Boston speech, there is a question whether Barack would be . . . [president] today. His public image changed because of that speech."[11]

REMARKS OF STATE SENATOR BARACK OBAMA: KEYNOTE ADDRESS AT THE 2004 DEMOCRATIC NATIONAL CONVENTION

On behalf of the great state of Illinois, crossroads of a nation, land of Lincoln, let me express my deep gratitude for the privilege of addressing this convention. Tonight is a particular honor for me because, let's face it, my presence on this stage is pretty unlikely. My father was a foreign student, born and raised in a small village in Kenya. He grew up herding goats, went to school in a tin-roof shack. His father, my grandfather, was a cook, a domestic servant.

But my grandfather had larger dreams for his son. Through hard work and perseverance my father got a scholarship to study in a magical place: America, which stood as a beacon of freedom and opportunity to so many who had come before. While studying here, my father met my mother. She was born in a town on the other side of the world, in Kansas. Her father worked on oil rigs and farms through most of the Depression. The day after Pearl Harbor he signed up for duty, joined Patton's army and marched across Europe. Back home, my grandmother raised their baby and went to work on a bomber assembly line. After the war, they studied on the G.I. Bill, bought a house through FHA, and moved west in search of opportunity.

And they too had big dreams for their daughter, a common dream, born of two continents. My parents shared not only an improbable love; they shared an abiding faith in the possibilities of this nation. They would give me an African name, Barack, or "blessed," believing that in a tolerant America your name is no barrier to success. They imagined me going to the best schools in the land, even though they weren't rich, because in a generous America you don't have to be rich to achieve your potential. They are both passed away now. Yet, I know that, on this night, they look down on me with pride.

I stand here today, grateful for the diversity of my heritage, aware that my parents' dreams live on in my precious daughters. I stand here knowing that my story is part of the larger American story, that I owe a debt to all of those who came before me, and that in no other country on earth is my story even possible. Tonight, we gather to affirm the greatness of our nation, not because of the height of our skyscrapers, or the power of our military, or the size of our economy. Our pride is based on a very simple premise, summed up in a declaration made over two hundred years ago, "We hold these truths to be self-evident, that all men are created equal. That they are endowed by their Creator with certain inalienable rights. That among these are life, liberty, and the pursuit of happiness."

That is the true genius of America, a faith in the simple dreams of its people, the insistence on small miracles. That we can tuck in our children at night and know they are fed and clothed and safe from harm. That we can say what we think, write what we think, without hearing a sudden knock on the door. That we can have an idea and start our own business without paying a bribe or hiring somebody's son. That we can participate in the political process without fear of retribution, and that our votes will be counted—or at least, most of the time.

This year, in this election, we are called to reaffirm our values and commitments, to hold them against a hard reality and see how we are measuring up, to the legacy of our forebearers, and the promise of future generations. And fellow Americans—Democrats, Republicans, independents—I say to you tonight: we have more work to do. More to do for the workers I met in Galesburg, Illinois, who are losing their union jobs at the Maytag plant that's moving to Mexico, and now are having to compete with their own children for jobs that pay seven bucks an hour. More to do for the father I met who was losing his job and choking back tears, wondering how he would pay $4,500 a month for the drugs his son needs without the health benefits he counted on. More to do for the young woman in East St. Louis, and thousands more like her, who has the grades, has the drive, has the will, but doesn't have the money to go to college.

Don't get me wrong. The people I meet in small towns and big cities, in diners and office parks, they don't expect government to solve all their problems. They know they have to work hard to get ahead and they want to. Go into the collar counties around Chicago, and people will tell you they don't want their tax money wasted by a welfare agency or the Pentagon. Go into any inner city neighborhood, and folks will tell you that government alone can't teach kids to learn. They know that parents have to parent, that children can't achieve unless we raise their expectations and turn off the television sets and eradicate the slander that says a black youth with a book is acting white. No, people don't expect government to solve all their problems. But they sense, deep in their bones, that with just a change in priorities, we can make sure that every child in America has a decent shot at life, and that the doors of opportunity remain open to all. They know we can do better. And they want that choice.

In this election, we offer that choice. Our party has chosen a man to lead us who embodies the best this country has to offer. That man is John Kerry. John Kerry understands the ideals of community, faith, and sacrifice, because they've defined his life. From his heroic service in Vietnam to his years as prosecutor and lieutenant governor, through two decades in the United States Senate, he has devoted himself to this country. Again and again, we've seen him make tough choices when easier ones were available. His values and his record affirm what is best in us.

John Kerry believes in an America where hard work is rewarded. So instead of offering tax breaks to companies shipping jobs overseas, he'll offer them to companies creating jobs here at home. John Kerry believes in an America where all Americans can afford the same health coverage our politicians in Washington have for themselves. John Kerry believes in energy independence, so we aren't held hostage to the profits of oil companies or the sabotage of foreign oil fields. John Kerry believes in the constitutional freedoms that have made our country the envy of the world, and he will never sacrifice our basic liberties nor use faith as a wedge to divide us. And John Kerry believes that in a dangerous world, war must be an option, but it should never be the first option.

A while back, I met a young man named Shamus at the VFW Hall in East Moline, Illinois. He was a good-looking kid, six-two or six-three, clear-eyed, with an easy smile. He told me he'd joined the Marines and was heading to Iraq the following week. As I listened to him explain why he'd enlisted, his absolute faith in our country and its leaders, his devotion to duty and service, I thought this young man was all any of us might hope for in a child. But then I asked myself: Are we serving Shamus as well as he was serving us? I thought of more than nine hundred servicemen and -women, sons and daughters, husbands and wives, friends and neighbors, who will not be returning to their hometowns. I thought of families I had met who were struggling to get by without a loved one's full income, or whose loved ones had returned with a limb missing or with nerves shattered, but who still lacked long-term health benefits because they were reservists. When we send our young men and women into harm's way, we have a solemn obligation not to fudge the numbers or shade the truth about why they're going, to care for their families while they're gone, to tend to the soldiers upon their return, and to never ever go to war without enough troops to win the war, secure the peace, and earn the respect of the world.

Now let me be clear. We have real enemies in the world. These enemies must be found. They must be pursued and they must be defeated. John Kerry knows this. And just as Lieutenant Kerry did not hesitate to risk his life to protect the men who served with him in Vietnam, President Kerry will not hesitate one moment to use our military might to keep America safe and secure. John Kerry believes in America. And he knows it's not enough for just some of us to prosper. For alongside our famous individualism, there's another ingredient in the American saga.

A belief that we are connected as one people. If there's a child on the South Side of Chicago who can't read, that matters to me, even if it's not my child. If there's a senior citizen somewhere who can't pay for her prescription and has to choose between medicine and the rent, that makes my life poorer, even if it's not my grandmother. If there's an Arab American family being rounded up without benefit of an attorney or due process, that threatens my civil liberties. It's that fundamental belief—I am my brother's keeper, I am my sister's keeper—that makes this country work. It's what allows us to pursue our individual dreams, yet still come together as a single American family. "E pluribus unum." Out of many, one.

Yet even as we speak, there are those who are preparing to divide us, the spin masters and negative ad peddlers who embrace the politics of anything goes. Well, I say to them tonight, there's not a liberal America and a conservative America—there's the United States of America. There's not a black America and white America and Latino America and Asian America; there's the United States of America. The pundits like to slice and dice our country into red states and blue states; red states for Republicans, blue states for Democrats. But I've got news for them, too. We worship an awesome God in the blue states, and we don't like federal agents poking around our libraries in the red states. We coach Little League in the blue states and have gay friends in the red states. There are patriots who opposed the war in Iraq and patriots who supported it. We are one people, all of us pledging allegiance to the stars and stripes, all of us defending the United States of America.

In the end, that's what this election is about. Do we participate in a politics of cynicism or a politics of hope? John Kerry calls on us to hope. John Edwards calls on us to hope. I'm not talking about blind optimism here—the almost willful ignorance that thinks unemployment will go away if we just don't talk about it, or the health care crisis will solve itself if we just ignore it. No, I'm talking about something more substantial. It's the hope of slaves sitting around a fire singing freedom songs; the hope of immigrants setting out for distant shores; the hope of a young naval lieutenant bravely patrolling the Mekong Delta; the hope of a millworker's son who dares to defy the odds; the hope of a skinny kid with a funny name who believes that America has a place for him, too. The audacity of hope!

In the end, that is God's greatest gift to us, the bedrock of this nation; the belief in things not seen; the belief that there are better days ahead. I believe we can give our middle class relief and provide working families with a road to opportunity. I believe we can provide jobs to the jobless, homes to the homeless, and reclaim young people in cities across America from violence and despair. I believe that as we stand on the crossroads of history, we can make the right choices, and meet the challenges that face us. America!

Tonight, if you feel the same energy I do, the same urgency I do, the same passion I do, the same hopefulness I do—if we do what we must do, then I have no doubt that all across the country, from Florida to Oregon, from Washington to Maine, the people will rise up in November, and John Kerry will be sworn in as president, and John Edwards will be sworn in as vice president, and this country will reclaim its promise, and out of this long political darkness a brighter day will come. Thank you and God bless you.

3

UNITED STATES SENATE VICTORY SPEECH

November 2, 2004 • Hyatt Ballroom, Chicago, Illinois

*And for those skeptics who believe that we can't accomplish
what we set out to accomplish, if our minds are clear and our heart is pure
and we believe in a just and merciful God, I say to them
look at this crowd tonight, look at this election today, and I have
three words for them ... Yes, we can.*

In many ways Barack Obama's Senate victory speech was anticlimactic.
By Election Day 2004, it was clear that he would win the election—and
would do so with comfortable margins.

What was significant about the night was that he was standing at the
rostrum at all. Earlier that year, few believed that the three-term state
senator and law school professor would spend the evening of November 2,
2004, surrounded by hundreds of adoring supporters, his wife, Michelle,
and his two young daughters, as the senator-elect from Illinois.

Few had turned out for his announcement speech in a small room at
the Hotel Allegro on January 21, 2003. At that point, no one thought
he'd win the Democratic primary—or even make a competitive showing.
Early on there had been rumors that former senator Carol Moseley-Braun
wanted to recapture her seat from the sitting Republican senator, Peter
Fitzgerald, who had bested her six years earlier. Moseley-Braun had been
the first African American woman in the Senate, but her first term was
marred by scandal. Her boyfriend, Kgosie Matthews, had been accused of
sexual harassment; there were rumors that she had spent taxpayer money
on clothing and jewelry and that she had met with the former dictator of
Nigeria, Sani Abacha, despite U.S. sanctions forbidding doing so. Still, if
Moseley-Braun ran, she would have a lock on liberals and blacks, preclud-
ing any chance of an Obama victory.

Fitzgerald was in trouble early on. He had spent $13 million in 1998
to become the youngest member of the U.S. Senate. But since then, he

had alienated large swaths of the Republican Party establishment with, as one author put it, his "maverick, outspoken approach."[1] Lacking party support and unwilling, for the second time, to invest millions of his own money into a campaign, Fitzgerald announced in April 2003 that he would not seek re-election.

On January 17, 2003, after weeks of deliberation, Moseley-Braun decided to skip the Senate and make a run for the presidency. The young and impatient Obama saw an opportunity. As his Harvard Law School classmate Christine Spurell noted, "It was clear to me from the day I met him that he was thinking of politics."[2] This was his moment.

Still, some close to Obama thought it was unwise and urged him to wait. After all, four years earlier he had decided to run against the incumbent, Bobby Rush, for Illinois's First Congressional District seat, and had lost by more than thirty percentage points. At the time, one Chicago political reporter asked on the radio, "Is Obama dead?"[3]

According to Obama's biographer David Mendell, back then Obama had miscalculated what it would take to win. Rush was well liked in his district. Obama had assumed that Rush was vulnerable as a result of Obama's support from high-profile members of the liberal establishment, including the well-connected federal judge Abner Mikva, and of Rush's poor showing in the 1999 Chicago mayoral race against Richard Daley. But Obama hadn't yet achieved enough in Springfield or "curried enough favor with the right interests" in the state legislature.[4]

After he announced his candidacy, Obama conducted a poll; Rush's name recognition was 90 percent, Obama's just 11. Rush's approval rating was close to 70 percent, Obama's was 8. As Obama later wrote in *The Audacity of Hope,* "I learned one of the cardinal rules of modern politics: Do the poll before you announce."

Mendell summarized Obama's weaknesses at that time in his political career: "Obama was too fond of reciting his impressive resume, too often mentioned that he had forsaken a high-priced law firm for public office and too often spoke in the high-minded prose of a constitutional law lecturer, all of which would make him appear condescending to his audience." This approach might have worked in wealthier areas such as Hyde Park, but it didn't resonate with the working-class sections of the city. In the end he was "spanked," commented Mendell.[5]

Still, despite his failure in 2000, a number of Obama's colleagues in the legislature argued that he should make a run for the Senate. But it wasn't their support he needed—it was Michelle's. Without her firmly in his corner, there would be no campaign. After all, he was just settling back into normal family life after a tumultuous congressional campaign that had strained their marriage. Plus, he had accrued massive credit card debt, and he and Michelle both still had unpaid law school loans. But the window was open now, much as it would be for the presidency several years later. What would he get from waiting?

For his Senate run, unlike his run for the House, Obama spent a good deal of time mapping out his path. He returned to the state senate, put his head down, and went to work on the issues that would help him in a statewide race. In 2000, for the first time in a decade, Democrats had taken charge of the state legislature, and Obama now had a chance to shine. He networked with the key members of the General Assembly, including Terry Link, Larry Walsh, and others in the Black Caucus, such as his political mentor Emil Jones Jr., a powerful Democratic leader. He told Jones, "I want to work." Jones noted, "He's always someone who has wanted . . . to champion causes. He's always been that way."[6]

With Jones's help, Obama cosponsored nearly eight hundred bills, many of which would help him win over key constituency groups in the Senate campaign. The legislation spanned the gamut, from tough anticrime bills to those that improved health care for children and the elderly. It didn't hurt that Obama had already spent several years reaching across the aisle, making friends and building coalitions at a weekly bipartisan poker game. This was particularly important when he first arrived in Springfield, since Democrats were then in the minority, in a state controlled by a Republican governor. His early outreach helped him get votes throughout his time in Springfield.

But ultimately, it was his relationship with Jones that helped Obama seal the deal in his Senate race. Jones gave Obama the street credibility he needed with the African American community, which had been a vulnerability in his race against Rush. But Obama knew that wouldn't be enough to win—he'd need to earn widespread support from whites as well. Rush doubted his former opponent could do so and actually endorsed one of Obama's white Senate opponents, Blair Hull, because, as he put it, he "no longer believes that being black is a necessary criteria for representing a largely black constituency. . . . The [criterion] is whether or not we can be successful on Election Day. . . . I try to not lead my people off a cliff or into a roadblock"[7]

It was an understandable choice, given that Obama's legislative district covered largely tonier white areas of Chicago, including Hyde Park and the University of Chicago, and much of his financial support came from the likes of Bettylu Saltzman and others in the city's liberal white establishment. Rush had demeaned these connections during his own campaign against Obama, telling one reporter, "Barack Obama went to Harvard and became an educated fool. Barack is a person who read about the civil rights protests and thinks he knows all about it."[8] He wasn't alone in this assessment. Laura Washington in the *Chicago Sun-Times* asked whether Obama was "too smart, too reserved, and perceived as too elitist for regular black folk. . . . Some of the black nationalists are whispering that 'Barack is not black enough. . . . He's of mixed race, he hangs out in Hyde Park, and is a darling of white progressives.'"[9]

Given that one in five primary voters was African American, Obama knew that he would have to nail down most of the liberal and black voters in the Democratic primary, something he had failed to do during his campaign against Rush.

The other necessary ingredient to his success was securing the media consultant David Axelrod to work with him. "Ax," as his friends called him, was a former *Chicago Tribune* reporter who had transitioned into political consulting. Not only did Ax know everyone in the media and the liberal establishment, but his involvement represented a certain political seal of approval. He had also helped other African American candidates— Deval Patrick in Massachusetts and Michael White in Cleveland—win over broad white support in their winning campaigns.

As he later admitted, Axelrod almost signed on to work for one of Obama's chief primary opponents, the multimillionaire and political newcomer Blair Hull. Hull amassed his fortune as a professional blackjack player and later as a securities trader on Wall Street, and he committed early on to spending tens of millions of his own dollars on his campaign. He wasn't shy about spending money: he hired numerous consultants (twenty-eight in all), paid his staff far beyond market rate (his campaign manager earned

$20,000 a month), and purchased large blocks of television time, billboards, and Internet space to run campaign ads; ultimately he spent $28.6 million of his own fortune. Hull's strategy was to drive his polling numbers to at least 30 percent early on and force his competitors out of the race.

The other serious contenders were Gery Chico, the former president of the Chicago Board of Education and an ex-aide to Mayor Richard Daley; Maria Pappas, the Cook County treasurer; Joyce Washington, a health care consultant; Nancy Skinner, host of a show on liberal talk radio; and Illinois's comptroller, Dan Hynes, the son of a powerful ward alderman. Hynes was the presumptive frontrunner going into the race, although Hull was on his tail from the very beginning. Hynes had been the youngest comptroller in the state's history and had an early lock on labor support, including the endorsement of nearly every trade union in Illinois.

The one missing arrow in Hull's quiver was Axelrod. The problem was that despite the millions Axelrod would have made off of Hull's campaign, he and Hull just didn't click. Hull was cold and awkward and consistently evaded Axelrod's questions. Moreover, Axelrod was nervous about the skeletons rumored to be in Hull's closet—secrets that ultimately destroyed his campaign: Hull, it was reported, had used cocaine, sought treatment for alcohol abuse, and physically and emotionally abused his ex-wife (he had been married three times). One of his ex-wives, Brenda Sexton, filed for and was a granted a restraining order against him.[10]

Axelrod signed on with Obama and put his Rolodex to work in Illinois and in Washington. He also convinced the Beltway direct-mail guru Pete Giangreco to join the operation. The campaign's first full-time hire was Nate Tamarin, the son of a Chicago union organizer. Soon thereafter Obama hired Jim Cauley as his campaign manager. Raised in Kentucky's Pike County, Cauley had managed Baltimore Mayor Martin O'Malley's campaign and had worked at the Democratic Congressional Campaign Committee.

The campaign set up shop in a modest office in Chicago's Loop district. Soon, Obama had the support of Reverend Jesse Jackson Sr., who called Obama "the light that challenges the darkness." Then, in what was a major boost to his campaign, the Service Employees International Union (SEIU) endorsed him. Obama had developed a working relationship with the SEIU leadership as chairman of the State Senate's Health

Committee. After the nod from SEIU, Obama received endorsements from the American Federation of State, County and Municipal Employees and the Chicago Teachers' Union. This was a major blow to Hynes, who was already under pressure from voters for his support of President Bush and the decision to invade Iraq.

It wasn't an easy primary fight. Obama was in third place from the outset, and in December 2003, just four months before the primary, he was still ten points behind Hynes in the polls. Hull, only a couple of points behind Hynes, continued to spend his fortune on television commercials. Obama was barely mentioned as a serious contender.

But even as he trailed, Obama remained a formidable fund-raiser, tapping members of the Pritzker family, worth billions of dollars, and the philanthropist Newton Minow, who had advised Presidents Kennedy and Johnson. In all, Obama raised $14 million during the campaign (in his 1998 congressional race he had amassed an impressive $500,000).

As the saying goes, in politics, anything can change overnight. After Mendell and a fellow *Tribune* writer, Eric Zorn, published stories detailing accounts of Hull's divorce, a growing chorus demanded that the candidate unseal his divorce records, which Hull petitioned the court to preempt. When it was clear that he would lose his petition in court, Hull released the documents—and it wasn't a pretty picture. In one account, Hull's ex-wife alleged that he "hung on the canopy bar of my bed, leered at me and stated, 'Do you want to die? I am going to kill you.'"[11] Then there was the cocaine and alcohol abuse (ironically, Obama had admitted to cocaine use, but had "inoculated" himself politically against a scandal by admitting it years earlier in *Dreams from My Father*). Hull didn't drop out of the race right away, but his candidacy was clearly over.

That left Hynes as the front-runner and Obama as the only remaining serious contender. Hynes's strategy was to play it safe, keeping his head below the parapet and out of the press and hoping he could coast into the primary. The problem was that after Obama's labor endorsements, his star was on the rise. Axelrod was playing hard and playing for keeps. And together, they were running a very smart campaign.

Obama's primary message was perfectly suited to Illinois Democrats. In his announcement speech, he invoked the biblical story of David and

Goliath, which was appropriate given his newcomer "David" status on the statewide political scene.

Obama captured the sentiment of the moment: "I don't have personal wealth or a famous name," he said, referring to Hull and Hynes, "but I have a fire in my belly for fairness and justice. . . . I believe with all my heart, we would have a far better chance to bring about such change with a United States Senate that truly reflects the people—all the people—it's elected to serve."

He also spoke of his strong record of "standing up for people who most need a voice," noting, "In the Illinois Senate, I led the fight for tax relief for the working poor. I fought for and won greater funding and legislation to combat juvenile crime. I have been the leader in working to extend health coverage to the uninsured, and move people from welfare to work."

He echoed this same point in a speech several months later: "When it comes to Washington, we just assume that the game is fixed for the powerful, for the special interests. . . . The essence of this campaign is for us to no longer accept the unacceptable, to raise the bar, to set a new set of standards, to start thinking differently about what is possible in our communities and in our politics."

Few journalists had covered Obama's announcement speech back in January 2003. So now, late in the primary process, with Hull out of the race, Obama was suddenly a fresh face—and reporters weren't tired of him as they were of Hynes. They had someone new to fall in love with.

Axelrod gave them plenty to like. With internal campaign polling in hand, Axelrod honed Obama's message. According to Mendell, Axelrod realized that Obama's résumé was chock full of information that would resonate with journalists and voters. The fact that Obama was the first black president of the *Harvard Law Review* resonated with white voters; his record of reaching across the aisle to Republicans appealed to downstate conservatives; his experience as a community organizer and his legislative work on health care for underprivileged children appealed to African Americans.[12]

Axelrod captured Obama's story and his vision in a theme that the candidate would repeat time and again on the stump and would appear in countless television ads: "Yes, we can." After all, Obama embodied the impossible—a black community organizer who could rise up from obscurity and win a United States Senate seat. Interestingly, Obama was actually opposed to the concept at first; he thought it was a bit of a cliché. But he eventually came around, finishing his political ads with, "Now they say we can't change Washington? I'm Barack Obama and I am running for the United States Senate to say, 'Yes, we can.'"

In one ad, he used footage of the former Illinois senator Paul Simon, who died just days before a planned public endorsement. Simon was beloved in the state and seen as a true reformer. Axelrod's ad overlaid images of Simon with the following narration: "There have been moments in our history when hope defeated cynicism, when the power of people triumphed over money and machines. . . . [Barack Obama has a] proven record of spirited, principled and effective leadership." His message to voters in that ad was almost identical to the one Obama would use in his presidential campaign years later, when he would once again employ phrases such as "when hope defeated cynicism."

Thanks in part to this new series of paid media and to a bevy of free press, Obama's poll numbers skyrocketed, particularly among African Americans (according to Mendell, his favorability numbers went from 15 to 50 percent in one week). The Obama campaign could scarcely handle the influx of college-age volunteers—the leading edge of a continuing trend. Hynes, on the other hand, was stagnating. His cautious approach and a series of ineffective ads weren't helping. And with each day, with each speech, Obama's popularity only continued to climb.

On the night of the primary, Obama paced anxiously around the room in the downtown Hyatt Hotel. Hundreds of his friends and supporters approached him to shake his hand and offer a congratulatory hug, but Obama wasn't ready to celebrate just yet. As the results came in, however, it was clear that he didn't have much to worry about. He wasn't just winning; he was doing so convincingly. To the surprise of the media and his staff, he captured white wards and precincts across the city and in the suburbs. When all was said and done, he took 53 percent of the vote to Hynes's 24 percent and Hull's 11. It was a blowout—and Obama didn't just win over big-city blacks and liberals; he took one in four Democratic votes outside of the city. Obama told his supporters that night, "At its best, the idea of this party has been that we are going to expand opportunity and include people that have not been included . . . and embrace people from the outside and bring them inside, and give them a piece of the American dream."

Within days, Obama's star began to rise in the national firmament. His former nemesis, Congressman Bobby Rush, came out to support him. He was on the cover of the *New Republic* and the main attraction on the Washington fund-raising circuit, including at the home of his future rival for the Democratic presidential nomination, Senator Hillary Clinton.

His chief Republican opponent in the general election was Jack Ryan, a young, handsome, and independently wealthy businessman. Obama quickly moved toward the center, in the hope of wooing moderates as well as liberals. He also hired a new troop of professional campaign staffers, including Robert Gibbs as his communications director; Gibbs had recently left the Kerry presidential campaign.

In yet another serendipitous circumstance for the Obama campaign, Ryan, like Hull, also had a divorce mess on his hands. He and his ex-wife, the Hollywood starlet Jeri Ryan, had sealed a section of their divorce papers, claiming it was to protect their young son. But other rumors about Ryan's sexual proclivities started to circulate. The public pressure was too much, and like Hull months earlier, Ryan was forced to release court papers relating to his divorce during a press conference. The files showed that he had voyeuristic tendencies and regularly tried to coerce his wife to "have sex with him . . . with another couple watching." Within weeks, the Republican establishment forced Ryan out of the race. One Illinois paper declared, "Press digs in and Ryan pulls out of Senate race."[13]

It's no wonder that some years later, a *Washington Post* headline labeled this phase of Obama's rise and his ascent to presidential candidate "A Series of Fortunate Events." David Axelrod told the *Washingtonian,* "He knows that he may be the best politician in America, but he also knows that in 2004 he was one of the luckiest."[14]

After weeks of public infighting over who would replace Ryan as the Republican candidate, the Illinois GOP turned to another African American political activist, Alan Keyes, a right-wing talk show host who had twice run for president. Keyes was a true firebrand who relied on faith-based moralistic and often inflammatory language to court voters. He immediately launched a bitter attack against Obama, questioning his commitment to Christianity and even accusing him of "genocide," because of his position on abortion.

But no amount of bombast would slow Obama down. The momentum was undoubtedly on Obama's side. After some lobbying in early June, Obama received a call from John Kerry's campaign manager, Mary Beth Cahill, inviting him to deliver the keynote address at the 2004 Democratic Convention. This was a huge opportunity for the soon-to-be junior senator from Illinois to launch himself on to the national stage. When July rolled around, he batted the ball out of the park.

Literally overnight—on July 28, the day after the speech—Obama was a national phenomenon. Crowds surfaced everywhere he went. The Democratic establishment and the media couldn't get enough of him. After Boston, the autobiography that he had published in 1995 became an immediate best seller; in fact, his publisher ordered a new print run of 85,000 copies within days of his speech.

But Obama didn't let up. After returning from Boston, he and his family embarked on a grueling sixteen-hundred-mile tour across Illinois, covering thirty-nine cities in just five days, making eight stops a day. At every stop, he was mobbed. Hundreds of people were showing up at campaign stops in small towns where only dozens had appeared before. But the state senator and his team didn't let all the hoopla go to their heads. They were careful to remember that he was running for a seat in Illinois, not for national office. "The reason I was there [in Boston] was because of you, the voters of Illinois," he said on the stump in one small, rural town.

By the time he got to Chicago for Election Day, polling showed that that two-thirds of Illinois voters supported him; Keyes was pulling less than one quarter. Obama's numbers were so strong in the weeks leading up to the election that he was able to spend part of the fall campaigning around the country for other candidates. So it ultimately wasn't much of a surprise that he won, though his margin of victory—70-to-29-percent—marked the largest margin in Illinois Senate history.

Obama spent most of election night waiting for the returns in a hotel room with his wife and two daughters until it was time to snake his way down to the packed Hyatt ballroom to thank his supporters and declare victory. Dozens of reporters packed the media risers in the back of the room, including journalists from as far away as Kenya. Michelle Obama and their pastor, the Reverend Jeremiah Wright, were the only ones to speak before him.

As he had done for most of the campaign, Obama drafted his own remarks. His speech didn't include much new rhetoric—it was mainly a rehash of his best language from the stump—and he spent a good chunk of his opening moments thanking a long list of friends and family, beginning with Wright. Many of the television stations actually cut away before the senator-elect even got to the body of his remarks.

Unlike many other politicians, Obama had a firm grip on his vision; he could clearly articulate why he was running and what he hoped to accomplish. That is what he spent the bulk of his address doing. He started by calling for a new approach in Washington—for unity across partisan lines. This was a theme that would become the core of his presidential campaign message: "We've show[n] . . . that all of us can disagree without being disagreeable; that we can set aside the scorched-earth politics, the slash and burn of the politics of the past. . . . We can look forward to the future. We can build step by step to ensure that we arrive at the practical common sense solutions that all of us hope for."

Of course, it didn't hurt that, given the circumstances, Obama had the luxury of running a completely positive campaign, as he put it, "without negative ads and without the normal partisan politics and just focusing on the issues that matter." Part of that, of course, was the fortuity of the race—a scandal-ridden primary opponent and a flaccid general election foe. Obama never had to use a battering ram and was able, as he said, paraphrasing Abraham Lincoln, "to appeal to the better angels of our nature." Many agreed with political scientist Ron Walters's assessment: "How many people get elected to the U.S. Senate without having a single negative ad against them? You could argue that if the Republicans had had a viable candidate, there would be no Barack."[15]

The policy agenda Obama outlined that night and that he had discussed throughout the campaign presaged the agenda of his presidential campaign two years later. He spoke about access to and affordability of health care, about the need to create more good-paying jobs for Americans and ship fewer jobs overseas, about restoring America's reputation in the world, and about the importance of improving education for all children.

As he would often do in the years ahead, Obama emphasized the balance between personal responsibility and the proper role for government: "We don't expect government to solve all our problems. . . . [W]e have to teach our own children initiative and self-respect and a sense of family and faith and community. But what we also know is that government can help provide us with the basic tools we need to live out the American dream."

Obama, then forty-three, told his well-wishers about a 104-year-old African American woman named Margaret Lewis whom he had met on the campaign trail. He spoke about how, over the course of Mrs. Lewis's life, America had changed in ways that no one could have predicted in 1899, when she was born "in the shadow of slavery . . . in the midst of Jim Crow." Over the years, Margaret had witnessed the advent of the automobile, the Great Depression, two world wars, bus boycotts, the end of legal segregation, and passage of the Civil Rights and Voting Rights Acts in 1964 and 1965. "She still believes," Obama said, "that her voice matters, that her life counts, that her story is sacred, just like the story of every person in this room. . . . The history of so many people building calloused hand by calloused hand, brick by brick, a better future for our children."

Obama used Margaret's story to make a larger point: "There are people today right now who are as skeptical about the future as they were at the outset of this campaign. There are people who are saying that the country is too divided, that the special interests are too entrenched. That there is no possibility that one person in the Senate can ever make a difference." (Four years later, on election night, he struck similar themes in reference to 106-year-old Ann Nixon Cooper.) With that set-up, he concluded his remarks with the phrase Axelrod had penned for him: "And for those skeptics who believe that we can't accomplish what we set out to accomplish . . . I have three words for them. The same three words that we started the campaign, the same three words that we finished the primary, the same three words that are going to carry us . . . yes, we can."

He would use those same three words in his final rally on the eve of the Iowa caucus. And he would use them again after his defeat in the New Hampshire primary. In those remarks to millions watching on television, he preached, "For when we have faced down impossible odds, when we've been told we're not ready or that we shouldn't try or that we can't, generations of Americans have responded with a simple creed that sums up the spirit of a people: Yes, we can. Yes, we can. Yes, we can."

After that night, "Yes, we can" would become a regular rallying cry from the stump throughout his campaign for the presidency. As in his Senate run, Obama would use the phrase as a vehicle to show that he and his supporters could overcome seemingly impossible obstacles. In fact, years later, the night he won the presidency, as his staff and volunteers watched on with tears in their eyes, he declared triumphantly, "Where we are met with cynicism and doubts and those who tell us that we can't, we will respond with that timeless creed that sums up the spirit of a people: yes, we can."

Obama's message that November 2004 evening was consistent with what he had said during his 1999 congressional run and would ultimately track—almost word for word—with the rhetoric of his presidential campaign. It also tracked the stump speech he had delivered throughout the Senate campaign: an opening joke about his name, a summation of his biography ("Barack means 'blessed by God'"), and his policy priorities and philosophy of government, which inevitability criticized the Republican approach. His discipline and consistency throughout his early political career were remarkable.

Obama often loaded his Senate campaign remarks, as he did that night at the Hyatt Regency, with values language, including his belief—steeped in the Bible—in our common responsibility for one another, "a belief that we are brothers and sisters—and that we have mutual obligations towards each other." He had used similar language in his 2004 convention speech: "It is that fundamental belief: I am my brother's keeper, I am my sister's keeper that makes this country work. It's what allows us to . . . come together as one American family." Voters heard similar language during his presidential campaign.

For instance, time and again, when he was running for president, he finished with a quote that Martin Luther King Jr. had borrowed from an antislavery Unitarian minister in New England, Theodore Parker: "The arc of the moral universe is long, but it bends toward justice." In fact, Obama often drew on King's words during his presidential race, including during his concession speech in New Hampshire and more subtly at the 2008 convention.

Obama and his family left the stage "in a hail of blue and white confetti which rained down on revelers."[16] Not surprisingly, the day after his victory, he was showered with national attention. The *New York Times* led with the headline, "Convention Star Obama Wins Illinois Senate Seat." Even before he officially resigned the state senate seat he had held since 1997, political commentators and journalists were already speculating about Obama's next move. Would he run for president, and if so, when? Despite his low rank in the Senate's seniority, ninety-ninth out of one hundred, already he was more than just the junior senator from the state of Illinois.

REMARKS BY SENATOR-ELECT BARACK OBAMA: UNITED STATES SENATE VICTORY SPEECH

Thank you, Illinois. Let me begin by thanking all of the people who have been involved in this effort. From downstate to upstate, city, suburb, from every community throughout the state. Let me say how grateful I am to all of you for the extraordinary privilege of standing here this evening. Let me thank, because I will forget later on, it is a thankless task, let me thank the best political staff that there has been put together in this state.

They are wonderful. You know who you are. You guys have been outstanding. I appreciate all of you. Let me thank my pastor, Jeremiah A. Wright Jr. of Trinity United Church of Christ. Fellow Trinitarians out there. Let me thank all the elected officials that stood by me through thick and thin. But most of all let me thank my family. I am so grateful to my nephew Avery, my niece Leslie, my mother-in-law Mary, my brother-in-law Craig Robinson. His wonderful girlfriend, Kelly. My sister Maya, my new niece Suhaila right there, my brother-in-law Conrad. And most of all my two precious daughters, Malia Obama and Sasha Obama. And the biggest star in the Obama family until the two girls grow up, the love of my life, Michelle Obama—give it up to Michelle. Give it up!

Before I begin let me also thank the service of the person whose seat I'm going to be replacing. Peter Fitzgerald comes from another party, yet he served ably and with integrity and I'm grateful for his service and we shall applaud the service that he provided to us.

Six hundred fifty-six days ago I announced in a room a little smaller than this—it was a lot smaller—that I was announcing for the United States Senate. At the time, as many of you know, people were respectful but nevertheless skeptical. They knew the work we had done to provide health insurance to children who didn't have it, to help make the tax system more fair, to reform a death penalty system that was broken. But they felt that in a nation as divided as ours there was no possibility that someone who looked like me could ever aspire to United States Senate. They felt that in a fearful nation like this someone named Barack Obama couldn't hope to win an election.

Yet here we stand because we had a different concept and notion of the American people. We understood that there was a core of decency to the American people. That there was a set of shared values that extended beyond race and region, extended beyond income and ethnicity. A belief that every child in America should have a decent shot at life. A belief that we are brothers and sisters. And that we have mutual obligations towards each other, and that those mutual obligations express themselves not only in our family, not only in our workplaces, not only in our places of worship, but also through our government. We believed in the possibility of a government that was just as decent as the American people are. And we knew that despite the misinformation, despite the bitterness, despite the partisan politics, that when you talk to people those common values would come out. That the innate instincts of the American people would surface, if we could speak to them, if we could connect to them, if we could talk to them directly.

And because of the efforts of so many of you in this room, we had the resources, we had the manpower, we had the capacity to touch each and every one of those hearts throughout the state.

And so as a consequence, I had a chance to hear the stories of people. And they would tell me we don't expect our government to solve all our problems. We know that we have to teach all our own children initiative and self-respect and a sense of family and faith and community. But what we also know is that government can help provide us with the basic tools we need to live out the American dream. And we also know that we're tired of politicians who are attacking each other instead of attacking problems. And that if we can come together as one people that we can make progress and close the gap between the ideal of America and its reality.

And today we stand here in the land of Lincoln, the man who once called for us to appeal to the better angels of our nature, we stand here as testimony to that belief that Lincoln articulated: the possibilities of appealing to those better angels. We stand here as one people, as one nation, proclaiming ourselves to be one America with a capacity to work together to create a better future for each other. And what a magnificent gift that is to the nation. How wonderful it is that we have been able to accomplish this without negative ads and without the normal partisan politics and just focusing on the issues that matter to people: health care, and jobs and education.

And it is because of you that I have been able to do that. Because you created a protective garment over this campaign. Your spirit allowed us to run the kind of campaign that we've been able to run. We have had some good breaks in this campaign. There is no doubt about it. And I am under no illusion that we come out of this assuming that all people throughout the state of Illinois agree with me on every single position. But I think that what we've showed is that all of us can disagree without being disagreeable; that we can set aside the scorched-earth politics, the slash and burn politics of the past. We can consign that to the past. We can look forward to the future.

We can build step by step to ensure that we arrive at the practical common sense solutions that all of us hope for. That's what this campaign has been about.

But we also have to remind ourselves that this is really just the end of the beginning. This is not the end itself. In the ultimate equation we will not be measured by the margin of our victory, but we will be measured by whether we are able to deliver concrete improvements to the lives of so many people all across the state who are struggling.

We will be measured by whether those men all across the state in Galesburg, in Rockford and Decatur and Alton, those folks who have been laid off their jobs, seen their jobs move to Mexico or China, lost their health care, their pensions threatened, whether they are able to find jobs that allow them to support a family and maintain their dignity. We are going to be measured by how well we deliver the resources to the school districts all across the state who are in deficit spending. To make sure that our children have the teachers and the programs they need to excel. We are going to be measured by whether or not we can provide access and affordability to health care so that no families in Illinois are bankrupt when they get sick. We are going to be measured by whether our senior citizens can retire with some dignity and some respect. We are going to be measured by the degree to which we can craft a foreign policy in which we are not simply feared in the world but we are also respected. That's what we are going to be measured by.

I told some of you about a story a couple of days ago where during a rally that the clergy had organized on the South Side of Chicago I was asked to meet with a woman who had attended a reception beforehand. And she was a woman who had voted absentee for me already and wanted to shake my hand and take a picture with me. And she came to the reception and she was very gracious and said how proud she was to have voted for me and how proud she was of the campaign that we had run. We shook hands, we hugged, we took a picture and all of this would be unexceptional except for the fact that she was born in 1899. Her name was Margaret Lewis. She may be watching television tonight. She's one hundred four. She will be one hundred five on November twenty-fourth.

And I have had much occasion over the last several days to think about Margaret Lewis. Trying to imagine what it would be like for this woman, an African American woman born in 1899, born in the shadow of slavery. Born in the midst of Jim Crow. Born before there were automobiles or roads to carry those automobiles. Born before there were airplanes in the sky, before telephones and televisions and cameras. Born before there were cell phones and the Internet. Imagining her life spanning three centuries, she lived to see World War One; she lived to see the Great Depression; she lived to see World War Two; and she lived to see her brothers and uncles and nephews and cousins coming home and still sitting in the back of a bus.

She lived to see women get the right to vote. She lived to see FDR drag this nation out of its own fear and establish the G.I. Bill and Social Security and all the programs that we now take for granted. She saw unions rising up and she saw immigrant families coming from every direction making a better life for themselves in this nation.

And yet she still was held back by her status until finally she saw hope breaking through the horizon and the civil rights movement. And women who were willing to walk instead of riding the bus after long day's work doing somebody else's laundry and looking after somebody else's children. And she saw young people of every race and every creed take a bus down to Mississippi and Alabama to register voters and some of them never coming back. And she saw four little girls die in a Sunday school and catalyze a nation. And then she saw the Civil Rights Act of 1964 passed and the Voting Rights Act of 1965 passed.

And she saw people lining up to vote for the first time and she was among those voters and she never forgot it. And she kept on voting each and every election, each and every election she kept voting thinking that there was a better future ahead despite her trials, despite her tribulations, continually believing in this nation and its possibilities. Margaret Lewis believed. And she still believes at the age of one hundred four that her voice matters, that her life counts, that her story is sacred, just like the story of every person in this room and the stories of their parents and grandparents, the legacy that we've established. The history of so many people building, calloused hand by calloused hand, brick by brick, a better future for our children.

That's what America understands, that we don't just inherit the world from our parents, but we also borrow it from our children. And that is why tonight, as we stand here, we have to understand that we have another journey ahead and it is going to be a journey even more challenging than the one we have already embarked on. There are people today right now who are as skeptical about the future as they were at the outset of this campaign. There are people who are saying that the country is too divided, that the special interests are too entrenched. That there is no possibility that one person in the Senate can ever make a difference. They don't believe that we can provide affordable health care to families across the state of Illinois. They are not convinced we can provide economic development for rural communities that have been forgotten. They don't really ascribe to the notion that in this competitive global economy we can still assure that every person gets a living wage. They are skeptical of the possibilities that our children can enjoy a better future than we had.

And for those skeptics who believe that we can't accomplish what we set out to accomplish, if our minds are clear and our heart is pure and we believe in a just and merciful God, I say to them look at this crowd tonight, look at this election today, and I have three words for them.

The same three words that we started the campaign, the same three words that we finished the primary, the same three words that are going to carry us, because as Dr. King said, "The arc of the moral universe is long but it bends toward justice as long as we help bend it that way."

I have three words for them. What are those words? Yes, we can. Thank you, Illinois, and I love you. Thank you. Thank you, Illinois.

4

JOHN LEWIS'S
SIXTY-FIFTH BIRTHDAY GALA

February 21, 2005
Georgia Tech Hotel and Conference Center, Atlanta, Georgia

Thank you for reminding us that in America,
ordinary citizens can somehow find in their hearts
the courage to do extraordinary things. That in the face
of the fiercest resistance and the most crushing oppression,
one voice can be willing to stand up and say that's wrong
and this is right and here's why. And say it again.
And say it louder. And keep saying it until other voices
join the chorus to sing the songs that set us free.

When Barack Obama first announced his run for president, Congressman John Lewis, of Atlanta, an icon of the civil rights movement, was firmly in the camp of Obama's chief opponent, Senator Hillary Clinton. That was no surprise. For nearly two decades, Lewis had been close friends with and a staunch supporter of both Bill and Hillary Clinton. Back when Governor Bill Clinton was considering a run for the presidency, he met with Congressman Lewis to seek his support. Lewis would become one of the first black leaders to endorse Clinton. In fact, Lewis later recounted a conversation he had with his staff, where they all agreed, "Bill Clinton acts more like a brother than a lot of brothers."[1]

In *The Battle for America 2008,* Dan Balz and Haynes Johnson wrote about a conversation they had with Lewis in 2008, shortly after the South Carolina primary. The congressman told them how Bill Clinton would say that he loved him and Lewis would respond, "I love you and Hillary, too." When Hillary Clinton was deciding whether to make her own run for the presidency, Lewis told Bill Clinton, "Hillary is really smart, she's smarter than you. She'd be a great president." Soon thereafter, he endorsed her, "because that was in my soul."[2]

This was no small endorsement for Hillary Clinton. John Lewis was a titan in the black community. Lewis grew up the son of a sharecropper in the Jim Crow South. He used to leave school during harvest time to help his parents pick the cotton, peanuts, and corn on their family farm in Pike County, Alabama. Growing up, he never had electricity or running water. At a young age, Lewis realized he had a predilection for preaching. In his teens, he relates in his autobiography, *Walking with the Wind,* how he preached to the animals on his farm, baptized the young chickens, and performed funerals for the dead ones.[3]

Lewis never missed a Sunday with his Bible and his radio, which was always tuned into WRMA, a Montgomery, Alabama, gospel-music station. It was on this station that he first heard the voice of a young Baptist minister from Atlanta named Dr. Martin Luther King Jr. Soon thereafter, at the age of seventeen, Lewis joined King's organization, the Southern Christian Leadership Conference, and became active in the group. He led sit-ins and attended nonviolence workshops, and joined the first Freedom Rides. From there, he attended Fisk University, from which he holds a BA in religion and philosophy, and went on to graduate from the American Baptist Theological Seminary, both in Nashville, Tennessee. King quickly became his friend and mentor. In 1963, King invited Lewis to speak at the March on Washington.

Two years later, Lewis was nearly beaten to death by Alabama state troopers as he led a group of protesters across the Edmund Pettus Bridge at the start of a planned Selma-to-Montgomery march. After seeing television news clips of Lewis and nearly ninety others being beaten, President Lyndon Johnson went to Congress declaring "We shall overcome" and won passage of the 1965 Voting Rights Act. After a failed congressional run in 1977, Lewis defeated a fellow activist, Julian Bond, to secure his seat in the Fifth Congressional District, representing the people of Atlanta.

By the ripe age of thirty, Lewis had earned a spot in the history books, so it's understandable that his backing of Hillary Clinton sent a clear signal to other African Americans that it was acceptable to support her, even though Barack Obama was the first truly viable black presidential candidate. But Lewis was under great pressure to change his endorsement.

Many of his constituents back home and his friends in the Congressional
Black Caucus didn't understand how he could stay with Clinton.

The pressure only built up after Obama won the Iowa caucus, coupled
with reports that Bill Clinton was intentionally making racially charged
comments to court southern white voters. On January 7, 2008, the eve of
the New Hampshire primary, Bill Clinton told a crowd at a rally, "Give
me a break. This whole thing is the biggest fairy tale I've ever seen."
Clinton later claimed he was accusing Obama of distorting his stance on
the Iraq War, although many others, including those in the mainstream
media, believed he was referring to Obama's candidacy.

A couple of weeks later, on January 26, the day that Obama swept the
South Carolina primary, President Clinton downplayed the significance
of his win. To a group of reporters he credited the state's demographics
and the Illinois senator's heavy African American support with the victory. "Jesse Jackson won South Carolina in eighty-four and eighty-eight,"
Clinton said near a rally in Columbia. "Jackson ran a good campaign.
And Obama ran a good campaign here."

The media and senior Democratic Party officials began questioning
Bill Clinton's tactics. Some whispered privately that Clinton was showing his true colors and was willing to play racial politics to help his wife
win the nomination.

It did not help that earlier in the month, Hillary Clinton, on NBC's *Meet
the Press*, had said, "Dr. King's dream began to be realized when President
Johnson passed the Civil Rights Act. . . . It took a president to get it done."
Clinton was responding to a speech Obama had made comparing himself
to President Kennedy and Dr. King. Historically speaking, Clinton was
correct; it took President Johnson, after Kennedy's assassination, to translate the protestors' goals into legislation. Critics, however, interpreted her
comments as minimizing King's importance in the civil rights movement.

These incidents—along with rumors about Bill Clinton's tactics and
threats from Lewis's constituents to challenge him in his next election—
chipped away at Lewis's once-strong support from his district. Eventually the elder statesman from the civil rights era announced that he was
supporting Barack Obama, although he denied any connection between
his decision and Bill Clinton's comments and the responses to them. He
even went so far as to pronounce "the stuff about King . . . horrible, awful
bullshit" and saying that Bill Clinton was "misunderstood."[4]

Lewis later explained his decision to Dan Balz and Haynes Johnson. After listening to Obama's victory and concession speeches in Iowa and New Hampshire, he realized that "something's happening here." This was reinforced when he was campaigning for Hillary in South Carolina, and he found himself "besieged by conflicting emotions." After having an "executive session with [himself]," Lewis decided that he couldn't let the moment pass him by. As he put it, "Sometimes you have to be on the right side of history."[5]

Lewis admitted that it was a very difficult decision to leave Clinton. He felt like he had "turn[ed] my back on a member of my family," adding, "The political thing to do would have been to do nothing, to not endorse anyone." But on February 28, 2008, weeks before the Ohio and Texas primaries, he finalized his decision. Referencing Obama and recognizing the historical significance of Obama's candidacy, he declared that "people are prepared and ready to make that great leap. . . . This is a movement. It's a spiritual event." He told the *Atlanta Journal Constitution* that Obama was "the heir apparent to the racial progress [he] himself had spent his life fighting for."[6]

In an interview with the *New York Times*, Lewis indicated that he could "never, ever do anything to reverse the action of the voters of his [Atlanta] district," who overwhelmingly supported Obama. He added, "I've been very impressed with the campaign of Senator Obama. He's getting better and better every day." He also offered to help mediate between the warring Obama and Clinton camps.[7]

Hillary Clinton quickly issued a statement: "Congressman Lewis is a true American hero, and we have the utmost respect for him and understand the great pressure he faced." Hillary Clinton also told reporters, "We were friends before this campaign and we'll be friends after this campaign." The former president was similarly conciliatory.[8]

Barack Obama was over the moon, to say the least, at having gained Lewis's support, and his comments reflected that. "John Lewis is an American hero and a gift of the civil rights movement, and I am deeply honored to have his support," he said. Obama had looked up to the congressman for, among other things, paving the way in America for him and his contemporaries: "There is a direct line between his courage and my current situation."

Obama's admiration for Lewis in 2008 was nothing new; he had expressed his respect publicly for the congressman many times over the years. In fact, in February 2005, just a month before entering the Senate and years before announcing his presidential bid, Obama delivered a sixty-fifth birthday tribute for Lewis at the Georgia Tech Hotel and Conference Center in Atlanta. The Illinois senator was the headliner that evening, and Bill Clinton, Coretta Scott King, and Harry Belafonte presented video messages with their birthday greetings. Obama sat between Mrs. King and Ethel Kennedy at the $500-a-plate dinner. The event raised $200,000 for Lewis's campaign fund.

This speech was the first major address Jon Favreau had crafted for his new boss, so he was understandably nervous. Obama tried to put his new apprentice at ease, telling him that "sometimes these relationships take time—so don't stay up all night worrying about it." In what would later become their routine, the two met in Obama's Senate office and the senator downloaded his extemporaneous thoughts to Favreau as Favreau pecked away on his laptop.

The message Obama wanted to convey—one of discipline and personal responsibility—was, even then, vintage Obama. It was a theme that would carry through to his run for the presidency and ultimately to the White House. The senator wanted his audience to understand the level of commitment and effort leaders like Lewis had put into the civil rights movement, from the bus boycotts in Montgomery to the Voting Rights March in Selma. Every step was meticulously planned. "People think [the civil rights movement] was all inspiring rhetoric," Obama told Favreau during their initial sit-down. "But these people were disciplined. They woke up every day, worked hard, and sacrificed. They had to be organized and responsible every step of the way, otherwise people wouldn't take them seriously."

Favreau distilled what Senator Obama had shared with him, adding material he had gleaned from Lewis's autobiography, and wrote a first draft. Obama liked what he read, telling Favreau, "I'll take it from here." Obama preserved most of the original draft, adding several personal anecdotes when he actually delivered the speech at the party in Atlanta.

Ultimately, Favreau's first speech process with Obama was a success. The two clicked right off the bat; it didn't "take time," as Obama had initially warned. Part of it was Jon's talent—and part was that Obama was a writer himself; he had spent many hours at the computer writing his autobiography after law school. So he appreciated how difficult Favreau's job was and was careful to give his writer the time and fodder he needed to accomplish his task. Words mattered to Obama; that appreciation is a gift to any speechwriter.

Obama's remarks centered on Lewis's lifelong courage and service to his country, in spite of the obstacles he faced. "He was often forced to leave school to work in the fields and the public library was off-limits to his kind, and yet young John Lewis sought knowledge. . . . And so he organized, even when so many tried to stop his efforts. He spoke truths, even when they tried to silence his words. And he marched, even when they tried to knock him down again and again and again."

The senator finished that thought with a line that would become a trademark theme: "The road John chose for himself was not easy. But the road to change never is." He added, "But the most amazing thing of all is that after that day—after John Lewis was beaten within an inch of his life, after people's heads were gashed open . . . after all that, they went back to march again. . . . They crossed the bridge. . . . And so it was, in a story as old as our beginnings and as timeless as our hopes, that change came about because the good people of a great nation willed it so. . . . Change is never easy, but always possible."

Obama then pivoted to an uncanny summary of what would become his presidential campaign message, capturing his beliefs in unity, organization, responsibility, and hope: "Change . . . comes not from violence or militancy or the kind of politics that pits us against each other and plays on our worst fears, but from great discipline and organization, from a strong message of hope, and from the courage to turn against the tide so that the tide eventually may be turned." Complementing that, Obama added a rundown of his policy positions on issues ranging from poverty—"It's wrong that one out of every five children is born into poverty in the richest country on earth"—to education, housing, and health care—"It's wrong to tell hardworking families who are earning less and paying more in taxes that we can't do anything to help them buy their own home or send their kids to college or care for them when they're sick."

The senator then retold a story about a trip he had taken during his 2004 Senate campaign with Illinois senator Dick Durbin to Cairo, Illinois, a city known for its abysmal racial climate in the sixties and seventies. It was a tale he had told often on the stump, and was a personal favorite of Robert Gibbs, his Senate communications director. Favreau knew he couldn't capture it on the page as well as Obama could deliver it from memory, so he left a placeholder in the draft that read "tell Dick Durbin story." As always, the story was a hit with the audience.

As he would often do, Obama also quoted Dr. Martin Luther King Jr.: "The arc of the moral universe is long, but it bends towards justice." Recognizing Lewis's accomplishments, Senator Obama stated that justice doesn't happen by accident—it takes passionate commitment and courageous leadership.

Obama closed his remarks by crediting Lewis with opening up opportunities for African Americans like himself; he and countless others "stood on that bridge and lived to cross it." He compared his path to the Senate as his own trip across the Edmund Pettus Bridge.

Obama had touched the crowd; you could hear a pin drop in the room.

Nearly three years later, on the eve of Obama's inauguration, Lewis told David Remnick of the *New Yorker* that Obama "has absorbed the lessons and spirit of the civil rights movement. But, at the same time, he doesn't have the scars of the movement."[9]

With that, Lewis turned and told a visitor in his congressional office, "Barack Obama is what comes at the end of that bridge in Selma."

Remarks by Senator Barack Obama: John Lewis's Sixty-fifth Birthday Gala

Thank you. It's an honor to be here tonight to celebrate one of the most courageous and compassionate Americans of our time. Happy birthday, John.

When I was first asked to speak here, I thought to myself, never in a million years would I have guessed that I'd be serving in Congress with John Lewis.

And then I thought, you know, there was once a time when John Lewis might never have guessed that he'd be serving in Congress. And there was a time not long before that when people might never have guessed that someday African Americans would be able to go to the polls, pick up a ballot, make their voice heard, and elect that Congress.

But we can, and I'm here because people like John Lewis believed. Because people like John Lewis feared nothing and risked everything for those beliefs. Because they were willing to spend sleepless nights in lonely jail cells, endure the searing pain of billy clubs cracked against their bones, and face down death simply so that all of us could share equally in the joys of life.

How far we've come because of your courage, John.

How far we've come from the days when the son of sharecroppers would huddle by the radio as the crackle of Dr. King's dreams filled his heart with hope. He was often forced to leave school to work in the fields and the public library was off-limits to his kind, and yet young John Lewis sought knowledge. His parents were never the type to complain or try to stir up any trouble, and yet their son sought justice.

And so he organized, even when so many tried to stop his efforts. He spoke truths, even when they tried to silence his words. And he marched, even when they tried to knock him down again and again and again.

The road John chose for himself was not easy. But the road to change never is.

I think it's simple for us to look back forty years and think that it was all so clear then. That while there may be room for moral ambiguity in the issues we debate today, civil rights was different. That people generally knew what was right and what was wrong, who the good guys and the bad guys were. But the moral certainties we now take for granted—that separate can never be equal, that the blessings of liberty enshrined in our Constitution belong to all of us, that our children should be able to go to school together and play together and grow up together—were anything but certain when John Lewis was a boy.

And so there was struggle and sacrifice, discipline and tremendous courage. And there was the culmination of it all one Sunday afternoon on a bridge in Alabama.

I've often thought about the people on the Edmund Pettus Bridge that day. Not only John and Hosea Williams leading the march but the hundreds of everyday Americans who left their homes and their churches to join it. Blacks and whites, teenagers and children, teachers and bankers and shopkeepers—a beloved community of God's children ready to stand for freedom.

And I wonder, Where did they find that kind of courage? When you're facing row after row of state troopers on horseback armed with billy clubs and tear gas . . . when they're coming toward you spewing hatred and violence, how do you simply stop, kneel down, and pray to the Lord for salvation? Truly, this is the audacity of hope.

But the most amazing thing of all is that after that day—after John Lewis was beaten within an inch of his life, after people's heads were gashed open and their eyes were burned and they watched their children's innocence literally beaten out of them—after all that, they went back to march again.

They marched again. They crossed the bridge. They awakened a nation's conscience, and not five months later, the Voting Rights Act of 1965 was signed into law.

And so it was, in a story as old as our beginnings and as timeless as our hopes, that change came about because the good people of a great nation willed it so.

Thank you, John, for going back. Thank you for marching again.

Thank you for reminding us that in America, ordinary citizens can somehow find in their hearts the courage to do extraordinary things. That in the face of the fiercest resistance and the most crushing oppression, one voice can be willing to stand up and say that's wrong and this is right and here's why. And say it again. And say it louder. And keep saying it until other voices join the chorus to sing the songs that set us free.

Today, I'm sure you'll all agree that we have songs left to sing and bridges left to cross. And if there's anything we can learn from this living saint sitting beside me, it is that change is never easy, but always possible. That it comes not from violence or militancy or the kind of politics that pits us against each other and plays on our worst fears; but from great discipline and organization, from a strong message of hope, and from the courage to turn against the tide so that the tide eventually may be turned.

Today, we need that courage. We need the courage to say that it's wrong that one out of every five children is born into poverty in the richest country on earth. And it's right to do whatever necessary to provide our children the care and the education they need to live up to their God-given potential.

It's wrong to tell hard-working families who are earning less and paying more in taxes that we can't do anything to help them buy their own home or send their kids to college or care for them when they're sick. And it's right to expect that if you're willing to work hard in this country of American Dreamers, the sky is the limit on what you can achieve.

It's wrong to tell those brave men and women who are willing to fight and die for this country that when they come home, we may not have room for them at the VA hospitals or the benefits we promised them. And it's right to always provide the very best care for the very best of America.

My friends, we have not come this far as a people and a nation because we believe that we're better off simply fending for ourselves. We are here because we believe that all men are created equal, and that we are all connected to each other as one people. And we need to say that more. And say it again. And keep saying it.

And where will our courage come from to speak these truths? When we stand on our own Edmund Pettus Bridge, what hope will sustain us?

I believe it is the hope of knowing that people like John Lewis have stood on that same bridge and lived to cross it.

For me, this kind of hope often comes from a memory of a trip I took during the campaign. About a week after the primary, Dick Durbin and I embarked on a nineteen city tour of southern Illinois. And one of the towns we went to was a place called Cairo, which, as many of you might know, achieved a certain notoriety during the late sixties and early seventies as having one of the worst racial climates in the country. You had an active White Citizens' Council there, you had cross burnings, Jewish families were being harassed, you had segregated schools, race riots, you name it—it was going on in Cairo.

And we're riding down to Cairo and Dick Durbin turns to me and says, "Let me tell you about the first time I went to Cairo. It was about thirty years ago. I was twenty-three years old, and Paul Simon, who was lieutenant governor at the time, sent me down there to investigate what could be done to improve the racial climate in Cairo."

And Dick tells me how he diligently goes down there and gets picked up by a local resident who takes him to his motel. And as Dick's getting out of the car, the driver says, "Excuse me, let me just give you a piece of advice. Don't use the phone in your motel room because the switchboard operator is a member of the White Citizens' Council, and they'll report on anything you do."

Well, this obviously makes Dick Durbin upset, but he's a brave young man, so he checks in to his room, unpacks his bags, and a few minutes later he hears a knock on the door. He opens up the door and there's a guy standing there who just stares at Dick for a second and then says, "What the hell are you doing here?" and walks away.

Well, now Dick is really feeling concerned, and so am I because as he's telling me this story, we're pulling in to Cairo. So I'm wondering what kind of reception we're going to get. And we wind our way through the town and we go past the old courthouse, take a turn and suddenly we're in a big parking lot and about three hundred people are standing there. About a fourth of them are black and three fourths are white and they all are about the age where they would have been active participants in the epic struggle that had taken place thirty years earlier.

And as we pull closer, I see something. All of these people are wearing these little buttons that say "Obama for U.S. Senate." And they start smiling. And they start waving. And Dick and I looked at each other and didn't have to say a thing. Because if you told Dick thirty years ago that he—the son of Lithuanian immigrants born into very modest means in East St. Louis— would be returning to Cairo as a sitting United States senator, and that he would have in tow a black guy born in Hawaii with a father from Kenya and a mother from Kansas named Barack Obama, no one would have believed it.

But it happened. And it happened because John Lewis and scores of brave Americans stood on that bridge and lived to cross it.

You know, two weeks after Bloody Sunday, when the march finally reached Montgomery, Martin Luther King Jr. spoke to the crowd of thousands and said, "The arc of the moral universe is long, but it bends towards justice." He's right, but you know what? It doesn't bend on its own. It bends because we help it bend that way. Because people like John Lewis and Hosea Williams and Martin Luther King and Coretta Scott King and Rosa Parks and thousands of ordinary Americans with extraordinary courage have helped bend it that way. And as their examples call out to us from across the generations, we continue to progress as a people because they inspire us to take our own two hands and bend that arc. Thank you, John. May God bless you, and may God bless these United States of America.

5

Knox College
Commencement Address
June 4, 2005 • *Galesburg, Illinois*

*The true test of the American ideal is whether we are able to
recognize our failings and then rise together to meet the challenges of our time. . . .
Whether chance of birth or circumstance decides life's big winners and losers,
or whether we build a community where, at the very least,
everyone has a chance to work hard, get ahead, and reach their dreams.*

It still looked as though the skies were going to open up when Barack
Obama's car pulled up to the South Lawn of the building known as Old
Main at Knox College, a small liberal arts school in Western Illinois.
There was no entourage, no Secret Service, no police motorcade. The
thunderheads seemed appropriate: Obama was admittedly nervous. After
all, this was his first major address since he had been elected to the United
States Senate just six months earlier.

The junior senator and his staff didn't take their assignment that day
lightly. Knox College had not only played host to important figures over
the course of history, but also was also the main site for the Underground
Railroad in Illinois and was the location of the fifth senatorial debate
between Abraham Lincoln and Stephen Douglas in 1858. It was there
that Lincoln for the very first time denounced slavery on moral grounds.
(Lincoln later received his first honorary degree from Knox College, proclaiming, as, for effect, he squeezed his narrow frame through a window
to get to the podium, "At last, I have finally gone through college.")[1]
Obama would be delivering his speech only feet from where Lincoln and
Douglas had stood.

As the only African American in the Senate, the issue of race was always in the background for Obama. But he wasn't there that afternoon to

deliver an address on civil rights. Instead, he wanted to use the moment as an opportunity to offer his philosophy on the role of government, anchored in a simple principle: "Everyone [should have] a chance to work, get ahead, and reach their dreams."

This was no minor event. Ever since his grand launch onto the national stage at the Democratic National Convention almost a year earlier, Obama had become of a political rock star. He graced the cover of *Newsweek* in January, his book *Dreams from My Father* was a national best seller, and as early as the fall of 2004, his name was being bandied about as a possible presidential candidate in 2008.

This was all a bit overwhelming for a man who had just left the Illinois state senate and was next to last in seniority in the U.S. Senate in Washington. But Obama was no ordinary senator. So even though only a few local reporters showed up that day, his speech would quickly be circulated via the Internet.

When Obama first sat down with his speechwriter, Jon Favreau, to discuss the speech, one thing was for certain: he didn't want to fill his twenty minutes that day with commencement platitudes. Instead, Obama thought Knox would offer him an opportunity to do what he had hoped to do when he got elected—use his platform as a national figure in the Senate to deliver major, thought-provoking speeches.

He already had a few big themes in mind. The one that immediately took priority was an address on how America would *and should* make its way in the new, global economy. Obama had a clear point of view on how our country and its citizens should behave—and thrive—in the new world order and what pitfalls of globalization we should avoid.

Galesburg was the perfect setting for this topic. The city had been devastated a year earlier when its largest employer, Maytag, closed its plant and moved to Mexico. Obama had visited Galesburg a number of times during his Senate campaign; it was a favorite story of his on the stump. Coupled with city's connection to the Underground Railroad and its linkage to Lincoln, Obama decided that Galesburg would be the perfect place to discuss the future of the American economy.

In fact, Favreau later credited the Knox commencement address as the foundation for Obama's broader economic philosophy and the language he used to describe it. Obama's consistency in this area is something that often goes unrecognized, but it is just one example of his impressive message discipline during his political campaigns.

Obama began his speech in Galesburg by presenting his perspective on why the American experiment had been so successful for so many people, a concept he ultimately described in his speech as "a journey to be shared and shaped and remade by people who had the gall, the temerity to believe that, against all odds, they could form 'a more perfect union' on this new frontier."

This theme of building "a more perfect union" would later appear often in his presidential campaign stump speeches. It was the central theme of his speech on race in Philadelphia and appeared in nearly every primary victory speech, including on election night and during the presidential inauguration. "For that is the true genius of America—that America can change," he said the night he won the presidency. "Our union can be perfected. And what we have already achieved gives us hope for what we can and must achieve tomorrow."

Favreau said that the Knox commencement address was actually the foundation for many ideas and themes, and Obama's broader economic philosophy, which he would touch on consistently throughout the 2008 campaign.

Favreau met with Senator Obama in his Senate office nearly a week before the speech. Afterward, he went back to his apartment and typed up the first draft. Obama read it the Thursday before the commencement and sent his edits back to Favreau on Friday. It was revised and written in less than a week, with a few edits on the road from Gibbs.

One thing Obama did was to add details that would become commonplace in his forthcoming speeches, including his election night speech: "And yet, brick by brick, rail by rail, calloused hand by calloused hand, people kept dreaming, and building, and working, and marching, and petitioning their government, until they made America."

The speech not only inspired his immediate audience, the 220-person graduating class of 2005, but also captured the attention of a national audience.

His central thesis was simply put, yet remarkably complex. It was also deeply revealing. Obama argued that America's success was built on and "depended on our sense of mutual regard for each other." He believed that "we're all in it together and everybody's got a shot at opportunity" and "that has produced [America's] unrivaled political stability." These were themes that later reappeared in his book *The Audacity of Hope.*

This was a significant contrast to George Bush and the Republican Party, which championed the "ownership society"; Obama compared this notion to Social Darwinism—"every man and woman for him- or herself." (He debated this idea at length as an undergraduate in Professor Roger Boesche's class at Occidental College.) Theirs was a hands-off philosophy with a small role for government and little regulatory intervention. Hyperbolically, Obama summarized Bush's eight-year approach: "It allows us to say to those whose health care or tuition may rise faster than they can afford—tough luck. . . . It lets us say to the child born into poverty—pull yourself up by your bootstraps."

Unsurprisingly, Obama stated flatly, "There is a problem. It won't work. It ignores our history."

Interestingly, Obama first discussed the "ownership society" at a speech at the Press Club in Washington, D.C., on the anniversary of the passage of the legislation that created Social Security. It was one of the first events he attended as a senator; he was joined by Franklin Roosevelt's grandson, Curtis Roosevelt.

Obama used his remarks at Knox College to outline his perspective on the role of government and regulation and the "opportunity" all Americans deserved. "Instead of doing nothing or simply defending twentieth-century solutions, let's imagine what we can do to give every American a fighting chance in the twenty-first century."

First, Obama argued that all children in America should have the education and skills they need to compete in the new economy; you cannot have opportunity without education. This was particularly critical given the "quiet revolution" of globalization that was "breaking down" traditional barriers and "connecting the world's economies." A highly skilled, educated workforce was essential to any country's success.

Obama used the background of Knox College that day to buttress his argument. Knox's founders believed that the college should be accessible to all students, regardless of their financial means, so its doors had been opened to hard-pressed students for generations. Obama also pointed to the town of Galesburg, the home of the college, to illustrate the effects of globalization. If America didn't focus more on educating its youth for better-paying jobs, the effects of globalization and the availability of low-cost labor in other countries would devastate the U.S. economy.

Second, Obama stressed the importance of good health care and reliable pensions, and expounded on the importance of portability to the American workforce. Third, he touched on innovation and the critical need for more research and development in the United States. In particular, he focused on green jobs—a topic that would be a mainstay of his presidential campaign speeches.

And he used this opportunity to raise another theme that would run through his campaign and his early presidency: responsibility (in his Inaugural Address he discussed a "new era of responsibility"). He exhorted his audience to "read more . . . slough off bad habits—like driving gas guzzlers. . . . Put away the video games." In a nod to bipartisanship, he added, "Republicans will have to recognize our collective responsibilities, even as Democrats recognize that we have to do more than just defend the old programs."

This was classic Obama—acknowledging America's shortcomings, but emphasizing our ability to remedy them. America has never been perfect—take, for instance, the period when Lincoln debated on campus and slavery was still legal. But as he put it, the "true test of the American ideal" isn't perfection; it's "whether we are able to recognize our failings and then rise together to meet the challenges of our time."

To make this point, Obama reached deep into the nation's past, from the Industrial Revolution to the Great Depression to the Second World War. "When the irrational exuberance of the Roaring Twenties came crashing down with the stock market, we had to decide: do we follow the call of leaders who would do nothing, or the call of a leader who, perhaps because of his physical paralysis, refused to accept political paralysis? We chose to act . . . and together we rose."

In short, he was talking about the responsibility earlier generations took to build a more perfect union, going back to the "lanky, raw-boned man" who "took the stage at Old Main," excoriated slavery, and reminded his audience about the American principles of "freedom and equality"— the same responsibility the citizens in Galesburg took when they helped slaves escape through the Underground Railroad.

The speech was well received. After a processional led by Professor Whitlatch and President Taylor, Obama received an honorary degree from the college and got an ovation from the graduates, their families, and Galesburg residents. The *Peoria Journal Star* headline crowed, "Providing Inspiration—Obama Urges Graduates to Accept Challenges of Future."[2] The liberal netroots crowd—the rapidly growing network of online commentators—also added their perspective: "Not impressed? Read any speech given by the current Democratic leadership. Understand now?" Democratic strategist Ken Baer wrote on Talking Points Memo: "Send Obama's speech to your friends. Their reactions may be like those of the 10 or so Democratic operatives I sent it to yesterday: sign me up."[3]

The best news of all: the weather cooperated with Knox College's commencement plans. Aside from a drizzle, the rain held off.

REMARKS BY SENATOR BARACK OBAMA: KNOX COLLEGE COMMENCEMENT ADDRESS

Good morning, President Taylor, the board of trustees, faculty, parents, family, friends, and the class of 2005. Congratulations on your graduation, and thank you for allowing me the honor to be a part of it.

Well, it's been about six months now since you sent me to Washington as your U.S. senator. And for those of you muttering under your breath, "I didn't send you anywhere," that's okay too—maybe we'll hold a little pump handle after the ceremony and I can change your mind for next time.

So far it's been a fascinating journey. Each time I walk onto the Senate floor, I'm reminded of the history, for good and for ill, that has been made there. But there have also been a few surreal moments. For example, I remember the day before I was sworn in, when we decided to hold a press conference in our office. Now, here I am, ninety-ninth in seniority—which, I was proud wasn't dead last until I found out that the only reason we aren't hundredth is because Illinois is bigger than Colorado. So I'm ninety-ninth in seniority, and the reporters are all cramped into our tiny transition office that was somewhere near the janitor's closet in the basement of the Dirksen Building. It's my first day in the building, I hadn't taken one vote, I hadn't introduced one bill, I hadn't even sat down at my desk, and this very earnest reporter asks:

"Senator Obama, what's your place in history?"

I laughed out loud. Place in history? I thought he was kidding! At that point, I wasn't even sure the other senators would save me a place at the cool lunch table.

But as I was thinking about what words I could share with this class, about what's next, what's possible, and what opportunities lay ahead, I think it's not a bad question to ask yourselves:

"What will be my place in history?"

In other eras, across distant lands, this is a question that could be answered with relative ease and certainty. As a servant of Rome, you knew you would spend your life forced to build somebody else's empire. As a peasant in eleventh-century China, you knew that no matter how hard you worked, the local warlord might take everything you had—and that famine might come knocking on your door any day. As a subject of King George, you knew that your freedom to worship and speak and build your own life would be ultimately limited by the throne.

And then, America happened.

A place where destiny was not a destination, but a journey to be shared and shaped and remade by people who had the gall, the temerity to believe that, against all odds, they could form "a more perfect union" on this new frontier.

And as people around the world began to hear the tale of the lowly colonists who overthrew an empire for the sake of an idea, they came. Across the oceans and the ages, they settled in Boston and Charleston, Chicago and St. Louis, Kalamazoo and Galesburg, to try and build their own American Dream. This collective dream moved forward imperfectly—it was scarred by our treatment of native peoples, betrayed by slavery, clouded by the subjugation of women, shaken by war and depression. And yet, brick by brick, rail by rail, calloused hand by calloused hand, people kept dreaming, and building, and working, and marching, and petitioning their government, until they made America a land where the question of our place in history is not answered for us, but by us.

Have we failed at times? Absolutely. Will you occasionally fail when you embark on your own American journey? Surely. But the test is not perfection.

The true test of the American ideal is whether we are able to recognize our failings and then rise together to meet the challenges of our time. Whether we allow ourselves to be shaped by events and history, or whether we act to shape them. Whether chance of birth or circumstance decides life's big winners and losers, or whether we build a community where, at the very least, everyone has a chance to work hard, get ahead, and reach their dreams.

We have faced this choice before.

At the end of the Civil War, when farmers and their families began moving into the cities to work in the big factories that were sprouting up all across America, we had to decide: Do we do nothing and allow the captains of industry and robber barons to run roughshod over the economy and workers by competing to see who can pay the lowest wage at the worst working conditions?

Or do we try to make the system work by setting up basic rules for the market, and instituting the first public schools, and busting up monopolies, and letting workers organize into unions?

We chose to act, and we rose together.

When the irrational exuberance of the Roaring Twenties came crashing down with the stock market, we had to decide: do we follow the call of leaders who would do nothing, or the call of a leader who, perhaps because of his physical paralysis, refused to accept political paralysis?

We chose to act—regulating the market, putting people back to work, expanding bargaining rights to include health care and a secure retirement—and together we rose.

When World War II required the most massive home-front mobilization in history and we needed every single American to lend a hand, we had to decide: Do we listen to the skeptics who told us it wasn't possible to produce that many tanks and planes?

Or, did we build Roosevelt's Arsenal of Democracy and grow our economy even further by providing our returning heroes with a chance to go to college and own their own home?

Again, we chose to act, and again, we rose together.

Today, at the beginning of this young century, we have to decide again. But this time, it's your turn to choose.

Here in Galesburg, you know what this new challenge is. You've seen it.

You see it when you drive by the old Maytag plant around lunchtime and no one walks out anymore. I saw it during the campaign when I met the union guys who use to work at the plant and now wonder what they're gonna do at fifty-five years old without a pension or health care; when I met the man who's son needs a new liver but doesn't know if he can afford when the kid gets to the top of the transplant list.

It's as if someone changed the rules in the middle of the game and no one bothered to tell these people. And, in reality, the rules have changed.

It started with technology and automation that rendered entire occupations obsolete—when was the last time anybody here stood in line for the bank teller instead of going to the ATM, or talked to a switchboard operator? Then companies like Maytag being able to pick up and move their factories to some third world country where workers are a lot cheaper than they are in the U.S.

As Tom Friedman points out in his new book, *The World Is Flat*, over the last decade or so, these forces—technology and globalization—have combined like never before. So that while most of us have been paying attention to how much easier technology has made our lives—sending e-mails on Blackberries, surfing the Web on our cell phones, instant messaging with friends across the world—a quiet revolution has been breaking down barriers and connecting the world's economies. Now, businesses not only have the ability to move jobs wherever there's a factory, but wherever there's an Internet connection.

Countries like India and China realized this. They understood that now they need not just be a source of cheap labor or cheap exports. They can compete with us on a global scale. The one resource they still needed was a skilled, educated labor force. So they started schooling their kids earlier, longer, and with a greater emphasis on math, science, and technology, until their most talented students realized they don't have to immigrate to America to have a decent life—they can stay right where they are.

The result? China is graduating four times the number of engineers that the United States is graduating. Not only are those Maytag employees competing with Chinese and Indonesian and Mexican workers, now you are too. Today, accounting firms are e-mailing your tax returns to workers in India who will figure them out and send them back as fast as any worker in Indiana could.

When you lose your luggage in a Boston airport, tracking it down may involve a call to an agent in Bangalore, who will find it by making a phone call to Baltimore. Even the Associated Press has outsourced some of their jobs to writers all over the world who can send in a story with the click of a mouse.

As British prime minister Tony Blair has said, in this new economy, "Talent is twenty-first-century wealth." If you've got the skills, you've got the education, and you have the opportunity to upgrade and improve both, you'll be able to compete and win anywhere. If not, the fall will be further and harder than ever before.

So what do we do about this? How does America find our way in this new, global economy? What will our place in history be?

Like so much of the American story, once again, we face a choice. Once again, there are those who believe that there isn't much we can do about this as a nation. That the best idea is to give everyone one big refund on their government—divvy it up into individual portions, hand it out, and encourage everyone to use their share to go buy their own health care, their own retirement plan, their own child care, education, and so forth.

In Washington, they call this the "ownership society." But in our past there has been another term for it—Social Darwinism, every man and woman for him or herself. It's a tempting idea, because it doesn't require much thought or ingenuity. It allows us to say to those whose health care or tuition may rise faster than they can afford—tough luck. It allows us to say to the Maytag workers who have lost their job—life isn't fair. It lets us say to the child born into poverty—pull yourself up by your bootstraps. And it is especially tempting because each of us believes that we will always be the winner in life's lottery, that we will be Donald Trump, or at least that we won't be the chump that he tells: "You're fired!"

But there a problem. It won't work. It ignores our history. It ignores the fact that it has been government research and investment that made the railways and the Internet possible. It has been the creation of a massive middle class, through decent wages and benefits and public schools—that has allowed all of us to prosper. Our economic dominance has depended on individual initiative and belief in the free market; but it has also depended on our sense of mutual regard for each other, the idea that everybody has a stake in the country, that we're all in it together and everybody's got a shot at opportunity—that has produced our unrivaled political stability.

And so if we do nothing in the face of globalization, more people will continue to lose their health care. Fewer kids will be able to afford this diploma you're about to receive.

More companies like United won't be able to provide pensions for their employees. And those Maytag workers will be joined in the unemployment line by any worker whose skill can be bought and sold on the global market.

Today, I'm here to tell you what most of you already know. This isn't us. This isn't how our story ends—not in this country. America is a land of big dreamers and big hopes.

It is this hope that has sustained us through revolution and civil war, depression and world war, a struggle for civil and social rights and the brink of nuclear crisis. And it is because of our dreamers that we have emerged from each challenge more united, more prosperous, and more admired than ever before.

So let's dream. Instead of doing nothing or simply defending twentieth-century solutions, let's imagine what we can do to give every American a fighting chance in the twenty-first century.

What if we prepared every child in America with the education and skills they need to compete in this new economy? If we made sure college was affordable for everyone who wanted to go? If we walked up to those Maytag workers and told them that their old job wasn't coming back, but that the new jobs will be there because of the serious job re-training and lifelong education that is waiting for them—the sorts of opportunities Knox has created with the strong future scholarship program?

What if no matter where you worked or how many times you switched jobs, you had health care and a pension that stayed with you always, so that each of us had the flexibility to move to a better job or start a new business?

And what if instead of cutting budgets for research and development and science, we fueled the genius and the innovation that will lead to the new jobs and new industries of the future?

Right now, all across America, there are amazing discoveries being made. If we supported these discoveries on a national level, if we committed ourselves to investing in these possibilities, just imagine what it could do for a town like Galesburg. Ten or twenty years down the road, that old Maytag plant could reopen its doors as an ethanol refinery that turns corn into fuel.

Down the street, a biotechnology research lab could open that's on the cusp of discovering a cure for cancer. And across the way, a new auto company could be busy churning out electric cars. The new jobs created would be filled by American workers trained with new skills and a world-class education.

None of this will come easy. Every one of us will have to work more, read more, train more, think more. We will have to slough off bad habits—like driving gas guzzlers that weaken our economy and feed our enemies abroad. Our kids will have to turn off the TV sets and put away the video games and start hitting the books. We will have to reform institutions, like our public schools, that were designed for an earlier time. Republicans will have to recognize our collective responsibilities, even as Democrats recognize that we have to do more than just defend the old programs.

It won't be easy, but it can be done. It can be our future. We have the talent and the resources and the brainpower. But now we need the political will. We need a national commitment.

And we need you.

Now, no one can force you to meet these challenges. If you want, it will be pretty easy for you to leave here today and not give another thought to towns like Galesburg and the challenges they face. There is no community service requirement in the real world; no one's forcing you to care. You can take your diploma, walk off this stage, and go chasing after the big house, and the nice suits, and all the other things that our money culture says you can buy.

But I hope you don't. Focusing your life solely on making a buck shows a poverty of ambition. It asks too little of yourself. You need to take up the challenges that we face as a nation and make them your own, not because you have an obligation to those who are less fortunate, although you do have that obligation. Not because you have a debt to all of those who helped you get to where you are, although you do have that debt. Not because you have an obligation to those who are less fortunate, although you do have that obligation. You need to take on the challenge because you have an obligation to yourself. Because our individual salvation depends on collective salvation. Because it's only when you hitch your wagon to something larger than yourself that you will realize your true potential. And if we're willing to share the risks and the rewards this new century offers, it will be a victory for each of you, and for every American.

You're wondering how you'll do this. The challenges are so big. And it seems so difficult for one person to make a difference.

But we know it can be done. Because where you're sitting, in this very place, in this town, it's happened before.

Nearly two centuries ago, before civil rights and voting rights, before Abraham Lincoln and the Civil War, before all of that, America was stained with the sin of slavery. In the sweltering heat of southern plantations, men and women who looked like me would dream of the day they could escape the life of pain and servitude into which they were sold like cattle. And yet, year after year, as this moral cancer ate away at the American ideals of liberty and equality, the nation was silent.

But its people would not stay silent for long.

One by one, abolitionists emerged to tell their fellow Americans that this would not be our place in history. That this was not the America that had captured the imagination of so many around the world.

The resistance they met was fierce, and some paid with their lives. But they would not be deterred, and they soon spread out across the country to fight for their cause. One man from New York went west, all the way to the prairies of Illinois to start a colony.

And here in Galesburg, freedom found a home.

Here in Galesburg, the main depot for the Underground Railroad in Illinois, escaped slaves could freely roam the streets and take shelter in people's homes. And when their masters or the police would come for them, the people of this town would help them escape north, some literally carrying them in their arms.

Think about the risks that involved—if they were caught abetting these fugitives, they could have been jailed or lynched. It would have been so easy for these simple townspeople to just turn the other way; to go on living their lives in a private peace.

And yet, they carried them. Why?

Perhaps it is because they knew that they were all Americans; that they were all brothers and sisters; and in the end, their own salvation would be forever linked to the salvation of this land they called home.

The same reason that a century later, young men and women your age would take a Freedom Ride down south, to work for the civil rights movement. The same reason that black women across the South chose to walk instead of ride the bus after a long day's work doing other people's laundry, cleaning other people's kitchens.

Today, on this day of possibility, we stand in the shadow of a lanky, raw-boned man with little formal education who once took the stage at Old Main and told the nation that if anyone did not believe the American principles of freedom and equality were timeless and all-inclusive, they should go rip that page out of the Declaration of Independence.

My hope for all of you is that you leave here today with the will to keep these principles alive in your own life and the life of this country. They will be tested by the challenges of this new century, and at times we may fail to live up to them. But know that you have it within your power to try. That generations who have come before you faced these same fears and uncertainties in their own time. And that though our labor, and God's providence, and our willingness to shoulder each other's burdens, America will continue on its precious journey towards that distant horizon, and a better day.

Thank you, and congratulations on your graduation.

6

CALL TO RENEWAL KEYNOTE ADDRESS

June 28, 2006 • *National City Church, Washington, D.C.*

*If we truly hope to speak to people where they're at, to communicate
our hopes and values in a way that's relevant to their own,
then as progressives, we cannot abandon the field of religious discourse.*

After John Kerry lost the presidential election in 2004, a debate exploded in Democratic circles over the language the candidate, and the party,
had used throughout the campaign. Scholars such as George Lakoff, the
author of *Don't Think of an Elephant: Know Your Values and Frame the Debate*, argued that Democrats, time and again, had conceded values-laden
language, especially rhetoric steeped in religion, to Republicans. In doing so, they had let Republicans take the moral high ground, twist the
Bible for their own purposes, and capture large swaths of the American
electorate. Given their economic circumstances, these people should have
been voting Democratic, the argument went, but in giving short shrift to
religious values in their words and policy-making, the party had simply
let them go.

Barack Obama agreed with the Lakoff school of thought. As he later
wrote, "The single biggest gap in party affiliation among white Americans is not between men and women, or between those who reside in
so-called red states and those who reside in blue states, but between those
who attend church regularly and those who don't." [1]

Obama didn't think there was any reason why Republicans should
own the debate over values or God. After all, Democrats, not Republicans, were the ones who traditionally favored the hard-pressed over the
well-off, fighting for poverty and workers' rights. They were the ones
who "loved thy neighbor," and championed inclusion and kindness at
every turn. On top of that, Democrats made up a significant portion of

the 95 percent of Americans who believe in God; 44 percent of those who practice some form of Christianity call themselves Democrats; and 38 percent of this latter group attend church every week.

Why had Democrats conceded the space to evangelicals and Bible thumpers? Why had they allowed themselves to get swept up by a small minority on the political left who rejected any role for religion in government or political discourse? It just didn't add up for the Illinois senator. Obama believed deeply that it was time for a course correction – or, at the very least, for a serious debate about the issue.

As he had on other issues, Obama decided to cash in some of the currency he had earned with his newly found prominence and national stature and take on the religion issue. After all, he was the up-and-comer in the Democratic Party; he had earned his stripes with his iconoclastic speech on Iraq and his convention keynote address in Boston. So, after consulting with his chief of staff, Pete Rouse, and his communications director, Robert Gibbs, Obama decided to accept a speaking invitation to the Call to Renewal, a conference held by a progressive Washington, D.C., faith-based organization committed to overcoming poverty. It was the perfect setting. Their conference theme, "building a new covenant for a new America," was an ideal occasion for an address on piety in the Democratic Party.

Obama agreed to speak on religion knowing that, ultimately, he'd be lecturing his fellow Democrats. He understood that not everyone would be pleased with what he would have to say or about the liberal tenets he would question. And he was right. His remarks that morning would unleash a firestorm in various segments of the party.

After he spoke, scores of Democrat bloggers such as Michelle Goldberg of Huffington Post scolded him for "perpetuat[ing] the fantasy that there really is a liberal war on faith" and "reinforcing Republican myths about liberal Godlessness instead of challenging them." Goldberg titled her post "What's the Matter with Barack Obama?"[2]

But Obama knew what he was doing. And his views on the issues were far more nuanced than the response would suggest. Like many Democrats, he too had struggled with the role of religion in public life and had been conflicted about his own faith.

Obama wasn't raised in a particularly religious household; unlike

many Americans, he hadn't gone to church every Sunday or to Sunday
school as child. His father, who returned to Kenya when he was only two
years old, was born Muslim, but later became an atheist. His mother's
parents were a nonpracticing Baptist and a nonpracticing Methodist. She
grew up, Obama said, "with a healthy skepticism of organized religion."
In fact, he acknowledged, "As [a] consequence, so did I."

Yet, Obama explained, "For all her professed secularism, my mother
was in many ways the most spiritually awakened person that I've ever
known. She had an unswerving instinct for kindness, charity and love.
. . . She worked mightily to instill in me the values that many Americans
learn in Sunday school: honesty, empathy, discipline, delayed gratifica-
tion, and hard work." [3] Beyond that, she insisted that her son and daughter have a working knowledge of the world's religions and put copies of
the Bible, the Koran, and the Bhagavad-Gita on their bookshelves.

In short, Obama's relationship with religion during his youth was
complicated. It wasn't until later in his life, when he returned to Chicago
after law school, that Obama developed a formal connection to a particular
church. It was then that he discovered the "power of the African American religious tradition" and saw the black church as a place that could
"spur social change." Moreover, as his views evolved, he began to see faith
"as an active, palpable agent in the world . . . as a source of hope."

This was a critical epiphany for the young community organizer and
one that would affect his personal and political views for years to come.
He no longer saw religion as "something [Americans] set apart from the
rest of their beliefs and values." On the contrary, it was "often what drives
their beliefs and values." Because of that, he believed, the left couldn't
force religion out of the political discourse; it was simply too much a part
of public life.

Obama documented this metamorphosis and his spiritual journey in
The Audacity of Hope, his political vision for the country, which he wrote
shortly after his Senate victory. It was clear from the book that he spent a
good deal of time struggling with the issue.

When he decided to speak at the Call to Renewal conference, Obama
asked his chief speechwriter, Jon Favreau, to turn his book's chapter on
faith into a speech. As Favreau later said, this wasn't as simple as flipping
a switch, but it certainly made his task easier than usual. In fact, he re-

counted, the hardest part of the process was keeping the draft to a reasonable length. With each exchange of drafts, Obama kept adding language Favreau had taken out. "Over the two weeks we wrote, I would cut and he would put more in," Favreau recalled. "He had spent a good deal of time and thought writing the chapter in his book; he didn't want to lose anything. But the reality was that he only had thirty minutes to speak."

It was also evident in the book that one of the defining moments in Obama's spiritual journey was his campaign for the Illinois senate in 2004.

In that contest, Alan Keyes, a two-time presidential candidate, a former ambassador to the United Nations, and an African American favorite of the evangelical right, unabashedly questioned Obama's character and competence in terms of his belief—or lack of it—in God. Keyes thought nothing of announcing to his supporters and the media that "Jesus Christ would not vote for Barack Obama . . . because Barack Obama has behaved in a way that is inconceivable for Christ to have behaved."[4] One of Obama's Republican friends explained Keyes's strategy: "We got our own Harvard-educated conservative black guy to go up against the Harvard-educated liberal black guy. He may not win, but a least he can knock that halo off your head."[5]

Time and again during the campaign, Keyes railed against Obama, beginning with his position on same-sex marriage: "Mr. Obama says he's a Christian . . . and yet he supports a lifestyle that the Bible calls an abomination." Later, he seized on the issue of choice, declaring: "Mr. Obama says he's a Christian, but supports the destruction of innocent and sacred life."[6]

Keyes had taken off the gloves. He was using any tactic possible to drum up attention. This was part of his strategy—and Obama knew it. He described Keyes as someone that was "well-versed in the Jerry Falwell–Pat Robertson style of rhetoric" that stirred up his supporters. There was little reason for Obama to engage Keyes or afford him any attention because, right up until the very end, Obama was besting his opponent by more than forty points in the polls.

Yet, despite all this, Keyes succeeded in getting under Obama's skin. He just couldn't let it go. "I had to take Mr. Keyes seriously," he told those at the Call to Renewal event, "for he claimed to speak for my religion, and my God. He claimed knowledge of certain truths." Like other

conservatives, Keyes had exploited religion for political gain, using it as
a disingenuous cue to "evangelical Christians that Democrats disrespect
their values and dislike their church."

Obama knew that Keyes's approach wasn't exactly groundbreaking.
For years, according to Obama, Republicans—for example, Ronald Reagan, Pat Robertson, Ralph Reed, and Karl Rove—had emphasized "family values, tradition, and order" to "harvest this crop of politically awakened evangelicals . . . against the liberal orthodoxy." They had mobilized
the pulpits on Sunday in churches and via right-wing media to communicate with their followers. Obama didn't blame Americans for responding to these tactics, because, as he pointed out in *The Audacity of Hope,*
"[People] want a sense of purpose, a narrative arc to their lives, something
that will relieve a chronic loneliness or lift them above the exhausting,
relentless toll of daily life."[7]

In retrospect, what troubled Obama even more than what Keyes said
about him was his own response to Keyes's accusations. Rather than fighting back, he ran away from a discussion of faith, with the intention of re-
fusing to energize Keyes. Instead of challenging his fundamental premise,
Obama responded with the typical liberal party line: "We live in a pluralistic society. . . . I can't impose my own religious views on another. . . . I
[am] running to be the U.S. senator from Illinois and not the minister
of Illinois." [8] He did what so many other Democrats do, as he noted in
The Audacity of Hope—he avoided "the conversation about religious values
altogether, fearful of offending anyone and claim[ed] that—regardless of
[our] personal beliefs—constitutional principles tie our hands."[9]

Obama's response to Keyes helped shape the message he delivered to
Democrats at the Call to Renewal conference that day: "As progressives
we cannot abandon the field of religious discourse." Rather, Democrats
needed to embrace it.

First and foremost, Obama told his fellow progressives, that they
shouldn't avoid religious venues and pious language. For too long, he
believed, Democrats had framed religion in a negative context—how "it
should not be practiced," instead of "a positive sense of what it tells us about
our obligations." As a consequence, he warned them, "If we don't reach
out to evangelical Christians and other religious Americans and tell them
what we stand for, then the Jerry Falwells . . . will continue to hold sway."

Democrats should not be uncomfortable with religious language and imagery in the public arena, Obama argued, because it is what "millions of Americans understand . . . [as] their personal morality and social justice." Obama saw this discomfort as a clear mistake. To make his point, he cited Abraham Lincoln's Second Inaugural Address—in which Lincoln spoke of "the judgments of the Lord"—and Frederick Douglass, William Jennings Bryan, Martin Luther King Jr., and other great reformers who embraced faith and "religious language to argue for their cause. . . . Secularists are wrong when they ask believers to leave their religion at the door before entering into the public square."

That said, Obama sympathized with Democrats for being hesitant. They feared sounding "preachy." In avoiding the language, however, they were ignoring an important reality: "values and culture" play a central role in addressing some of the nation's most pressing social problems. Poverty, unemployment, racism, and violence—all core Democratic issues —were rooted in what the Bible calls the "imperfections of man." He explained, "There's a hole . . . that the government alone cannot fix." This was a point he raised in *The Audacity of Hope*: "The discomfort of some progressives with any hint of religiosity has often inhibited us from effectively addressing issues in moral terms."[10]

Second, Obama insisted that avoiding religion was "just bad politics" for Democrats—a statement that some might view as crass. But Obama was matter-of-fact and unabashedly political on this point. "There are a whole lot of religious people in America, including the majority of Democrats," he noted, and went on to say in the book that Democrats must engage all people of faith, instead of conceding those voters and their issues to the political right.

Third, Obama argued that the absolute separation of church and state was anachronistic. While there was a line to be drawn, some liberals had gone too far in making the separation of church and state a black-and-white issue, with no shades of gray. He had written earlier, "To say that men and women should not inject their personal morality into public policy debates is a practical absurdity; our law is by definition a codification of morality, much of it grounded in the Judeo-Christian tradition." America's Founding Fathers were not atheists; rather, they were persecuted minorities who "didn't want state-sponsored religion hindering their ability to practice their faith as they understood it."[11] He encouraged his fellow Democrats to be circumspect but more accepting of some faith in public life. This was a strong statement, one that appeared to be aimed at the far left of his party.

Obama concluded his speech with a direct appeal for comity on both sides of the political aisle: "Not every mention of God in public is a breach to the wall of separation [between church and state]." As examples, he cited "under God" in the Pledge of Allegiance and voluntary prayer in high schools, which, he argued, "should not be a threat any more than [a school's] use by the high school Republicans should threaten Democrats."

As his rhetoric confirmed, Obama wasn't afraid to question the orthodoxy of his party. He had the political capital and was already a darling of the left. Cynics, however, may view his speech as a pragmatic play for the allegiance of political centrist voters, who tended to be more religious and less concerned about faith in the public sector.

Either way, his message at the National City Church was consistent with his long-standing call for greater "unity" in government and for an end to the traditional balkanization of American politics. This issue of religion was no different to him. He saw an opportunity to lessen the divide between the churchgoers and the less active. As he said in his speech, "I am hopeful that we can bridge the gaps that exist and overcome the prejudices that each of us bring[s] to this debate. . . . No matter how religious they may or may not be, people are tired of seeing faith used as a tool of attack. They don't want faith used to belittle or divide . . . because, in the end, that's not how they think about faith in their own lives."

Many viewed Obama's speech as courageous. He stepped into the lion's den on both sides of the religious issue and walked away with all of his limbs intact. The *Washington Post* summarized his remarks with the headline "Obama: Democrats Must Court Evangelicals," adding, "His speech included unusually personal references to religion, the type of remarks that usually come more readily from Republicans than Democrats."[12] Garrett Graff later wrote in the *Washingtonian* magazine that the speech was "perhaps the most important dissection of the political world and the role of faith made by any Democratic politician in a generation."[13]

In an interview on NPR a few weeks later, Obama described his intentions: "Part of my interest was to figure out how we can stop using reli-

gion as a divisive force in the body politic and how we can tap into
that sense that our values . . . can be harnessed to bring about changes that
might have been impossible." He went on to say that his remarks that day
were not politically calculating: "I can't really spend a lot of time worrying about how my words are interpreted."[14]

But, as much as he contended that he wasn't "calculating," it was
no surprise that in 2006, Obama was already highlighting the need for
"change" in our politics. In his eyes, as he would say in the years to come,
there were few places in the political system that didn't demand change.

Obama was the final Democrat to address the conference. His soon-
to-be rival, Senator Hillary Clinton, and the chairman of the Democratic
National Committee, Howard Dean, had addressed the participants earlier in the week. The chapel was packed for Obama's speech and he was
lifted by the energy of the crowd. Favreau, who was with him, described
it by saying, "He was clapping along in church and swaying as he spoke.
There was a preachy cadence to his voice. The parishioners were certainly
with Obama."

In the end, Obama was elated with the reaction to the speech. His
remarks that day would serve his speechwriters as a template for years to
come. It influenced the piece he wrote for the October 16 issue of *Time*
magazine later that year entitled "My Spiritual Journey." Adam Frankel
used it on the campaign trail to shape Obama's remarks at the United
Church of Christ's fiftieth-anniversary celebration—which Andrew Sullivan called "the best speech Obama has ever given"[15]—and then again
in the White House at the National Prayer Breakfast just weeks after his
inauguration.

Remarks by Senator Barack Obama:
Call to Renewal Keynote Address

Good morning. I appreciate the opportunity to speak here at the Call to Renewal's Building a Covenant for a New America conference. I've had the opportunity to take a look at your Covenant for a New America. It is filled with outstanding policies and prescriptions for much of what ails this country. So I'd like to congratulate you all on the thoughtful presentations you've given so far about poverty and justice in America, and for putting fire under the feet of the political leadership here in Washington.

But today I'd like to talk about the connection between religion and politics and perhaps offer some thoughts about how we can sort through some of the often bitter arguments that we've been seeing over the last several years.

I do so because, as you all know, we can affirm the importance of poverty in the Bible; and we can raise up and pass out this Covenant for a New America. We can talk to the press, and we can discuss the religious call to address poverty and environmental stewardship all we want, but it won't have an impact unless we tackle head-on the mutual suspicion that sometimes exists between religious America and secular America.

I want to give you an example that I think illustrates this fact. As some of you know, during the 2004 U.S. Senate general election I ran against a gentleman named Alan Keyes. Mr. Keyes is well-versed in the Jerry Falwell–Pat Robertson style of rhetoric that often labels progressives as both immoral and godless.

Indeed, Mr. Keyes announced towards the end of the campaign that "Jesus Christ would not vote for Barack Obama. Christ would not vote for Barack Obama because Barack Obama has behaved in a way that it is inconceivable for Christ to have behaved."

Jesus Christ would not vote for Barack Obama.

Now, I was urged by some of my liberal supporters not to take this statement seriously, to essentially ignore it. To them, Mr. Keyes was an extremist, and his arguments not worth entertaining. And since at the time, I was up forty points in the polls, it probably wasn't a bad piece of strategic advice.

But what they didn't understand, however, was that I had to take Mr. Keyes seriously, for he claimed to speak for my religion, and my God. He claimed knowledge of certain truths.

Mr. Obama says he's a Christian, he was saying, and yet he supports a lifestyle that the Bible calls an abomination.

Mr. Obama says he's a Christian, but supports the destruction of innocent and sacred life.

And so what would my supporters have me say? How should I respond? Should I say that a literalist reading of the Bible was folly? Should I say that Mr. Keyes, who is a Roman Catholic, should ignore the teachings of the Pope?

Unwilling to go there, I answered with what has come to be the typically liberal response in such debates—namely, I said that we live in a pluralistic society, that I can't impose my own religious views on another, that I was running to be the U.S. senator of Illinois and not the minister of Illinois.

But Mr. Keyes's implicit accusation that I was not a true Christian nagged at me, and I was also aware that my answer did not adequately address the role my faith has in guiding my own values and my own beliefs.

Now, my dilemma was by no means unique. In a way, it reflected the broader debate we've been having in this country for the last thirty years over the role of religion in politics.

For some time now, there has been plenty of talk among pundits and pollsters that the political divide in this country has fallen sharply along religious lines. Indeed, the single biggest "gap" in party affiliation among white Americans today is not between men and women, or those who reside in so-called red states and those who reside in blue, but between those who attend church regularly and those who don't.

Conservative leaders have been all too happy to exploit this gap, consistently reminding evangelical Christians that Democrats disrespect their values and dislike their church, while suggesting to the rest of the country that religious Americans care only about issues like abortion and gay marriage, school prayer and intelligent design.

Democrats, for the most part, have taken the bait. At best, we may try to avoid the conversation about religious values altogether, fearful of offending anyone and claiming that—regardless of our personal beliefs—constitutional principles tie our hands. At worst, there are some liberals who dismiss religion in the public square as inherently irrational or intolerant, insisting on a caricature of religious Americans that paints them as fanatical, or thinking that the very word "Christian" describes one's political opponents, not people of faith.

Now, such strategies of avoidance may work for progressives when our opponent is Alan Keyes. But over the long haul, I think we make a mistake when we fail to acknowledge the power of faith in people's lives, in the lives of the American people, and I think it's time that we join a serious debate about how to reconcile faith with our modern, pluralistic democracy.

And if we're going to do that then we first need to understand that Americans are a religious people: 90 percent of us believe in God, 70 percent affiliate themselves with an organized religion, 38 percent call themselves committed Christians, and substantially more people in America believe in angels than they do in evolution.

This religious tendency is not simply the result of successful marketing by skilled preachers or the draw of popular megachurches. In fact, it speaks to a hunger that's deeper than that—a hunger that goes beyond any particular issue or cause.

Each day, it seems, thousands of Americans are going about their daily rounds—dropping off the kids at school, driving to the office, flying to a business meeting, shopping at the mall, trying to stay on their diets—and they're coming to the realization that something is missing. They are deciding that their work, their possessions, their diversions, their sheer busyness, is not enough.

They want a sense of purpose, a narrative arc to their lives. They're looking to relieve a chronic loneliness, a feeling supported by a recent study that shows Americans have fewer close friends and confidants than ever before. And so they need an assurance that somebody out there cares about them, is listening to them—that they are not just destined to travel down that long highway towards nothingness.

And I speak with some experience on this matter. I was not raised in a particularly religious household, as undoubtedly many in the audience were. My father, who returned to Kenya when I was just two, was born Muslim but as an adult became an atheist. My mother, whose parents were nonpracticing Baptists and Methodists, was probably one of the most spiritual and kindest people I've ever known, but grew up with a healthy skepticism of organized religion herself. As a consequence, so did I.

It wasn't until after college, when I went to Chicago to work as a community organizer for a group of Christian churches, that I confronted my own spiritual dilemma.

I was working with churches, and the Christians who I worked with recognized themselves in me. They saw that I knew their Book and that I shared their values and sang their songs. But they sensed that a part of me remained removed, detached, that I was an observer in their midst.

And in time, I came to realize that something was missing as well—that without a vessel for my beliefs, without a commitment to a particular community of faith, at some level I would always remain apart, and alone.

And if it weren't for the particular attributes of the historically black church, I may have accepted this fate. But as the months passed in Chicago, I found myself drawn—not just to work with the church, but to be in the church.

For one thing, I believed and still believe in the power of the African American religious tradition to spur social change, a power made real by some of the leaders here today. Because of its past, the black church understands in an intimate way the biblical call to feed the hungry and clothe the naked and challenge powers and principalities. And in its historical struggles for freedom and the rights of man, I was able to see faith as more than just a comfort to the weary or a hedge against death, but rather as an active, palpable agent in the world. As a source of hope.

And perhaps it was out of this intimate knowledge of hardship—the grounding of faith in struggle—that the church offered me a second insight, one that I think is important to emphasize today.

Faith doesn't mean that you don't have doubts.

You need to come to church in the first place precisely because you are first of this world, not apart from it. You need to embrace Christ precisely because you have sins to wash away—because you are human and need an ally in this difficult journey.

It was because of these newfound understandings that I was finally able to walk down the aisle of Trinity United Church of Christ on Ninety-fifth Street in the South Side of Chicago one day and affirm my Christian faith.

It came about as a choice, and not an epiphany. I didn't fall out in church. The questions I had didn't magically disappear. But kneeling beneath that cross on the South Side, I felt that I heard God's spirit beckoning me. I submitted myself to His will, and dedicated myself to discovering His truth.

That's a path that has been shared by millions upon millions of Americans—evangelicals, Catholics, Protestants, Jews, and Muslims alike; some since birth, others at certain turning points in their lives. It is not something they set apart from the rest of their beliefs and values. In fact, it is often what drives their beliefs and their values.

And that is why that, if we truly hope to speak to people where they're at—to communicate our hopes and values in a way that's relevant to their own—then as progressives, we cannot abandon the field of religious discourse.

Because when we ignore the debate about what it means to be a good Christian or Muslim or Jew; when we discuss religion only in the negative sense of where or how it should not be practiced, rather than in the positive sense of what it tells us about our obligations towards one another; when we shy away from religious venues and religious broadcasts because we assume that we will be unwelcome—others will fill the vacuum, those with the most insular views of faith, or those who cynically use religion to justify partisan ends.

In other words, if we don't reach out to evangelical Christians and other religious Americans and tell them what we stand for, then the Jerry Falwells and Pat Robertsons and Alan Keyeses will continue to hold sway.

More fundamentally, the discomfort of some progressives with any hint of religion has often prevented us from effectively addressing issues in moral terms. Some of the problem here is rhetorical—if we scrub language of all religious content, we forfeit the imagery and terminology through which millions of Americans understand both their personal morality and social justice.

Imagine Lincoln's Second Inaugural Address without reference to "the judgments of the Lord." Or King's 'I Have a Dream' speech without references to "all of God's children." Their summoning of a higher truth helped inspire what had seemed impossible, and move the nation to embrace a common destiny.

Our failure as progressives to tap into the moral underpinnings of the nation is not just rhetorical, though. Our fear of getting "preachy" may also lead us to discount the role that values and culture play in some of our most urgent social problems.

After all, the problems of poverty and racism, the uninsured and the unemployed, are not simply technical problems in search of the perfect ten point plan. They are rooted in both societal indifference and individual callousness—in the imperfections of man.

Solving these problems will require changes in government policy, but it will also require changes in hearts and a change in minds. I believe in keeping guns out of our inner cities, and that our leaders must say so in the face of the gun manufacturers' lobby—but I also believe that when a gang-banger shoots indiscriminately into a crowd because he feels somebody disrespected him, we've got a moral problem. There's a hole in that young man's heart—a hole that the government alone cannot fix.

I believe in vigorous enforcement of our nondiscrimination laws. But I also believe that a transformation of conscience and a genuine commitment to diversity on the part of the nation's CEOs could bring about quicker results than a battalion of lawyers. They have more lawyers than us anyway.

I think that we should put more of our tax dollars into educating poor girls and boys. I think that the work that Marian Wright Edelman has done all her life is absolutely how we should prioritize our resources in the wealthiest nation on earth. I also think that we should give them the information about contraception that can prevent unwanted pregnancies, lower abortion rates, and help assure that that every child is loved and cherished.

But, you know, my Bible tells me that if we train a child in the way he should go, when he is old he will not turn from it. So I think faith and guidance can help fortify a young woman's sense of self, a young man's sense of responsibility, and a sense of reverence that all young people should have for the act of sexual intimacy.

I am not suggesting that every progressive suddenly latch on to religious terminology—that can be dangerous. Nothing is more transparent than inauthentic expressions of faith. As Jim has mentioned, some politicians come and clap—off rhythm—to the choir. We don't need that.

In fact, because I do not believe that religious people have a monopoly on morality, I would rather have someone who is grounded in morality and ethics, and who is also secular, affirm their morality and ethics and values without pretending that they're something they're not. They don't need to do that. None of us need to do that.

But what I am suggesting is this—secularists are wrong when they ask believers to leave their religion at the door before entering into the public square. Frederick Douglass, Abraham Lincoln, Williams Jennings Bryan, Dorothy Day, Martin Luther King—indeed, the majority of great reformers in American history—were not only motivated by faith, but repeatedly used religious language to argue for their cause. So to say that men and women should not inject their "personal morality" into public policy debates is a practical absurdity. Our law is by definition a codification of morality, much of it grounded in the Judeo-Christian tradition.

Moreover, if we progressives shed some of these biases, we might recognize some overlapping values that both religious and secular people share when it comes to the moral and material direction of our country. We might recognize that the call to sacrifice on behalf of the next generation, the need to think in terms of "thou" and not just "I," resonates in religious congregations all across the country. And we might realize that we have the ability to reach out to the evangelical community and engage millions of religious Americans in the larger project of American renewal.

Some of this is already beginning to happen. Pastors, friends of mine like Rick Warren and T. D. Jakes, are wielding their enormous influences to confront AIDS, third world debt relief, and the genocide in Darfur. Religious thinkers and activists like our good friends Jim Wallis and Tony Campolo are lifting up the biblical injunction to help the poor as a means of mobilizing Christians against budget cuts to social programs and growing inequality.

And by the way, we need Christians on Capitol Hill, Jews on Capitol Hill, and Muslims on Capitol Hill talking about the estate tax. When you've got an estate tax debate that proposes a trillion dollars being taken out of social programs to go to a handful of folks who don't need and weren't even asking for it, you know that we need an injection of morality in our political debate.

Across the country, individual churches like my own and your own are sponsoring day-care programs, building senior centers, helping ex-offenders reclaim their lives, and rebuilding our Gulf Coast in the aftermath of Hurricane Katrina.

So the question is, How do we build on these still-tentative partnerships between religious and secular people of goodwill? It's going to take more work, a lot more work than we've done so far. The tensions and the suspicions on each side of the religious divide will have to be squarely addressed. And each side will need to accept some ground rules for collaboration.

While I've already laid out some of the work that progressive leaders need to do, I want to talk a little bit about what conservative leaders need to do—some truths they need to acknowledge.

For one, they need to understand the critical role that the separation of church and state has played in preserving not only our democracy, but the robustness of our religious practice. Folks tend to forget that during our founding, it wasn't the atheists or the civil libertarians who were the most effective champions of the First Amendment. It was the persecuted minorities, it was Baptists like John Leland who didn't want the established churches to impose their views on folks who were getting happy out in the fields and teaching the Scripture to slaves. It was the forebearers of the evangelicals who were the most adamant about not mingling government with religion, because they did not want state-sponsored religion hindering their ability to practice their faith as they understood it.

Moreover, given the increasing diversity of America's population, the dangers of sectarianism have never been greater. Whatever we once were, we are no longer just a Christian nation; we are also a Jewish nation, a Muslim nation, a Buddhist nation, a Hindu nation, and a nation of nonbelievers.

And even if we did have only Christians in our midst, if we expelled every non-Christian from the United States of America, whose Christianity would we teach in the schools? Would we go with James Dobson's, or Al Sharpton's? Which passages of Scripture should guide our public policy? Should we go with Leviticus, which suggests slavery is okay and that eating shellfish is abomination? How about Deuteronomy, which suggests stoning your child if he strays from the faith? Or should we just stick to the Sermon on the Mount—a passage that is so radical that it's doubtful that our own Defense Department would survive its application? So before we get carried away, let's read our Bibles. Folks haven't been reading their Bibles.

This brings me to my second point. Democracy demands that the religiously motivated translate their concerns into universal, rather than religion-specific, values. It requires that their proposals be subject to argument, and amenable to reason. I may be opposed to abortion for religious reasons, but if I seek to pass a law banning the practice, I cannot simply point to the teachings of my church or evoke God's will. I have to explain why abortion violates some principle that is accessible to people of all faiths, including those with no faith at all.

Now this is going to be difficult for some who believe in the inerrancy of the Bible, as many evangelicals do. But in a pluralistic democracy, we have no choice. Politics depends on our ability to persuade each other of common aims based on a common reality. It involves the compromise, the art of what's possible. At some fundamental level, religion does not allow for compromise. It's the art of the impossible. If God has spoken, then followers are expected to live up to God's edicts, regardless of the consequences. To base one's life on such uncompromising commitments may be sublime, but to base our policymaking on such commitments would be a dangerous thing. And if you doubt that, let me give you an example.

We all know the story of Abraham and Isaac. Abraham is ordered by God to offer up his only son, and without argument, he takes Isaac to the mountaintop, binds him to an altar, and raises his knife, prepared to act as God has commanded.

Of course, in the end God sends down an angel to intercede at the very last minute, and Abraham passes God's test of devotion.

But it's fair to say that if any of us leaving this church saw Abraham on a roof of a building raising his knife, we would, at the very least, call the police and expect the Department of Children and Family Services to take Isaac away from Abraham. We would do so because we do not hear what Abraham hears, do not see what Abraham sees, true as those experiences may be. So the best we can do is act in accordance with those things that we all see, and that we all hear, be it common laws or basic reason.

Finally, any reconciliation between faith and democratic pluralism requires some sense of proportion.

This goes for both sides.

Even those who claim the Bible's inerrancy make distinctions between scriptural edicts, sensing that some passages—the Ten Commandments, say, or a belief in Christ's divinity—are central to Christian faith, while others are more culturally specific and may be modified to accommodate modern life.

The American people intuitively understand this, which is why the majority of Catholics practice birth control and some of those opposed to gay marriage nevertheless are opposed to a constitutional amendment to ban it. Religious leadership need not accept such wisdom in counseling their flocks, but they should recognize this wisdom in their politics.

But a sense of proportion should also guide those who police the boundaries between church and state. Not every mention of God in public is a breach to the wall of separation—context matters. It is doubtful that children reciting the Pledge of Allegiance feel oppressed or brainwashed as a consequence of muttering the phrase "under God." I didn't. Having voluntary student prayer groups use school property to meet should not be a threat, any more than its use by the High School Republicans should threaten Democrats. And one can envision certain faith-based programs, targeting ex-offenders or substance abusers, that offer a uniquely powerful way of solving problems.

So we all have some work to do here. But I am hopeful that we can bridge the gaps that exist and overcome the prejudices each of us bring to this debate. And I have faith that millions of believing Americans want that to happen. No matter how religious they may or may not be, people are tired of seeing faith used as a tool of attack. They don't want faith used to belittle or to divide. They're tired of hearing folks deliver more screed than sermon. Because in the end, that's not how they think about faith in their own lives.

So let me end with just one other interaction I had during my campaign. A few days after I won the Democratic nomination in my U.S. Senate race, I received an e-mail from a doctor at the University of Chicago Medical School that said the following:

> Congratulations on your overwhelming and inspiring primary win. I was happy to vote for you, and I will tell you that I am seriously considering voting for you in the general election. I write to express my concerns that may, in the end, prevent me from supporting you.

The doctor described himself as a Christian who understood his commitments to be "totalizing." His faith led him to a strong opposition to abortion and gay marriage, although he said that his faith also led him to question the idolatry of the free market and quick resort to militarism that seemed to characterize much of the Republican agenda.

But the reason the doctor was considering not voting for me was not simply my position on abortion. Rather, he had read an entry that my campaign had posted on my Web site, which suggested that I would fight "right-wing ideologues who want to take away a woman's right to choose." The doctor went on to write:

> I sense that you have a strong sense of justice . . . and I also sense that you are a fair-minded person with a high regard for reason. . . . Whatever your convictions, if you truly believe that those who oppose abortion are all ideologues driven by perverse desires to inflict suffering on women, then you, in my judgment, are not fair-minded. . . . You know that we enter times that are fraught with possibilities for good and for harm, times when we are struggling to make sense of a common polity in the context of plurality, when we are unsure of what grounds we have for making any claims that involve others. . . . I do not ask at this point that you oppose abortion, only that you speak about this issue in fair-minded words.

Fair-minded words.

So I looked at my Web site and found the offending words. In fairness to them, my staff had written them using standard Democratic boilerplate language to summarize my pro-choice position during the Democratic primary, at a time when some of my opponents were questioning my commitment to protect *Roe v. Wade.*

Rereading the doctor's letter, though, I felt a pang of shame. It is people like him who are looking for a deeper, fuller conversation about religion in this country. They may not change their positions, but they are willing to listen and learn from those who are willing to speak in fair-minded words. Those who know of the central and awesome place that God holds in the lives of so many, and who refuse to treat faith as simply another political issue with which to score points.

So I wrote back to the doctor, and I thanked him for his advice. The next day, I circulated the e-mail to my staff and changed the language on my Web site to state in clear but simple terms my pro-choice position. And that night, before I went to bed, I said a prayer of my own—a prayer that I might extend the same presumption of good faith to others that the doctor had extended to me.

And that night, before I went to bed I said a prayer of my own. It's a prayer I think I share with a lot of Americans. A hope that we can live with one another in a way that reconciles the beliefs of each with the good of all. It's a prayer worth praying, and a conversation worth having in this country in the months and years to come.

Thank you.

7

"An Honest Government, A Hopeful Future"

August 28, 2006 • *University of Nairobi, Nairobi, Kenya*

Like many nations across this continent,
where Kenya is failing is in its ability to create
a government that is transparent and accountable.
One that serves its people and is free from corruption.

At the height of the power of the apartheid regime, in 1966, Senator Robert Kennedy and a few of his aides made a historic trip to South Africa. In a speech at University of Cape Town, before eighteen thousand students and activists, Kennedy eloquently described the struggle for freedom in South Africa and, in a controversial affront to the government, exhorted his audience to carry on their movement against discrimination. Historians have argued that the trip was an important catalyst in Kennedy's decision to seek the presidency in 1968.

Like Kennedy, political commentators have credited Obama's two-week voyage to the continent in the summer of 2006 as being critical to his decision to run for the presidency. There were several other parallels between his and Kennedy's trips.

Like Kennedy, Obama's journey received an intense amount of attention. In 1966, Kennedy, the brother of a former president, was a junior senator in the national spotlight. His trip was widely reported by the international media, and photos of him surrounded by Africans were widely disseminated. His "Ripples of Hope" speech at the University of Cape Town has been etched into the annals of civil rights history.

Similarly, by 2006, Barack Obama was no ordinary first-term senator. He too was a young, charismatic figure and a darling of the American press; he even had family roots in Africa. Obama had more media and speaking requests than his staff could possibly field. News crews jumped when Obama announced his trip with stops in South Africa, Rwanda, Kenya, Djibouti, Chad, and the Democratic Republic of the Congo. (In the end, Obama would visit South Africa, Kenya, and Chad, but scrapped plans to visit the other countries because of violence in those countries and visa issues.) The trip would bring to life the stories Obama told in his best-selling book *Dreams from My Father.*

A gaggle of reporters followed Obama to Africa and hung on his every word, including reporters from his hometown papers, the *Chicago Tribune* and *Chicago Sun Times,* and the *St. Louis-Dispatch,* Associated Press, *Time,* and *Newsweek.* There were also two documentary film crews, one of which was hired by Obama's campaign strategist, David Axelrod. The press couldn't get enough footage.[1]

Also like Kennedy's trip to Africa, Obama's journey, and the international attention it received, helped crystallize his decision to run for the presidency. The trip had been a key part of the two-year strategy he and his team of advisers—Axelrod; his communications director, Robert Gibbs; and his Senate chief of staff, Pete Rouse—had developed shortly after Obama was elected to the Senate. According to David Mendell, "The Plan" had several components, including constituent outreach, establishing a political action committee, and establishing his foreign policy credentials—this was where the Kenya trip came into play.[2]

In January 2005, Obama took an assignment on the Foreign Relations Committee, the perfect perch from which to burnish this part of his résumé. In his first year on the committee, he took trips to Russia, Eastern Europe, and the Middle East; he also successfully secured increased aid for the Republic of Congo, as part of his interest in drawing more attention to Africa. "The Plan" also outlined a trip to Kenya to visit his father's homeland. Doing so would "raise the senator's profile nationally and internationally; solidify his support among a key constituency, African Americans; and bulk up his foreign policy credentials."[3]

Obama's trip to Africa was a whirlwind tour; the senator and his traveling party, which included his foreign policy adviser, Mark Lippert, and Gibbs, never had a moment to rest or catch up on sleep. Their itinerary began with a visit to South Africa, where Obama visited a community health center and Robben Island Prison (where Nelson Mandela had been held for more than a quarter century), spent time with the Nobel Peace Prize winner Archbishop Desmond Tutu, and delivered a speech criticizing the country's handling of the AIDS epidemic. Then, it was off to Kenya for his first visit to the country since he had been there fourteen years earlier to research his memoir.

By the time Obama's plane taxied down the narrow landing strip at Jomo Kenyatta International Airport in Nairobi, the tarmac was teeming with government officials and thousands of locals. It was immediately clear that Kenya considered him both a native son and a powerful political figure who could carry Kenya's voice to the rest of the world. Street vendors sold T-shirts printed with "Obama in the House"; someone had produced a play based on his book; a school in rural Kenya was named in his honor; there was even a beer with his name on it. By all accounts, it was a mob scene.[4]

Obama's schedule included six days in Kenya, beginning with a visit with President Mwai Kibaki of the National Rainbow Coalition. Obama impressed on Kibaki the importance of ending corruption, a precursor to his speech later in the week. Kenya was a functioning democracy, but its political parties still broke along ethnic tribal lines.

After a few days in the country spent traveling with a twelve-car motorcade, Obama and his entourage flew to the rural area of Kolego in the Siaya District of Nyanza Province, about 175 miles east of Nairobi, to his family's homestead. To avoid what could be an eight-hour drive on dirt roads, Obama and the traveling press flew from Nairobi to Kisimu and drove from there. Kolego is dominated by the Luo tribe, a community that lives in mud huts and farmed their own land.[5]

When his flight arrived in Kisimu, throngs of people descended on Obama: Peace Corps workers, Lao tribal officials, and elated local onlookers. After traveling with Michelle to a hospital for an event focusing on AIDS—where he publicly took an HIV test—he finally visited his father's compound. Once there, he jumped out of his vehicle and embraced his eighty-three-year-old grandmother, who had tears in her eyes. Unfortunately, his visit with his family was cut short because of all the commotion, as reporters, security, and a cadre of local officials swarmed the property.

The next morning, back in Nairobi, Obama and Michelle went to

Kibera, one of the world's most desperate slums, located only a few miles from downtown Nairobi, and discussed education and AIDS prevention. This was his last stop before arriving at the University of Nairobi, where he would deliver his major address of the trip. Speaking in a simple auditorium before nearly a thousand people and reaching thousands more who listened on loudspeakers, Obama made his case to end the corruption that was plaguing his father's homeland.

When Obama's speechwriter, Jon Favreau, first sat down to draft this speech, Robert Kennedy and his 1966 "Ripples of Hope" speech was certainly on his mind. He had read extensively about Kennedy's trip to Africa decades earlier and wanted Obama's speech to have a similar historical impact. He and Obama had discussed Kennedy's trip at length when they had met in Obama's Senate office a few weeks before the trip.

When Obama read Favreau's first draft, during his flight to Africa, he wasn't surprised to find several quotes from Kennedy's speech. But Obama decided to take out the references. He wanted to leave his own, distinct mark and deliver his own message. He didn't need Kennedy to buttress his point. (Plus, the media would make the connection for him.) The core message he and Favreau had discussed back in Washington— transparency and ending corruption—would be enough to carry the day. Favreau ultimately agreed.

Obama also wanted to add to the speech references to something Kennedy lacked: an African family. Obama's father and grandfather were born in Kenya, and a majority of his family still lived there. He is a child of Africa, a point he made not only by delivering his speech in the country his father grew up in but also by including his family history in the text: "The first time I came to Kenya was in 1987. . . . I discovered the story of my father's life and the story of his father before him. . . . I learned that my grandfather had been a cook for the British, and although he was a respected elder in his village, he was called 'boy' by his employers. . . . I learned how my father had grown up in a tiny village called Alego."

Obama was right. His personal connection was enough to grab headlines. But it also afforded him the credibility to hit the corruption point hard, a topic that would have been difficult for another American politician. "For all the progress that has been made," he told his audience, "we must acknowledge that neither Kenya nor the African continent have yet fulfilled their potential." Obama proceeded to tick off a raft of missed opportunities and challenges, from economic development and parity to HIV/AIDS and education.

He then moved on to the central message of his speech: "It's more than just history and outside influences that explain why Kenya lags behind. Like many nations across this continent, where Kenya is failing is in its ability to create a government that is transparent and accountable. One that serves its people and is free from corruption."

Obama was quick to acknowledge that corruption wasn't just an African problem; it also plagued his hometown city, Chicago, and American politics in general. It was a "human problem." But, he added, "while corruption is a problem we all share, here in Kenya it is a crisis—a crisis that's robbing honest people of the opportunities they have fought for." It stood in the way of everything Africa needed to advance—health care, education, government, security, economic development, and innovation.

Although he offered faint praise for "signs of progress," Obama's words called into question the leadership of Mwai Kibaki, the very man he'd met with just days earlier. Kibaki was elected to clean up Kenyan corruption, but it was widely known that he had fallen into the trap of his predecessors: entanglement in financial impropriety, nepotism, misappropriation of funds, mismanagement, and corruption. Obama made his comments knowing that his speech was being broadcast to the entire nation. "If the people cannot trust their government to do the job for which it exists—to protect them and to promote their common welfare—all else is lost."

Although some claimed that Obama could have taken his argument further, Obama was careful not to say anything that would give ammunition to Kenyan politicians who might seek to use his speech for political gain; he was particularly concerned not to give encouragement to officials in his father's tribe, the Luo.

The solutions Obama presented were akin to those he suggested back home and ones that would resurface during his presidential run: "The Kenyan people are crying out for real change. . . . An accountable transparent government can break this cycle."

Like Kennedy years earlier, Obama's language was artful and inspiring. He issued a call to all Kenyans, especially the young, to stand up to corruption in all areas—in the government bureaucracy, in the judicial system, and in business. He called for regulatory reform, accountability from the country's leadership, and an end to ethnic-based tribal politics. His words echoed in the hall: "In the end, one of the strongest weapons your country has against corruption is the ability of you, the people, to stand up and speak out about the injustices you see. The Kenyan people are the ultimate guardians against abuses." Students clapped and, when appropriate, laughed throughout the speech.

The speech was a resounding success, and its effects—and his message—were felt across the country for weeks after he left. Jeffrey Gettleman in the *New York Times* noted that Obama was "using all the rapturous attention to spotlight serious issues that are too often ignored in Africa." He added that Obama called on Kenyans to "accept responsibility" for their actions, a common theme in the senator's public life.[6] Local newspapers chimed in, too. East Africa's largest paper, the *Daily Nation,* ran the headline "Village Beats the Drums for Returning Son."[7]

David Mendell, who was present in Kenya during Obama's trip, wrote extensively about the speech itself, noting that Obama exuded "presence, confidence, and moral clarity." Students he interviewed commented on Obama's "charisma" and "eloquence," although they "wanted him to take a harder line on the current political leadership." Mendell summarized his experience that day by saying, "It was hard not to witness this kind of speech by Obama and not envision a presidential run."[8]

According to Gettleman, when one African reporter asked Obama whether he harbored presidential ambitions and whether he would run for president in 2008, according to Gettleman, he simply answered, "I don't know what to do with these two questions."[9]

Shortly after returning from his final stop in Chad, and basking in the flood of post-Africa attention—which included stories in *Men's Vogue, New York* magazine, *Ebony,* and an appearance on the *Tonight Show,* Obama met again with the architects of "The Plan." They all agreed that he should begin in earnest to explore a run for the presidency.

Remarks by Senator Barack Obama:
"An Honest Government, A Hopeful Future"

The first time I came to Kenya was in 1987. I had just finished three years of work as a community organizer in low-income neighborhoods of Chicago, and was about to enroll in law school. My sister, Auma, was teaching that year at this university, and so I came to stay with her for a month.

My experience then was very different than it has been on this trip. Instead of a motorcade, we traveled in my sister's old VW Beetle, which even then was already ten years old. When it broke down in front of Uhuru Park, we had to push until some *joakalis* came to fix it by the side of the road. I slept on the couch of my sister's apartment, not a fancy hotel, and often took my meals at a small tea house in downtown Nairobi. When we went up-country, we traveled by train and *matatu* [a type of minibus taxi], with chickens and collard greens and sometimes babies placed in my lap.

But it was a magical trip. To begin with, I discovered the warmth and sense of community that the people of Kenya possess—their sense of hopefulness even in the face of great difficulty. I discovered the beauty of the land, a beauty that haunts you long after you've left.

And most importantly for me, I discovered the story of my father's life, and the story of his father before him.

I learned that my grandfather had been a cook for the British and, although he was a respected elder in his village, he was called "boy" by his employers for most of his life. I learned about the brutal repression of Operation Anvil, the days of rape and torture in the "Pipeline" camps, the lives that so many gave, and how my grandfather had been arrested briefly during this period, despite being at the periphery of Kenya's liberation struggles.

I learned how my father had grown up in a tiny village called Alego, near Siaya, during this period of tumult. I began to understand and appreciate the distance he had traveled—from being a boy herding goats to a student at the University of Hawaii and Harvard University to the respected economist that he was upon his return to Kenya. In many ways, he embodied the new Africa of the early sixties, a man who had obtained the knowledge of the Western world and sought to bring it back home, where he hoped he could help create a new nation.

And yet, I discovered that for all his education, my father's life ended up being filled with disappointments. His ideas about how Kenya should progress often put him at odds with the politics of tribe and patronage, and because he spoke his mind, sometimes to a fault, he ended up being fired from his job and prevented from finding work in the country for many, many years. And on a more personal level, because he never fully reconciled the traditions of his village with more modern conceptions of family—because he related to women as his father had, expecting them to obey him no matter what he did—his family life was unstable, and his children never knew him well.

In many ways, then, my family's life reflects some of the contradictions of Kenya, and indeed, the African continent as a whole. The history of Africa is a history of ancient kingdoms and great traditions; the story of people fighting to be free from colonial rule; the heroism not only of great men like Nkrumah and Kenyatta and Mandela, but also ordinary people who endured great hardship, from Ghana to South Africa, to secure self-determination in the face of great odds.

But for all the progress that has been made, we must surely acknowledge that neither Kenya nor the African continent have yet fulfilled their potential—that the hopefulness of the postcolonial era has been replaced by cynicism and sometimes despair, and that true freedom has not yet been won for those struggling to live on less than a few shillings a day, for those who have fallen prey to HIV/AIDS or malaria, to those ordinary citizens who continue to find themselves trapped in the crossfire of war or ethnic conflict.

One statistic powerfully describes this unfulfilled promise. In the early 1960s, as Kenya was gaining its independence, its gross national product was not very different from that of South Korea. Today, South Korea's economy is forty times larger than Kenya's.

How can we explain this fact? Certainly it is not due to lack of effort on the part of ordinary Kenyans—we know how hard Kenyans are willing to work, the tremendous sacrifices that Kenyan mothers make for their children, the Herculean efforts that Kenyan fathers make for their families. We know as well the talent, the intelligence, and the creativity that exists in this country. And we know how much this land is blessed—just as the entire African continent is blessed—with great gifts and riches.

So what explains this? I believe there are a number of factors at work.

Kenya, like many African nations, did not come of age under the best historical circumstances. It suffers from the legacy of colonialism, of national boundaries that were drawn without regard to the political and tribal alignments of indigenous peoples, and that therefore fed conflict and tribal strife.

Kenya was also forced to rapidly move from a highly agrarian to a more urban, industrialized nation. This means that the education and health care systems—issues that my own nation, more than two hundred years old, still struggles with—lag behind, impacting its development.

Third, Kenya is hurt from factors unique to Africa's geography and place in the world—disease, distance from viable markets, and especially terms of trade. When African nations were just gaining independence, industrialized nations had decades of experience building their domestic economies and navigating the international financial system. And, as Frederick Douglass once stated: "Power concedes nothing without a demand. It never did, and it never will." As a result, many African nations have been asked to liberalize their markets without reciprocal concessions from mature economies. This lack of access for Africa's agriculture and commodities has restricted an important engine of economic growth. Other issues, such as resource extraction and the drain of human capital, have also been major factors.

As a senator from the United States, I believe that my country, and other nations, have an obligation and self-interest in being full partners with Kenya and with Africa. And I will do my part to shape an intelligent foreign policy that promotes peace and prosperity. A foreign policy that gives hope and opportunity to the people of this great continent.

But Kenya must do its part. It cannot wait for other nations to act first. The hard truth is that nations, by and large, will act in their self-interest and if Kenya does not act, it will fall behind.

It's more than just history and outside influences that explain why Kenya lags behind. Like many nations across this continent, where Kenya is failing is in its ability to create a government that is transparent and accountable. One that serves its people and is free from corruption.

There is no doubt that what Kenyans have accomplished with this independence is both impressive and inspiring. Among African nations, Kenya remains a model for representative democracy—a place where many different ethnic factions have found a way to live and work together in peace and stability. You enjoy a robust civil society; a press that's free, fair, and honest; and a strong partnership with my own country that has resulted in critical cooperation on terrorist issues, real strides in fighting disease and poverty, and an important alliance on fostering regional stability.

And yet, the reason I speak of the freedom that you fought so hard to win is because today that freedom is in jeopardy. It is being threatened by corruption.

Corruption is not a new problem. It's not just a Kenyan problem, or an African problem. It's a human problem, and it has existed in some form in almost every society. My own city of Chicago has been the home of some of the most corrupt local politics in American history, from patronage machines to questionable elections. In just the last year, our own U.S. Congress has seen a representative resign after taking bribes, and several others fall under investigation for using their public office for private gain.

But while corruption is a problem we all share, here in Kenya it is a crisis—a crisis that's robbing an honest people of the opportunities they have fought for—the opportunity they deserve.

I know that while recent reports have pointed to strong economic growth in this country, fifty-six percent of Kenyans still live in poverty. And I know that the vast majority of people in this country desperately want to change this.

It is painfully obvious that corruption stifles development—it siphons off scarce resources that could improve infrastructure, bolster education systems, and strengthen public health. It stacks the deck so high against entrepreneurs that they cannot get their job-creating ideas off the ground. In fact, one recent survey showed that corruption in Kenya costs local firms six percent of their revenues, the difference between good-paying jobs in Kenya or somewhere else. And corruption also erodes the state from the inside out, sickening the justice system until there is no justice to be found, poisoning the police forces until their presence becomes a source of insecurity rather than comfort.

Corruption has a way of magnifying the very worst twists of fate. It makes it impossible to respond effectively to crises—whether it's the HIV/AIDS pandemic or malaria or crippling drought.

What's worse, corruption can also provide opportunities for those who would harness the fear and hatred of others to their agenda and ambitions.

It can shield a war criminal—even one like Felicien Kabuga, suspected of helping to finance and orchestrate the Rwandan genocide—by allowing him to purchase safe haven for a time and robbing all humanity of the opportunity to bring the criminal to justice.

Terrorist attacks—like those that have shed Kenyan blood and struck at the heart of the Kenyan economy—are facilitated by customs and border officers who can be paid off, by police forces so crippled by corruption that they do not protect the personal safety of Kenyans walking the streets of Nairobi, and by forged documents that are easy to find in a climate where graft and fraud thrive.

Some of the worst actors on the international stage can also take advantage of the collective exhaustion and outrage that people feel with official corruption, as we've seen with Islamic extremists who promise purification, but deliver totalitarianism. Endemic corruption opens the door to this kind of movement, and in its wake comes a new set of distortions and betrayals of public trust.

In the end, if the people cannot trust their government to do the job for which it exists—to protect them and to promote their common welfare—all else is lost. And this is why the struggle against corruption is one of the great struggles of our time.

The good news is that there are already signs of progress here. Willingness to report corruption is increasingly significantly in Kenya. The Kenyan media has been courageous in uncovering and reporting on some of the most blatant abuses of the system, and there has been a growing recognition among people and politicians that this is a critical issue.

Among other things, this recognition resulted in the coalition that came to power in the December elections of 2002. This coalition succeeded by promising change, and their early gestures—the dismissal of the shaky judges, the renewed vigor of the investigation into the Goldenberg scandal, the calls for real disclosure of elected officials' personal wealth—were all promising.

But elections are not enough. In a true democracy, it is what happens between elections that is the true measure of how a government treats its people.

Today, we're starting to see that the Kenyan people want more than a simple changing of the guard, more than piecemeal reforms to a crisis that's crippling their country. The Kenyan people are crying out for real change, and whether one voted orange or banana in last year's referendum, the message that many Kenyans seemed to be sending was one of dissatisfaction with the pace of reform, and real frustration with continued tolerance of corruption at high levels.

And so we know that there is more work to be done—more reforms to be made. I don't have all the solutions or think that they'll be easy, but there are a few places that a country truly committed to reform could start.

We know that the temptation to take a bribe is greater when you're not making enough on the job. And we also know that the more people there are on the government payroll, the more likely it is that someone will be encouraged to take a bribe. So if the government found ways to downsize the bureaucracy—to cut out the positions that aren't necessary or useful—it could use the extra money to increase the salary of other government officials.

Of course, the best way to reduce bureaucracy and increase pay is to create more private-sector jobs. And the way to create good jobs is when the rules of a society are transparent—when there's a clear and advertised set of laws and regulations regarding how to start a business, what it takes to own property, how to go about getting a loan—there is less of a chance that some corrupt bureaucrat will make up his own rules that suit only his interests. Clarifying these rules and focusing resources on building a judicial system that can enforce them and resolve disputes should be a primary goal of any government suffering from corruption.

In addition, we know that the more information the public is provided, the easier it will be for your Kenyan brothers and sisters out in the villages to evaluate whether they are being treated fairly by their public servants or not. Wealth declarations do little good if no one can access them, and accountability in government spending is not possible if no one knows how much was available and allocated to a given project in the first place.

Finally, ethnic-based tribal politics has to stop. It is rooted in the bankrupt idea that the goal of politics or business is to funnel as much of the pie as possible to one's family, tribe, or circle with little regard for the public good. It stifles innovation and fractures the fabric of the society. Instead of opening businesses and engaging in commerce, people come to rely on patronage and payback as a means of advancing. Instead of unifying the country to move forward on solving problems, it divides neighbor from neighbor.

An accountable, transparent government can break this cycle. When people are judged by merit, not connections, then the best and brightest can lead the country, people will work hard, and the entire economy will grow—everyone will benefit and more resources will be available for all, not just select groups.

Of course, in the end, one of the strongest weapons your country has against corruption is the ability of you, the people, to stand up and speak out about the injustices you see. The Kenyan people are the ultimate guardians against abuses.

The world knows the names of Wangari Maathai and John Githongo, who are fighting against the insidious corruption that has weakened Kenya. But there are so many others, some of whom I'm meeting during my visit here—Betty Murungi, Ken Njau, Jane Onyango, Maina Kiai, Milly Odhiombo, and Hussein Khalid. As well as numerous Kenyan men and women who have refused to pay bribes to get civil servants to perform their duties; the auditors and inspectors general who have done the job before them accurately and fairly, regardless of where the facts have led; the journalists who asked questions and pushed for answers when it may have been more lucrative to look the other way, or whip up a convenient fiction. And then there are anonymous Kenyan whistleblowers who show us what is, so that we can all work together to demand what should be.

By rejecting the insulting idea that corruption is somehow a part of Kenyan culture, these heroes reveal the very opposite—they reveal a strength and integrity of character that can build a great country, a great future. By focusing on building strong, independent institutions—like an anticorruption commission with real authority—rather than cults of personality, they make a contribution to their country that will last longer than their own lives. They fight the fight of our time.

Looking out at this crowd of young people, I have faith that you will fight this fight too.

You will decide if your leaders will be held accountable, or if you will look the other way.

You will decide if the standards and the rules will be the same for everyone—regardless of ethnicity or of wealth.

And you will determine the direction of this country in the twenty-first century—whether the hard work of the many is lost to the selfish desires of a few, or whether you build an open, honest, stronger Kenya where everyone rises together.

This is the Kenya that so many who came before you envisioned—all those men and women who struggled and sacrificed and fought for the freedom you enjoy today.

I know that honoring their memory and making that freedom real may seem like an impossible task—an effort bigger than you can imagine—but sometimes all it takes to move us there is doing what little you can to right the wrongs you see.

As I said at the outset, I did not know my father well—he returned to Kenya from America when I was still young. Since that time I have known him through stories—those my mother would tell and those I heard from my relatives here in Kenya on my last trip to this country.

I know from these stories that my father was not a perfect man—that he made his share of mistakes and disappointed his share of people in his lifetime.

As our parents' children, we have the opportunity to learn from these mistakes and disappointments. We have the opportunity to muster the courage to fulfill the promise of our forefathers and lead our great nations towards a better future.

In today's Kenya—a Kenya already more open and less repressive than in my father's day—it is that courage that will bring the reform so many of you so desperately want and deserve. I wish all of you luck in finding this courage in the days and months to come, and I want you to know that as your ally, your friend, and your brother, I will be there to help in any way I can. Thank you.

8

Presidential Announcement Speech

February 10, 2007 • *Old State Capitol, Springfield, Illinois*

*The life of a tall, gangly, self-made Springfield lawyer
tells us that a different future is possible.
He tells us that there is power in words.
He tells us that there is power in conviction.
That beneath all the differences of race and religion, faith and station,
we are one people. He tells us that there is power in hope.*

Standing in a single-digit morning chill before a crowd of about sixteen thousand well-wishers, wearing an overcoat but no gloves, the first-term Democratic senator from Illinois announced his campaign for president of the United States.

The choice of Springfield, the state capital, to make his announcement had been made carefully. For seven years Obama had cut his political teeth in the small, sleepy town. It was where, as a state senator, he had fought for health care and lobbying reform—two issues central to his campaign—and where Abraham Lincoln, another Washington outsider and former Illinois legislator, had launched his candidacy for the White House.

Just as important, Springfield wasn't the South Side of Chicago, where Obama spent the early years of his career. Obama's advisers, particularly his chief strategist, David Axelrod, wanted to highlight Obama's "experience," but in a wholesome setting, not one that would suggest a Washington insider or a "pol" from the corrupt streets of Mayor Daley's Chicago. Despite Obama's years in the Illinois State House and the United States Senate, his handlers wanted their candidate to be seen as a change agent, running against the broken, partisan, divisive ways of Washington. According to his young speechwriter, Jon Favreau, this was the campaign thesis—not, as commentators asserted at the time, Obama's stance against the war in Iraq.

Consequently, his announcement speech stressed his pragmatic governing philosophy and his desire to work across party lines to take on tough and often politically unpopular issues that others had avoided.

This frame also separated Obama from his chief primary opponent, the then frontrunner, Senator Hillary Clinton, whose favorability in a CNN-WMUR poll at the time exceeded Obama's by seven points. To Obama's team, the former first lady and her husband epitomized the old-style, partisan Washington politics Obama was running against. This was a point they would regularly stress throughout the primary campaign and that they made clear in the announcement remarks: "I know I haven't spent a lot of time learning the ways of Washington. But I've been there long enough to know that the ways of Washington must change. . . . What's stopped us from meeting these challenges is not the absence of sound policies and sensible plans. What's stopped us is the failure of leadership, the smallness of our politics—the ease with which we're distracted by the petty and trivial, our chronic avoidance of tough decisions, our preference for scoring cheap political points instead of rolling up our sleeves and building a working consensus to tackle big problems."

By running against the "petty and trivial" of Washington, Obama strategically turned his lack of political experience into an asset and laid the argument for his candidacy—old versus new; change versus more of the same.

Similar to Senator John Kennedy in 1960 and Governor Bill Clinton in 1992, Obama positioned himself as a candidate of generational change. At age forty-five, Obama was fifteen years younger than Senator Hillary Clinton. This too was part of the shrewd attempt to turn Senator Clinton's experience into a liability instead of an asset. The political commentator Gwen Ifill recognized this on *Meet the Press* the weekend after Obama's announcement, saying, "I think [Obama] understands that if he can appeal to people who . . . are driven to the notion of hope and cause politics [and] that if he can emphasize the fact that he represents something new and fresh, then he can keep the momentum going."

Accompanied by his wife, Michelle, and their two young daughters, Obama spoke in front of Springfield's bunting-adorned Old State Capitol Building, where Lincoln made his famous "House Divided" speech, which launched his 1858 U.S. Senate campaign, and the site of his 1860 presidential campaign headquarters. The third-floor office where Lincoln practiced law and prepared his First Inaugural Address was less than two hundred feet from where Obama spoke. And the candidate made direct reference to the President in his remarks: "The life of a tall, gangly, self-made Springfield lawyer tells us that a different future is possible," Obama said. "He tells us that there is power in words. He tells us that there is power in conviction. That beneath all the differences of race and religion, faith and station, we are one people. He tells us that there is power in hope."

Lincoln was a personal hero of Obama's. Cass Sunstein, Obama's friend and a colleague on the faculty of the University of Chicago Law School, wrote of Lincoln's political creed: "In the legal culture, Lincoln is famous for believing that there are some principles that you can't compromise in terms of speaking, but in terms of what you do, there are pragmatic reasons and sometimes reasons of principle not to act on them."[1] Those words could have been written about Obama; it was clear why Obama held Lincoln in such esteem.

Ironically, Obama never mentioned race directly, and according to his speechwriter, there wasn't even a debate about whether he should. Obama never saw himself as the African American candidate. Yet, by wrapping himself in the mantle of the president credited with abolishing slavery, Obama underscored both the historic nature of the moment and his confidence that he too could lead a country torn by the moral and political conundrum of war.

Despite President Lincoln's emancipation of the slaves, race continued to divide Americans in the century and a half after the end of the Civil War. A full forty-five years after the Emancipation Proclamation, Springfield was the site of riots and mob violence that targeted African Americans. In 1908, a mob lynched two African American prisoners, William Donnegan and Scott Burton, less than a half mile from the Old State Capitol, while some in the crowd chanted, "Abe Lincoln brought them to Springfield and we will run them out."

Even as Obama downplayed the topic of race in his remarks, it was the elephant in the room. As the ABC News reporter Jake Tapper put it on the afternoon of Obama's speech, "It may be nice to think that as a nation we have moved beyond race. But some observers say Obama faces serious questions of whether America is ready to elect an African American president, or conversely whether he is 'black enough' as some African American columnists have alleged."[2] A columnist for the local *Journal Register*, Dave Bakke, captured the essence of the moment when he wrote, "What would those who were killed for the color of their skin think about a crowd that will come together today in the same place, but in a different mood and for such a different reason than that mob of 1908?"[3]

Obama's ideas were big, but Don Baer, Bill Clinton's former chief speechwriter, later remarked that Obama's language that day was more spare than in some of the loftier language of speeches that would come later in the campaign. "It was a direct and some ways expected speech," but Obama's use of Lincoln to "punctuate" the speech was "a deft, audacious, and bold stroke."

The evening before Obama's speech, his advance team was still hard at work, showing dozens of camera crews how to capture the Lincoln aura for their candidate and how best to frame the stage, with the columns of the Greek revival-style building decked out in red, white, and blue for the occasion.

At the same time, Obama was still putting the finishing touches on his speech. He hadn't started editing Favreau's draft until Wednesday night, just three days before he would take the podium. Given the crush of preparation, Favreau and Obama hadn't spoken much during the initial writing process, so Favreau wasn't sure what to expect when he received the senator's comments. The changes were relatively minor.

After a long night at the keyboard, Obama sent Favreau his edits at 4:00 a.m. on Thursday morning. "It was very long and it needed a few more applause lines and sound bites," Favreau said. So he tweaked the draft with the help of another speechwriter, Wendy Button, and the chief strategist, David Axelrod, and sent it back to Obama for another read-through later that afternoon. Obama made a few more minor changes and, according to Favreau, "by Thursday night at six p.m., it was done."

Early the next morning, Favreau and Obama's scheduler, Alyssa Mastromonaco, flew to Springfield to help with any last-minute issues. (Mastromonaco was a crucial member of the team, having planned the logistics for the speech, two stops in Iowa, and a trip to New Hampshire in the preceding two weeks.)

Favreau was shocked by the ease of the speechwriting process. A few weeks earlier, the senator's communications director and Favreau's men-

tor, Robert Gibbs, had pulled Favreau aside and told him that Obama
had decided to run for president, and he, Favreau, would be the head
speechwriter for the campaign. Favreau had just a couple of weeks to
pull together a writing team, draft an announcement speech, and prepare
his own move from Washington to Chicago, the campaign headquarters.
Favreau immediately called his friend and colleague from the Kerry campaign, Adam Frankel, and offered him a job. Then, working closely with
Button and Axelrod, he sat down and took a first crack at a draft of the
Springfield announcement. The good news, Favreau said, was that there
wasn't an army of consultants weighing in on the draft and mucking it
up; it was just a small group of editors, focused on crafting an impas-
sioned argument for Obama's candidacy.

When Favreau arrived in Springfield, he headed to the Old State House,
where Obama was to deliver his speech the next morning. Favreau, Axelrod,
and David Plouffe—a staffer for former congressional leader Dick Gephardt
of Iowa, who had been hired as campaign manager—had set aside the evening to rehearse the speech with Obama. They set up a TelePrompter in
a room in the basement while waiting for Obama to finish filming a 60
Minutes segment that would air on Sunday. It was 10:30 p.m. by the time
Obama's interview wrapped up and he walked over to the rehearsal—a little
more than twelve hours before the announcement. It was late and Obama
was exhausted. "It was his first and only night he'd have to practice and he
only wanted to do it twice," Favreau said. "And I remember telling him I
was worried. He had bumbled a bit through the first run through." Plus,
it was the first time Obama had used a TelePrompter since his Democratic
convention speech in 2004, and he was rusty.

Needless to say, after the first run-through, the soon-to-be-candidate
quickly extinguished his writer's concerns. "Don't worry about my diction. When I get up there I'll be fine. I'm just trying to get through it,"
he told Favreau.

Obama was much better in the second run-through, after which he
made a few minor edits. He wanted Favreau to put greater emphasis on
his background as a community organizer; Obama believed that his ability to activate grassroots support would make or break his campaign.
Favreau stressed this point in the speech, saying later, "He believed this
was the only way he could get around the Washington establishment."

The next day Obama delivered the speech that launched his ascent to the presidency. In the nearly twenty-minute address, with five hundred journalists looking on, Obama touched on a wide array of substantive issues Americans were facing that winter, ranging from ending the war in Iraq to achieving energy independence to the need for universal health care. These issues, and the economy, remained the ones Obama hammered on throughout the campaign. They were also the bread-and-butter topics Democratic primary voters had become accustomed to hearing about from their recent presidential candidates, beginning with Bill Clinton in 1991. Political consultants often call these the "do-no-harm lists": try to please as many constituencies as possible—including labor, teachers, and middle-class voters—and marginalize as few as you can.

Obama recognized that he couldn't accomplish his agenda as president without making the tough decisions—and the critical investments in our future. Consequently, he wasn't coy about his position on sustainability, declaring, "We've been told that climate change is a hoax" and "Let's be the generation that finally frees America from the tyranny of oil." His ambitious plan called for deeper investment in biofuels, a cap-and-trade system, and an expansive green-jobs platform. He also confronted health care reform, long Hillary Clinton's calling card, and demanded "universal health care" for all Americans in his first term.

In what became a signature issue, and later a challenge in his first months in office, Obama called for extensive lobbying reform to help weed out the special interests that have, as he put it, "turned our government into a game only they can afford to play. They write the checks and you get stuck with the bills, they get the access while you get to write a letter, they think they own this government, but we're here today to take it back." If Obama was going to clean up government and enact change, the special interests were ground zero.

Lobbying reform and transparency in government were not new issues and they certainly weren't politically popular with the Washington crowd. Jimmy Carter, in his 1974 announcement speech, made in the shadow of the Watergate scandal, called for "an all-inclusive sunshine law in Washington so that special interests will not retain their exclusive access behind closed doors" and insisted that the "activities of lobbyists must be more thoroughly revealed and controlled."[4] Bill Clinton had also

stumped for campaign finance reform in the early 1990s, but Obama took
it a step further. Lobbyists would be banned from donating to, collecting
money for, or even working on his campaign. It was, as Obama put it,
"time to turn the page."

Taken together, these policy proposals—and, in some case, the language—weren't radically different from those John Kerry had offered in
his announcement speech in 2004 or, interestingly, from those that Hillary Clinton put forth in her online statement announcing her own candidacy a few weeks later.

Speaking in Patriot's Point, South Carolina, in 2004, John Kerry
railed against the war in Iraq and called for energy reform and measures
to put an end to global warming. He had insisted that "the threats today
don't just come from gun barrels; they also come from oil barrels." Senator Kerry had hit the same notes on economic opportunity: "The most
powerful economic engine in this nation has always been opportunity—
the ability for anyone from any start in life, to get a good education, to go
to work, to start a business, to take an idea and change the world."[5]

Senator Clinton struck a similar chord in her announcement on the
economy, framing her opportunity agenda as striking a "basic bargain"
with the American people. In a speech "broadcast" online only, that borrowed heavily from her husband's announcement speech sixteen years earlier, Clinton said, "Our basic bargain [is] that no matter who you are or
where you live, if you work hard and play by the rules, you can build a
good life for yourself and your family. . . . I have spent a lifetime opening
opportunities for tens of millions who are working hard to raise a family:
new immigrants, families living in poverty, people who have no health
care or face an uncertain retirement. . . . The promise of America is that
all of us will have access to opportunity."[6]

Beyond the policy particulars, Obama also touched on familiar themes
such as the "opportunity-responsibility-community" troika that was the
centerpiece of Bill Clinton's 1991 presidential announcement speech
at the Old State House in Little Rock, Arkansas, where he said: "Make
no mistake—this election is about change: in our party, in our national
leadership, and in our country. . . . Government's responsibility is to create more opportunity. The people's responsibility is to make the most of

it. . . . In a Clinton administration, we are going to create opportunity for all."[7]

Obama's message echoed this idea, particularly the responsibility message: "Each of us, in our own lives, will have to accept responsibility—for instilling an ethic of achievement in our children, for adapting to a more competitive economy, for strengthening our communities, and sharing some measure of sacrifice." This theme would make a regular appearance on the campaign trail.

When Obama finished his remarks, the enthusiastic crowd chanted, "O-BA-MA, O-BA-MA." Dozens sported "Are You Ready to Barack?" sweatshirts over their sweaters and coats. Others held signs with the newly unveiled campaign logo featuring a blue "O," which also appeared on buttons, placards, and T-shirts.

Obama knew that ultimate victory would depend on a grassroots movement; he had to run against the establishment and enlist to his campaign disgruntled Americans of all political stripes—Democrats, independents, and Republicans—as he had done successfully in his run for the state senate. His closing remarks stressed that idea: "That is why this campaign can't only be about me. It must be about us—it must be about what we can do together."

The intensity and depth of his desire to do things differently cannot be overstated. His campaign staff saw it as the central theme to his candidacy, said Favreau: "I believed it; Axelrod believed that, [Obama] believed it. . . . He really thought that, and really that's how he thought was the only way he could get around the stuff in Washington."

Obama also knew that stubborn dogmatism or quixotic idealism would never get him to the White House; winning would take enlightened pragmatism. But this view was nothing new to Obama; it had helped shape his approach to governing as a state senator in Springfield. As a Republican Illinois state senator, Kirk Dillard, noted: "While Barack had principles, he was, importantly, practical and realistic."[8]

Obama's historic announcement launched a three-day wave of campaign events in Iowa and New Hampshire, with a Chicago fund-raiser in between. More important, it was the beginning of a long campaign that, like Lincoln's, ultimately led to the White House.

Remarks of Senator Barack Obama: Presidential Announcement Speech

Let me begin by saying thanks to all you who've traveled, from far and wide, to brave the cold today.

We all made this journey for a reason. It's humbling, but in my heart I know you didn't come here just for me, you came here because you believe in what this country can be. In the face of war, you believe there can be peace. In the face of despair, you believe there can be hope.

In the face of a politics that's shut you out, that's told you to settle, that's divided us for too long, you believe we can be one people, reaching for what's possible, building that more perfect union.

That's the journey we're on today. But let me tell you how I came to be here. As most of you know, I am not a native of this great state. I moved to Illinois over two decades ago. I was a young man then, just a year out of college; I knew no one in Chicago, was without money or family connections. But a group of churches had offered me a job as a community organizer for thirteen thousand dollars a year. And I accepted the job, sight unseen, motivated then by a single, simple, powerful idea—that I might play a small part in building a better America.

My work took me to some of Chicago's poorest neighborhoods. I joined with pastors and laypeople to deal with communities that had been ravaged by plant closings. I saw that the problems people faced weren't simply local in nature—that the decision to close a steel mill was made by distant executives; that the lack of textbooks and computers in schools could be traced to the skewed priorities of politicians a thousand miles away; and that when a child turns to violence, there's a hole in his heart no government could ever fill.

It was in these neighborhoods that I received the best education I ever had, and where I learned the true meaning of my Christian faith.

After three years of this work, I went to law school, because I wanted to understand how the law should work for those in need. I became a civil rights lawyer, and taught constitutional law, and after a time, I came to understand that our cherished rights of liberty and equality depend on the active participation of an awakened electorate. It was with these ideas in mind that I arrived in this capital city as a state senator.

It was here, in Springfield, where I saw all that is America converge—farmers and teachers, businessmen and laborers, all of them with a story to tell, all of them seeking a seat at the table, all of them clamoring to be heard. I made lasting friendships here—friends that I see in the audience today.

It was here we learned to disagree without being disagreeable—that it's possible to compromise so long as you know those principles that can never be compromised; and that so long as we're willing to listen to each other, we can assume the best in people instead of the worst.

That's why we were able to reform a death penalty system that was broken. That's why we were able to give health insurance to children in need. That's why we made the tax system more fair and just for working families, and that's why we passed ethics reforms that the cynics said could never, ever be passed.

It was here, in Springfield, where North, South, East, and West come together, that I was reminded of the essential decency of the American people—where I came to believe that through this decency, we can build a more hopeful America.

And that is why, in the shadow of the Old State Capitol, where Lincoln once called on a divided house to stand together, where common hopes and common dreams still live, I stand before you today to announce my candidacy for president of the United States.

I recognize there is a certain presumptuousness—a certain audacity—to this announcement. I know I haven't spent a lot of time learning the ways of Washington.

But I've been there long enough to know that the ways of Washington must change.

The genius of our founders is that they designed a system of government that can be changed. And we should take heart, because we've changed this country before. In the face of tyranny, a band of patriots brought an empire to its knees. In the face of secession, we unified a nation and set the captives free. In the face of depression, we put people back to work and lifted millions out of poverty. We welcomed immigrants to our shores, we opened railroads to the West, we landed a man on the moon, and we heard a King's call to let justice roll down like water, and righteousness like a mighty stream.

Each and every time, a new generation has risen up and done what's needed to be done. Today we are called once more—and it is time for our generation to answer that call.

For that is our unyielding faith—that in the face of impossible odds, people who love their country can change it.

That's what Abraham Lincoln understood. He had his doubts. He had his defeats. He had his setbacks. But through his will and his words, he moved a nation and helped free a people. It is because of the millions who rallied to his cause that we are no longer divided, North and South, slave and free. It is because men and women of every race, from every walk of life, continued to march for freedom long after Lincoln was laid to rest, that today we have the chance to face the challenges of this millennium together, as one people—as Americans.

All of us know what those challenges are today—a war with no end, a dependence on oil that threatens our future, schools where too many children aren't learning, and families struggling paycheck to paycheck despite working as hard as they can. We know the challenges. We've heard them. We've talked about them for years.

What's stopped us from meeting these challenges is not the absence of sound policies and sensible plans. What's stopped us is the failure of leadership, the smallness of our politics—the ease with which we're distracted by the petty and trivial, our chronic avoidance of tough decisions, our preference for scoring cheap political points instead of rolling up our sleeves and building a working consensus to tackle big problems.

For the last six years we've been told that our mounting debts don't matter, we've been told that the anxiety Americans feel about rising health care costs and stagnant wages are an illusion, we've been told that climate change is a hoax, and that tough talk and an ill-conceived war can replace diplomacy, and strategy, and foresight. And when all else fails, when Katrina happens, or the death toll in Iraq mounts, we've been told that our crises are somebody else's fault. We're distracted from our real failures, and told to blame the other party, or gay people, or immigrants.

And as people have looked away in disillusionment and frustration, we know what's filled the void. The cynics, and the lobbyists, and the special interests who've turned our government into a game only they can afford to play. They write the checks and you get stuck with the bills, they get the access while you get to write a letter, they think they own this government, but we're here today to take it back. The time for that politics is over. It's time to turn the page.

We've made some progress already. I was proud to help lead the fight in Congress that led to the most sweeping ethics reform since Watergate.

But Washington has a long way to go. And it won't be easy. That's why we'll have to set priorities. We'll have to make hard choices. And although government will play a crucial role in bringing about the changes we need, more money and programs alone will not get us where we need to go. Each of us, in our own lives, will have to accept responsibility—for instilling an ethic of achievement in our children, for adapting to a more competitive economy, for strengthening our communities, and sharing some measure of sacrifice. So let us begin. Let us begin this hard work together. Let us transform this nation.

Let us be the generation that reshapes our economy to compete in the digital age. Let's set high standards for our schools and give them the resources they need to succeed. Let's recruit a new army of teachers, and give them better pay and more support in exchange for more accountability. Let's make college more affordable, and let's invest in scientific research, and let's lay down broadband lines through the heart of inner cities and rural towns all across America.

And as our economy changes, let's be the generation that ensures our nation's workers are sharing in our prosperity. Let's protect the hard-earned benefits their companies have promised. Let's make it possible for hardworking Americans to save for retirement. And let's allow our unions and their organizers to lift up this country's middle class again.

Let's be the generation that ends poverty in America. Every single person willing to work should be able to get job training that leads to a job, and earn a living wage that can pay the bills, and afford child care so their kids have a safe place to go when they work. Let's do this.

Let's be the generation that finally tackles our health care crisis. We can control costs by focusing on prevention, by providing better treatment to the chronically ill, and using technology to cut the bureaucracy. Let's be the generation that says right here, right now, that we will have universal health care in America by the end of the next president's first term.

Let's be the generation that finally frees America from the tyranny of oil. We can harness home-grown alternative fuels like ethanol and spur the production of more fuel-efficient cars. We can set up a system for capping greenhouse gases. We can turn this crisis of global warming into a moment of opportunity for innovation, and job creation, and an incentive for businesses that will serve as a model for the world. Let's be the generation that makes future generations proud of what we did here.

Most of all, let's be the generation that never forgets what happened on that September day and confront the terrorists with everything we've got. Politics doesn't have to divide us on this anymore—we can work together to keep our country safe. I've worked with Republican senator Dick Lugar to pass a law that will secure and destroy some of the world's deadliest, unguarded weapons. We can work together to track terrorists down with a stronger military, we can tighten the net around their finances, and we can improve our intelligence capabilities. But let us also understand that ultimate victory against our enemies will come only by rebuilding our alliances and exporting those ideals that bring hope and opportunity to millions around the globe.

But all of this cannot come to pass until we bring an end to this war in Iraq. Most of you know I opposed this war from the start. I thought it was a tragic mistake. Today we grieve for the families who have lost loved ones, the hearts that have been broken, and the young lives that could have been. America, it's time to start bringing our troops home. It's time to admit that no amount of American lives can resolve the political disagreement that lies at the heart of someone else's civil war. That's why I have a plan that will bring our combat troops home by March of 2008. Letting the Iraqis know that we will not be there forever is our last, best hope to pressure the Sunni and Shia to come to the table and find peace.

Finally, there is one other thing that is not too late to get right about this war, and that is the homecoming of the men and women—our veterans—who have sacrificed the most. Let us honor their valor by providing the care they need and rebuilding the military they love. Let us be the generation that begins this work.

I know there are those who don't believe we can do all these things. I understand the skepticism. After all, every four years, candidates from both parties make similar promises, and I expect this year will be no different. All of us running for president will travel around the country offering ten-point plans and making grand speeches; all of us will trumpet those qualities we believe make us uniquely qualified to lead the country. But too many times, after the election is over, and the confetti is swept away, all those promises fade from memory, and the lobbyists and the special interests move in, and people turn away, disappointed as before, left to struggle on their own.

That is why this campaign can't only be about me. It must be about us—it must be about what we can do together. This campaign must be the occasion, the vehicle, of your hopes, and your dreams. It will take your time, your energy, and your advice—to push us forward when we're doing right, and to let us know when we're not. This campaign has to be about reclaiming the meaning of citizenship, restoring our sense of common purpose, and realizing that few obstacles can withstand the power of millions of voices calling for change.

By ourselves, this change will not happen. Divided, we are bound to fail.

But the life of a tall, gangly, self-made Springfield lawyer tells us that a different future is possible.

He tells us that there is power in words.

He tells us that there is power in conviction.

That beneath all the differences of race and region, faith and station, we are one people.

He tells us that there is power in hope.

As Lincoln organized the forces arrayed against slavery, he was heard to say: "Of strange, discordant, and even hostile elements, we gathered from the four winds, and formed and fought to battle through."

That is our purpose here today.

That's why I'm in this race.

Not just to hold an office, but to gather with you to transform a nation.

I want to win that next battle—for justice and opportunity.

I want to win that next battle—for better schools, and better jobs, and health care for all.

I want us to take up the unfinished business of perfecting our union, and building a better America.

And if you will join me in this improbable quest, if you feel destiny calling, and see as I see, a future of endless possibility stretching before us; if you sense, as I sense, that the time is now to shake off our slumber, and slough off our fear, and make good on the debt we owe past and future generations, then I'm ready to take up the cause, and march with you, and work with you. Together, starting today, let us finish the work that needs to be done, and usher in a new birth of freedom on this earth.

9

IOWA JEFFERSON-JACKSON DINNER

November 10, 2007

Veterans Memorial Auditorium, Des Moines, Iowa

*The same old Washington textbook campaigns just
won't do in this election. That's why not answering questions
'cause we are afraid our answers won't be popular just won't do. . . .
Triangulating and poll-driven positions because we're worried
about what Mitt or Rudy might say about us just won't do.*

The early fall of 2007 was not a high point for the Obama campaign. The candidate and his team had been hard at work for months, but the numbers were disappointing. A *Time* magazine poll released in the last week of August showed John Edwards leading Clinton by five points and Obama by seven—not exactly what the Illinois senator wanted. Clinton's own internal polls in late October had Clinton at 32 percent, Edwards at 31 percent, and Obama at 25 percent. Donors were getting restless; some even called for a change in the top management. Obama's performances in the countless debates were good, but not game-changing. Political columnists were asking whether Obama had what it took to overcome the Clinton machine; if Obama didn't win in the Iowa caucus, they reckoned, he would have trouble continuing his campaign. Chris Cillizza, a political blogger at the *Washington Post,* put it frankly in an October 2 post: "If Clinton wins Iowa, it's hard not to see her running away with New Hampshire. . . . And if she wins Iowa and New Hampshire, it's over [for Obama]."[1]

In a meeting with his senior staff, Obama pressed his team about the national polls; he wanted to know how they could turn Iowa around. His senior strategist, David Axelrod, said, "[Obama] wanted assurance that we knew what we were doing. . . . We said by the measure we apply, things are on the right track. The metrics in Iowa were good."[2] One thing was clear to all of them: they needed some new momentum; they needed a game-changer. The speech at the Iowa Jefferson-Jackson dinner offered just such an opportunity.

Most state Democratic organizations hold an annual fund-raising dinner they call the Jefferson-Jackson, named for two of the standard-bearers of the Democratic Party (Republicans traditionally hold Lincoln-Reagan dinners). Given Iowa's role in the presidential nominating process as the first of many primaries and caucuses, the state's Jefferson-Jackson dinner in 2007 carried particular significance. The attendees at the dinner were a who's who of the Iowa political establishment; along with other rank-and-file Democrats, they donned shirts and pins bearing their candidates' slogans and faces. The media, including, of course, the influential Iowa press, also attended.

The good news was that the Obama campaign had been working Iowa for more than two years; it was ground zero on their roadmap to victory. They understood Iowa's caucusing system inside and out, no easy feat given its complexity. The system works as follows: On caucus day, people from individual precincts "caucus" in local gymnasiums or armories to discuss the candidates. For the first round of public voting, the room is split, with, say, Obama supporters in one corner, Edwards supporters in another, Clinton supporters in a third, and so forth. After the first round of voting, any candidate with less than 15 percent of the vote is eliminated, and his or her supporters then switch to one of the remaining candidates. This was key to the Obama team's strategy: although they knew they couldn't prevail on the first round, they could pick up a sizable percentage in the second round if they could convince people to switch to their candidate.

Needless to say, in a state with such a confusing system, Iowa was all about organization, and in 2007, no campaign was better prepared than Obama's. With David Plouffe at the helm of his campaign, Obama held a chip that neither Clinton nor Edwards could match—a campaign manager who was a veteran of Iowa politics. Plouffe, along with Axelrod and deputy campaign manager Steve Hildebrand (both of whom also had extensive Iowa experience), built an unmatched army of volunteers that was able to canvas the entire state.

Whereas the Clinton campaign skimped on resources in Iowa, Obama bet the ranch on that contest. Rather than relying solely on paid campaign staff, as Clinton did, Obama had a cadre of young volunteers he could deploy, who lived on macaroni and cheese and were willing to work the precincts day in, day out to make sure that registered Democrats actually came to the caucuses. Plus, Obama personally had been on the ground in Iowa far more than Clinton, making forty-four visits and spending a total of eighty-nine days in the Hawkeye State between February 2007 and Election Day.[3]

In fact, up until May 2007, the Clinton campaign was still undecided as to whether Senator Clinton was even going to compete in the Iowa caucus. Technically, she didn't need to participate in the caucus—Clinton could win enough delegates in the other states to capture the nomination. But Iowa, as the first state to cast any votes in the primary season, was symbolically important. That said, Clinton knew she was out-organized and outspent, and Bill Clinton had skipped the state in his primary campaign in 1992 and won the nomination. As the campaign considered its options, a memorandum from Clinton's political director, Mike Henry, leaked to the *New York Times* in which Henry urged Clinton to skip Iowa, save resources, and focus on New Hampshire. It was a devastating development that put the Clinton campaign in the worst position possible: she couldn't bow out of Iowa gracefully and on her terms; she was boxed into participating in the caucus by her own staff. So, after acknowledging the authenticity of the memo, Clinton had no choice but to throw her hat into the ring. Her campaign poured tens of millions of dollars into the state, but the damage to the campaign was already done, as a large number of Iowans doubted Clinton's commitment to their state.

Clinton faced another obstacle leading up to the Jefferson-Jackson dinner. After a string of solid debate performances, Clinton flubbed an answer in a debate in Philadelphia on October 30. Asked whether illegal immigrants should be allowed to have driver's licenses, Clinton refused to take a clear position on the politically charged issue; her body language and answer showed that. Clearly the question had taken her by surprise.

The press pounced. Slate dubbed it "The Philadelphia Pile-On—Hillary Debates Her Opponents and Herself."[4] Although the rest of Clinton's performance that evening was gaffeless, the media coverage was all about her first major blunder and about the attacks she received from both Obama and Edwards because of it. The seemingly invincible Clinton operation was starting to show cracks.

Senior Obama aides smelled opportunity; they knew that a strong performance at the Jefferson-Jackson dinner could help formulate a new narrative. Obama could show Iowans once and for all that there were clear differences between him and Clinton; Hillary might not represent the "change" Democrats needed.

The J-J dinner is governed by a strict and—to many candidates—irksome set of rules. All major candidates are invited to speak, and they have to attend the entire dinner, which often drags on late into the night. The campaigns purchase tables for guests and cordon off sections of bleachers for their supporters; these guests are allowed, and to some degree expected, to participate in elaborate cheers. The cheers are often developed way in advance of the dinner, in part, because the candidates are required to memorize their speeches. There's neither a teleprompter, nor a podium (the event is in the round, with the audience on all sides), and candidates aren't allowed to bring a script or note cards onto stage.

Part of political lore, the J-J dinner is a challenge, and has made or broken candidates in the past. In 1999, Al Gore used the dinner to nudge aside his chief rival, Senator Bill Bradley. In 2003, John Kerry's ailing campaign came alive at the dinner, signaling the beginning of the end for the then frontrunner, Governor Howard Dean.

Leading up to the event, Obama and his senior team held a series of brainstorming conference calls. The topic of discussion was the Jefferson-Jackson, but it was actually about a much larger problem. Obama had been struggling to settle on a stump speech that he and his team were comfortable with. The stump he had been using was long and unfocused; Obama had fallen into "professor mode." In a forty-five-minute phone conversation with Favreau one afternoon, Obama both acknowledged that his stump was "broken" and asked his speechwriter what he envisioned for the J-J speech.

Favreau hoped that the J-J speech would not only be a success that evening, reinvigorating the Iowa campaign, but would also give the candidate a new, tightly scripted stump speech to use going forward—one with real spark. The campaign had been falling into the same trap: "We'd give him a stump speech, he'd practice and do great on the TelePrompter and then, if we didn't watch carefully, it would gradually lengthen," said Favreau.

But the J-J could solve this problem. Candidates only had ten minutes and they had to memorize their speeches. "It was perfect!" said Favreau. "If he liked what we wrote, we'd have a new, tight stump."

According to Dan Balz and Haynes Johnson, Obama's advisers argued for a speech that introduced a "new politics," in sharp contrast to the Washington status quo, where the average American had little voice in the political process. They wanted Obama to stress his opposition to the special interests, even if it wasn't what polls indicated people wanted to hear. All of these points provided a sharp contrast with Clinton, who would have a more difficult time portraying herself as a Washington outsider who stood up to the special interests.

Favreau, along with his fellow speechwriters, Adam Frankel and Ben Rhodes, understood the stakes. Favreau had lived through the Kerry campaign, and he knew that it was make-or-break time. In his eyes, this was the biggest speech of the cycle. The writing team holed up in the Chicago campaign headquarters late into the night for three days straight, cobbling together different drafts, unsure how the speech would be received.

The tension was starting to build; all eyes were on the J-J speech, and it seemed like everyone came out of the woodwork to offer the writers their opinion. Gibbs called Favreau with an idea to alleviate the pressure. Obama was set to give a speech in South Carolina a week before the dinner, on November 3, to mark the year out before the general election; they could use that speech as a test run for the Jefferson-Jackson. "We'll just slip it under the radar," Favreau remembered Gibbs telling him. "If Obama likes it, then we'll be done early."

The crowd in South Carolina loved the speech. Obama had them eating out of the palm of his hand. Gibbs called Favreau and Axelrod to let them know that the candidate loved it, too. Problem solved. Obama and Gibbs flew to New York right after the speech and met Axelrod at the set of *Saturday Night Live,* where Obama was appearing as a guest later that night. Favreau was at his Chicago apartment getting ready to watch with friends when he got a call from Axelrod, who was sitting in the green room with the candidate. He asked him to cut the draft in half and get it back to Obama by the morning.

Favreau looked at the clock and realized that he'd better get to work if he was to get the speech finished. "I kicked everyone out of my apartment, set my alarm for three thirty a.m., and went to bed," he recalled. "I was in the office and at the computer by four a.m. By eleven a.m., I'd cut the thirty-minute South Carolina speech to ten minutes and e-mailed it off to Obama, Axelrod, Frankel, and Rhodes." The speech was finished with a week to spare.

Obama sent a few final tweaks back to Favreau on Monday morning, and Axelrod added in a few more changes. That afternoon, Obama returned to the Chicago office, where he, Axelrod, Gibbs, and Favreau locked themselves in a room and practiced the speech on a TelePrompter. Obama was happy with the draft. Now, he had six days to memorize and practice it.

On Thursday, Favreau arrived in Des Moines for the first day of rehearsal for the dinner, but Obama canceled it, citing exhaustion after a long day of events. "Don't worry, the speech is Saturday," Obama told Favreau. Later that night, Gibbs heard Obama practicing the speech in his hotel room. Obama practiced the speech all week, testing paragraphs out on Iowa crowds in Cedar Rapids and Davenport.

Obama understood the importance of getting the speech just right. Friday morning, the day before the speech, he told reporters, "If you don't do well in Iowa, you're going to have problems catching up."

By Friday night he had it memorized. He ran through the speech in front of Axelrod, Gibbs, and Favreau at a table in his hotel room, even pausing when he thought there would be applause. Saturday morning, he delivered a final run-through. Everyone agreed that it was a hit.

Clinton and Obama had been assigned the last two slots of the night— Obama would be the final speaker. The Veterans Memorial Auditorium in Des Moines was packed with nearly nine thousand people. Speaker of the House Nancy Pelosi, who emceed the event, opened the evening. Lieutenant Governor Patty Judge and Governor Chet Culver also spoke briefly before Pelosi introduced the night's first candidate, John Edwards, who spoke mainly about his health care plan. Bill Richardson spoke next, followed by Senators Joe Biden and Chris Dodd.

The crowd was a bit weary when Clinton finally took the stage, just before 11:00 p.m. Clinton's base was older than most of Obama's supporters. Because of that, by the time she spoke, four hours after they had sat down, many of her supporters had already left the hall.

Clinton's speech was solid, but it certainly wasn't a home run. Characteristically, her campaign aides were still debating the speech content and her slogan just days before the speech. This did not make life any easier for her Iowa campaign staff—they needed to have signs printed and find rehearsal time—or for the candidate, who had to memorize and practice the speech. But despite their pleas, they couldn't get the senior staff in Washington to focus on her remarks early enough in the process—a sharp contrast to team Obama.

Clinton settled on the slogan "Turn up the heat," which, as Ruth Marcus wrote in the *Washington Post,* "slyly combines her toughness message with her gender appeal."[5] In a play on Harry Truman's famous aphorism "If you can't stand the heat, get out of the kitchen," Clinton exhorted the crowd, "I know as the campaign goes on that it's going to get a little hotter up here. But that's fine with me. I feel really comfortable in the kitchen." Not surprisingly, Clinton, as the front-runner, wanted Democrats to focus on the Republicans, not on her, saying, "We're going to turn up the heat on the Republicans and we're going to turn America around. . . . I'm not interested in attacking my opponents. I'm interested in attacking the problems of America."

Although she never mentioned Obama by name (likewise, Obama didn't mention her), Clinton took an indirect swipe at him and his "change" mantra, saying: "We are ready for change, [but] 'change' is just a word if you don't have the strength and experience to make it happen." She continued to hammer this point of differentiation, which she had been advancing for weeks, saying, "There are some who will say they don't know where I stand. Well, I think you know better than that. I stand where I have stood for thirty-five years. I stand with you, and with your children, and with every American who needs a fighter in their corner for a better life."[6]

When he finally took the podium, at 11:15, Obama's supporters erupted with cheers and applause. It's tradition that the campaigns purchase the tickets for their supporters, because, as Roger Simon noted in Politico: "If people are not willing to come out on a mild fall evening for a free dinner, they probably won't come out on a cold night to vote for you in the caucuses."[7] And the Obama campaign had shown its organizing muscle, claiming that three thousand of the nine thousand attendees in the Veterans Memorial Auditorium were their supporters.

Earlier that evening Obama had marched into the hall to a chorus of supporters who were shouting, "Fired up. Ready to go." His team had been practicing the campaign chant for days. Obama and Michelle had also rehearsed earlier that day with the Isiserettes Drill and Drum Corps, a nonprofit group from Des Moines.

Obama didn't take long to warm up; he came out swinging. His first target was the Bush administration, calling for an end to "the era of Scooter Libby justice" (a reference to Vice President Cheney's defrocked chief of staff), "Brownie incompetence" (a reference to Michael Brown, the director of FEMA during the Hurricane Katrina debacle), and "Karl Rove politics." From there, he aimed his sights on his chief opponent, Hillary Clinton, but did so gingerly. Like Clinton, he didn't attack by name, but he drew clear distinctions between their candidacies.

Obama reminded his audience that he was the only candidate to oppose the war in Iraq from the beginning—"a war that should never have been authorized and should have never been waged." He added, "I am sick and tired of Democrats thinking that the only way to look tough on national security is by talking, and acting, and voting like George Bush Republicans." Obama also made it clear that it was time to move beyond the partisanship that "festered long before George Bush ever took office"—a thinly veiled attack on the Bill Clinton presidency—and "bring the country together in a new majority."

He then declared, as his team wanted, that it was time to set aside the "same old Washington textbook campaigns." In Obama's eyes, Senator Clinton was one of the old-style politicians who told "the American people what we think they want to hear instead of telling the American people what they need to hear." Those campaigns, Obama asserted, were rooted in "triangulating and poll-driven positions"—a clear slap at Bill Clinton's presidency. Obama harkened to a rosier time for the Democrats, to "the party of Jefferson and Jackson; of Roosevelt and Kennedy . . . when we led, not by polls, but by principle; not by calculation, but by conviction."

He then drove the point home, saying that America needs "a party that doesn't just offer change as a slogan, but real, meaningful change— change that America can believe in." After he declared, "America, our moment is now," the crowd in the Des Moines hall roared.

From moment one, Obama had the audience eating out of his hand,

and Clinton knew it. She shifted uncomfortably in her seat throughout his speech and leaned over to speak to her campaign chairman, Terry Mcauliffe. At that moment, Clinton heard Obama take a final jab: "I am not in this race to fulfill some long-held ambitions or because I believe it's somehow owed to me." For months, Clinton had faced attacks about her air of "inevitability" and presumptions about the nomination.

Obama's Jefferson-Jackson speech was a barnburner and by all accounts a watershed moment in his campaign. Although Favreau was initially concerned that Obama was in the last slot, in the end he was thrilled with the sequence. After a long evening, Clinton had reawakened the crowd with her speech, just in time for Obama to deliver the closer and provide an opportunity for direct comparisons. All of the reporters Favreau ran into later that night commented that the crowd was "rapt" for Obama's speech and that he had "blown it out of the water."

The momentum in the race shifted almost overnight. David Yepsen, an influential columnist with the *Des Moines Register*, insisted, "The passion [Obama] showed should help him close the gap on Hillary Clinton by tipping some undecided caucus-goers his way. Should he come from behind to win the Iowa caucuses, Saturday's dinner will be remembered as one of the turning points in his campaign here."

Yepsen added, "For a lover of political oratory, it was a little like listening to a long Beethoven symphony while having some kid play a Tonette between movements."[8]

Political commentator David Gergen said, "This speech has changed the expectations and the sense—the sense of how this race is going."[9] One Obama aide noted, "The real question is . . . has [Clinton] just bloodied her nose or has she burst an artery? It is amazing that the dynamic has changed in a single week from she's inevitable to you can't believe a word that she says."[10]

The race certainly changed. Clinton's internal poll numbers plummeted, and by the end of the month Clinton and Obama were tied at 29 percent favorability in the *Des Moines Register*'s Iowa poll.[11] The tune played by the media followed, as did Obama's fund-raising.

Remarks by Senator Barack Obama: Jefferson-Jackson Dinner

Thank you so much. To the great governor of Iowa and lieutenant governor of Iowa, to my dear friend Tom Harkin for the outstanding work that he does, to the congressional delegation of Iowa that is doing outstanding work, and to Nancy Pelosi, Madam Speaker, thank you all for the wonderful welcome and the wonderful hospitality. [Responding to audience] I love you back.

A little less than one year from today, you will go into the voting booth and you will select the president of the United States of America.

Now, here's the good news—the name George W. Bush will not be on the ballot. The name of my cousin Dick Cheney will not be on the ballot. We've been trying to hide that for a long time. Everybody has a black sheep in the family. The era of Scooter Libby justice, and Brownie incompetence, and Karl Rove politics will finally be over.

But the question you're going to have to ask yourself when you caucus in January and you vote in November is, "What's next for America?"

We are in a defining moment in our history. Our nation is at war. The planet is in peril. The dream that so many generations fought for feels as if it's slowly slipping away. We are working harder for less. We've never paid more for health care or for college. It's harder to save and it's harder to retire. And most of all we've lost faith that our leaders can or will do anything about it.

We were promised compassionate conservatism and all we got was Katrina and wiretaps. We were promised a uniter, and we got a president who could not even lead the half of the country that voted for him. We were promised a more ethical and more efficient government, and instead we have a town called Washington that is more corrupt and more wasteful than it was before. And the only mission that was ever accomplished is to use fear and falsehood to take this country to a war that should have never been authorized and should have never been waged.

It is because of these failures that America is listening, intently, to what we say here today—not just Democrats, but Republicans and independents who've lost trust in their government, but want to believe again.

And it is because of these failures that we not only have a moment of great challenge, but also a moment of great opportunity. We have a chance to bring the country together in a new majority—to finally tackle problems that George Bush made far worse, but that had festered long before George Bush ever took office—problems that we've talked about year after year after year after year.

And that is why the same old Washington textbook campaigns just won't do in this election. That's why not answering questions 'cause we are afraid our answers won't be popular just won't do. That's why telling the American people what we think they want to hear instead of telling the American people what they need to hear just won't do. Triangulating and poll-driven positions because we're worried about what Mitt or Rudy might say about us just won't do. If we are really serious about winning this election, Democrats, we can't live in fear of losing it.

This party—the party of Jefferson and Jackson; of Roosevelt and Kennedy—has always made the biggest difference in the lives of the American people when we led, not by polls, but by principle; not by calculation, but by conviction; when we summoned the entire nation to a common purpose—a higher purpose. And I run for the presidency of the United States of America because that's the party America needs us to be right now.

A party that offers not just a difference in policies, but a difference in leadership.

A party that doesn't just focus on how to win but why we should.

A party that doesn't just offer change as a slogan, but real, meaningful change—change that America can believe in.

That's why I'm in this race. That's why I am running for the presidency of the United States of America—to offer change that we can believe in.

I am in this race to tell the corporate lobbyists that their days of setting the agenda in Washington are over. I have done more than any other candidate in this race to take on lobbyists—and won. They have not funded my campaign, they will not get a job in my White House, and they will not drown out the voices of the American people when I am president.

I'm in this race to take those tax breaks away from companies that are moving jobs overseas and put them in the pockets of hard working Americans who deserve it. And I won't raise the minimum wage every ten years—I will raise it to keep pace so that workers don't fall behind.

That is why I am in it. To protect the American worker. To fight for the American worker.

I'm in this race because I want to stop talking about the outrage of forty-seven million Americans without health care and start actually doing something about it. I expanded health care in Illinois by bringing Democrats and Republicans together. By taking on the insurance industry. And that is how I will make certain that every single American in this country has health care they can count on and I won't do it twenty years from now, I won't do it ten years from now, I will do it by the end of my first term as president of the United States of America.

I run for president to make sure that every American child has the best education that we have to offer—from the day they are born to the day they graduate from college. And I won't just talk about how great teachers are—as president I will reward them for their greatness, by raising salaries and giving them more support. That's why I'm in this race.

I am running for president because I am sick and tired of Democrats thinking that the only way to look tough on national security is by talking, and acting, and voting like George Bush Republicans.

When I am this party's nominee, my opponent will not be able to say that I voted for the war in Iraq; or that I gave George Bush the benefit of the doubt on Iran; or that I supported Bush-Cheney policies of not talking to leaders that we don't like. And he will not be able to say that I wavered on something as fundamental as whether or not it is okay for America to torture—because it is never okay. That's why I am in it.

As president, I will end the war in Iraq. We will have our troops home in sixteen months. I will close Guantánamo. I will restore habeas corpus. I will finish the fight against al Qaeda. And I will lead the world to combat the common threats of the twenty-first century—nuclear weapons and terrorism; climate change and poverty; genocide and disease. And I will send once more a message to those yearning faces beyond our shores that says, "You matter to us. Your future is our future. And our moment is now."

America, our moment is now.

Our moment is now.

I don't want to spend the next year or the next four years re-fighting the same fights that we had in the 1990s.

I don't want to pit red America against blue America; I want to be the president of the United States of America.

And if those Republicans come at me with the same fear-mongering and swift-boating that they usually do, then I will take them head-on. Because I believe the American people are tired of fear and tired of distractions and tired of diversions. We can make this election not about fear, but about the future. And that won't just be a Democratic victory; that will be an American victory.

And that is a victory America needs right now.

I am not in this race to fulfill some long-held ambitions or because I believe it's somehow owed to me. I never expected to be here, I always knew this journey was improbable. I've never been on a journey that wasn't.

I am running in this race because of what Dr. King called "the fierce urgency of now." Because I believe that there's such a thing as being too late. And that hour is almost upon us.

I don't want to wake up four years from now and find out that millions of Americans still lack health care because we couldn't take on the insurance industry.

I don't want to see that the oceans have risen a few more inches. The planet has reached a point of no return because we couldn't find a way to stop buying oil from dictators.

I don't want to see more American lives put at risk because no one had the judgment or the courage to stand up against a misguided war before we sent our troops into fight.

I don't want to see homeless veterans on the streets. I don't want to send another generation of American children to failing schools. I don't want that future for my daughters. I don't want that future for your sons. I do not want that future for America.

I'm in this race for the same reason that I fought for jobs for the jobless and hope for the hopeless on the streets of Chicago; for the same reason I fought for justice and equality as a civil rights lawyer; for the same reason that I fought for Illinois families for over a decade.

Because I will never forget that the only reason that I'm standing here today is because somebody, somewhere stood up for me when it was risky.

Stood up when it was hard. Stood up when it wasn't popular. And because that somebody stood up, a few more stood up. And then a few thousand stood up. And then a few million stood up. And standing up, with courage and clear purpose, they somehow managed to change the world.

That's why I'm running, Iowa—to give our children and grandchildren the same chances somebody gave me.

That's why I'm running, Democrats—to keep the American Dream alive for those who still hunger for opportunity, who still thirst for equality.

That's why I'm asking you to stand with me, that's why I'm asking you to caucus for me, that's why I am asking you to stop settling for what the cynics say we have to accept. In this election—in this moment—let us reach for what we know is possible. A nation healed. A world repaired. An America that believes again. Thank you very much, everybody.

10

NIGHT OF IOWA CAUCUS

January 3, 2008 • Hy-Vee Hall, Des Moines, Iowa

*In lines that stretched around schools and churches,
in small towns and big cities, you came together as
Democrats, Republicans, and independents to stand up
and say that we are one nation, we are one people,
and our time for change has come.*

Barack Obama's opening line said it all: "You know, they said this day would never come. They said our sights were set too high. They said this country was too divided; too disillusioned to ever come together around a common purpose. But on this January night—at this defining moment in history—you have done what the cynics said we couldn't do."

To say the least, Obama's victory in Iowa defied all conventional wisdom. A month earlier no one would have guessed that the junior senator from Illinois would be looking at the "inevitable" candidate, Senator Hillary Clinton, in his rearview mirror. No one would have guessed that he would have picked up seven points in the polls in a matter of weeks, while winning over a predominantly white electorate.

For a year, Obama's campaign team mapped out every county, every precinct, and every high school in the state of Iowa. While they were confident in their strategy, victory was never a guarantee.

From the outset, the team's goal was to significantly expand the number of caucus participants to numbers never seen before or imagined. They had trained an army of volunteers to make it a reality, and in the end they nearly doubled the number of Iowans participating in the 2008 caucus compared to 2004. The team had also worked their candidate to the bone—Obama spent more than eighty days in the state and attended so many events that he had lost his voice by caucus day. But above all else—more than the strategy, more than the man-hours, more than the sheer number of volunteers, handshakes, and phone calls—the Obama team members believed in their message of change over experience, of unity over division.

When the last of the 1,781 precincts had closed and the final caucus tallies were compiled, it was clear that their strategy had worked. Obama swung 37.6 percent, Clinton 29.5, and Edwards 29.8. The *Des Moines Register* had called the contest for Obama in its final pre-caucus poll, predicting that he would win 32 percent to Hillary's 24.

Obama's campaign team understood the Iowa caucus system inside and out. The caucus was a complicated affair. Unlike a primary, where a voter casts a single secret ballot, caucuses function more like town meetings. Beginning at eight in the evening, dozens—and sometimes hundreds—of people gather in school gymnasiums, living rooms, and church halls across the state. They organize themselves in preference groups around the candidate they support. After the initial sorting, if one candidate does not meet the threshold of 15 percent, the caucus-goers can shift their support to another candidate. Obama's key to success was not to just win the first round of voting, but to be a voter's second choice, too—to win in the second round.

The campaign leadership—the campaign manager, David Plouffe; the chief strategist, David Axelrod; and the Iowa campaign manager, Paul Tewes—understood early on that winning Iowa would take significant financial and organizational resources. Both the Clinton and Obama campaigns spent approximately $20 million in the state, but Obama's organizational structure—including his enormous army of volunteers—ran circles around his chief opponent.

Recognizing how essential it was for him to win Iowa, Obama invested heavily and early in the state, whereas up until May 23, 2007, the Clinton campaign was still debating whether Senator Clinton should even compete in Iowa. Her husband had skipped the state in 1992 and won the nomination. Clinton knew she hadn't spent the time necessary in the state, plus it would costs tens of millions of dollars to win—money her campaign could invest elsewhere. (According to the Campaign Media Analysis Group, in December 2007 alone, the presidential campaigns had spent $17 million on more than twenty thousand political ads in

Iowa.) Outside circumstances compelled a final decision when a confidential campaign memo debating this issue from her political director, Mike Henry, was leaked to the *New York Times* and Clinton was forced to commit publicly to competing in the state.[1]

Not only were Iowans now suspicious of her intentions, but Clinton had to spend even more resources to prove her genuine interest in letting Iowans weigh in on her candidacy. Eventually, she even sent her senior campaign staff from her Washington, D.C., headquarters to live in Iowa until the caucus was over.

The other reason for Obama's structural strength was his demographic appeal. From the start of his campaign, Senator Obama drew younger voters (and some would say more passionate supporters) than Senator Clinton. Many of these young voters made up the volunteer army that the Obama campaign built in the state, an asset no other candidate had. It allowed the Obama campaign to run an unmatched grassroots operation in every hamlet in Iowa. The volunteers were well trained, energetic, and dogged, and, unlike Clinton's staff, many, being young and having fewer responsibilities, could afford to work for little or no pay.

Ultimately, Obama's ground game helped to significantly expand the pool of caucus-goers. More people than ever before turned out to caucus in 2008, braving single-digit cold. More than half were first-time caucus-goers, and Obama captured 40 percent of the new voters.

Interestingly, 20 percent of the first-time caucus participants were under the age of thirty, a large number of whom had traveled home from college to caucus for Obama. Many more were high school students (the other campaigns claimed that Obama's team had bused students in from other states). Obama's team understood the importance of Iowa's youth to his victory. On the eve of the Iowa caucus, Obama held an event in Coralville, near the University of Iowa campus, during which he asked the nearly fifteen hundred energetic and youthful supporters packed into the room, "How many people are first-time caucus-goers?" Two-thirds raised their hands. On caucus night, Obama captured 57 percent of those younger voters (age eighteen to thirty) to Clinton's 11 percent; he also won voters age thirty to forty-four. Clinton, on the other hand, only just managed to capture the over-sixty voters.

The Clinton, Obama, and Edwards campaigns had all expected turnout to rise, but no one expected the final count of 239,000 voters. The carpools, free babysitting, and endless canvassing had worked. In 2000, 59,000 Iowans turned out to caucus. In 2004, 125,000 people showed up. In 2008, in the small northern Iowa town of Belmond, 214 people signed in to caucus at the local precinct, compared to 72 in 2004.[2]

Obama's message was fine-tuned to appeal to voters who wanted change, regardless of their party; Clinton's core message of "Ready on day one" was important, but it wasn't resonating to the degree that Obama's was. This trend was especially true for independent voters, who, under Iowa law, could caucus with either party. After eight years of George Bush, and decades of bickering and division in Washington, Iowans longed for a fresh voice that promised comity, not conflict. According to caucus night polls, half of Democrats said change was the top factor influencing their choice of candidate; only 20 percent said experience.

Since announcing his candidacy on February 7, 2007, in Springfield, Illinois, Obama had consistently courted Democrats, Republicans, and independents. As he said in Iowa, "You said the time has come to move beyond the bitterness and pettiness and anger that's consumed Washington; to end the political strategy that's been all about division . . . to build a coalition for change that stretches through red states and blue states."

In addition, Obama personally avoided negative attacks and refused to run negative ads—except for the occasional debate line on foreign policy or driver's licenses for illegal immigrants. This decision appealed to the Midwestern Iowan voter and it shrewdly hemmed in the Clinton operation that was champing at the bit to launch a negative assault on Obama.

It was no accident that when the votes were counted, Senator Obama had grabbed 41 percent of independent voters (who made up 20 percent of the caucus-goers) to Clinton's 17 percent. By careful design, the campaign had decided early on to go after any voter under forty, regardless of party.

In hindsight, the momentum in Iowa shifted after Senator Obama's rousing speech at the Jefferson-Jackson dinner. Clinton dropped from a seven-point lead over Obama to a dead heat with him.

Obama's chief speechwriter, Jon Favreau, spent a majority of November and December 2007 in the Chicago headquarters. In early December, to make sure he was getting good intelligence, he asked one his deputies, Adam Frankel, to go to Iowa and write from there. It was clear that Frankel had his ear to the ground, which was critical in the weeks leading up to the caucus. Two weeks before caucus night, Favreau flew to Des Moines to travel the state with Obama and help him develop his closing-argument speech. Until then, he largely had been using a version of his Iowa Jefferson-Jackson remarks.

On Sunday morning, four days before the caucus, Favreau and Frankel holed up in a backroom of the Village Bean coffee shop, a block from the Iowa campaign office, and began working on a version of the victory speech. They had kicked around a few ideas back at headquarters the day before—Favreau's first day off the road—but it wasn't until that morning that the speech began to gel and the duo wrote the now-famous draft that began, "They said this day would never come." Frankel had actually typed a version of that particular line on his computer the day before. As the two worked, a *Newsweek* reporter sat right outside the door, just out of earshot.

Over the course of the day, Favreau and Frankel took calls from Axelrod and Obama, who, said Favreau, "wanted to emphasize the role grassroots played in our effort. Instead of just thanking volunteers, they wanted the role of volunteers to be a big part of the speech." Favreau and Frankel also received ideas throughout the day via instant message from Ben Rhodes, one of the other speechwriters, who had been camped out in New Hampshire for several weeks. At one point, Frankel turned to Favreau and said, "What we need to capture here is the moment and spirit of Churchill, when he said, 'Let us therefore brace ourselves that, if the British Empire and its Commonwealth last for a thousand years, men will still say, "This was their finest hour."'"

Favreau and Frankel boldly only wrote one draft that day, for a victory speech, and then went to watch Senator Obama's final Iowa rally. They both felt that even if Obama came in second place, he could use most of the speech that they had written, with a few tweaks. As Favreau put it, "If we had lost, [we would have just] reassessed the speech and figured out what really needed to come out."

Favreau admitted that they hadn't even considered what they would have done if Obama had taken third place, but if worse came to worst, they would have drafted something on the fly. He added, "We were still fighting on if we came in third, so we at least knew the guts of the speech would be there—so to crash would not [have been] a big deal." But Axelrod and Obama hadn't even asked for another version; losing was never part of their discussions. It was all about how to frame just how much they had accomplished in their underdog performance.

Favreau sent Obama the speech on Monday night, but, given his campaign schedule, the candidate didn't have time to review it until hours before the caucus. He sent Favreau a few line edits, but he was so busy that he never had a chance to practice the speech.

After visiting a caucus site at Ankeny High School, the candidate and his wife settled down in the Hotel Fort Des Moines (where Clinton was staying, too) to await the results. Obama was confident going into the Iowa caucus. More than two thousand people had packed his last event, almost at midnight, in Dubuque, even though there was a half foot of snow on the ground. But, because of the unpredictable nature of the caucus, he wasn't counting his chickens just yet.

On caucus night, Favreau sat in a room in the hotel adjacent to the Obamas', with Plouffe, Robert Gibbs, and a press aide, Katie McCormick-Lelyveld. They all sat glued to the television as the results trickled in. According to Favreau, "Then they called [the caucus] and we just all erupted, shouting and screaming. A moment later, [Obama] and Michelle walked into the room and gave everyone hugs and high fives. We were all in disbelief."[3] Not only had they won, but it looked as though Clinton had taken third place. They were all floored.

Minutes after they heard the news, Favreau sat with his boss for a final read and a last-minute polish of the victory speech and then sent it to be loaded into the TelePrompTer. Senator Clinton called Senator Obama to congratulate him on his victory, mustered a positive disposition, and made her way out on a stage in the Hotel Fort Des Moines to deliver her concession speech. She struck the right tone and delivered the right words that evening. Yet the moment held an aura of the past, not of the future. Clinton was accompanied on a small, cramped stage by her husband and by Madeline Albright, the former secretary of state, who, though beloved figures in the party, communicated experience, not the promise of revolutionary change.

Shortly after 11:00 p.m. Eastern time, Obama came out onstage at Hy-

Vee Hall in downtown Des Moines with Michelle and their two daughters. He was grinning from ear to ear, clapping his hands and pumping his fists. Using brilliant theatrics, the Obama campaign had built a victory event in Iowa so far unseen in primary politics: before a packed room of nearly three thousand supporters, with dozens flanking him on the stage, Obama delivered a full-length speech that wowed the hundreds of accredited journalists who were present and the hundreds of thousands of citizens watching at home.

The energy in the room was palpable as he hit the notes that he had been playing for months now: "We are choosing hope over fear. We're choosing unity over division, and sending a powerful message that change is coming to Washington." Obama touched on the roster of issues, including health care, energy, and Iraq. But his bigger message was about what his long-shot campaign had accomplished—what a band of volunteers had made a reality in Iowa by making phone calls, canvassing, knocking on doors, and speaking to their neighbors. It was not just that he had toppled the inevitable candidate and the Washington establishment; it was the fact that he had done so as an African American in a state of three million people, only 2.5 percent of whom were black. The headline of Adam Nagourney's report in the January 4 *New York Times* said it all: "Obama Takes Iowa in a Big Turnout as Clinton Falters."

As he wound up his remarks, Obama asked his supporters to remember what they had done at that moment, saying: "Years from now, you'll look back and you'll say that this was the moment—this was the place—where America remembered what it means to hope. . . . This is what we started here in Iowa and that is the message we can now carry to New Hampshire and beyond; the one that can change this country brick by brick, block by block; calloused hand by calloused hand."

One voter, a fifty-six-year-old Lansing Democrat named John Rethwisch, captured the moment by commenting, "I have been seeing more and more something Kennedy-esque coming from Obama."[4]

Since the inception of the Iowa caucus in 1972, five of the eight Democratic caucuses victors have gone on to win the party's presidential nomination. Obama's ascent that evening triggered a nationwide movement that helped set him up for what would be a long and winding road to the nomination and later the White House. It was the first step in his campaign's original battle plan: make a strong showing in early states, but be prepared for a long haul to the convention.

As Obama's Iowa supporters left the hall that evening and flooded downtown to celebrate, they were handed slips of paper with one more request from the senator: please visit one of three campaign offices still open and start phone banking voters in New Hampshire and other Super Tuesday states. There was no time to waste.

REMARKS BY SENATOR BARACK OBAMA: NIGHT OF IOWA CAUCUS

Thank you, Iowa.

You know, they said this day would never come.

They said our sights were set too high.

They said this country was too divided, too disillusioned, to ever come together around a common purpose.

But on this January night—at this defining moment in history—you have done what the cynics said we couldn't do. You have done what the state of New Hampshire can do in five days. You have done what America can do in this New Year, 2008. In lines that stretched around schools and churches, in small towns and big cities, you came together as Democrats, Republicans, and independents to stand up and say that we are one nation, we are one people, and our time for change has come.

You said the time has come to move beyond the bitterness and pettiness and anger that's consumed Washington; to end the political strategy that's been all about division and instead make it about addition—to build a coalition for change that stretches through red states and blue states. Because that's how we'll win in November, and that's how we'll finally meet the challenges that we face as a nation.

We are choosing hope over fear. We're choosing unity over division, and sending a powerful message that change is coming to America.

You said the time has come to tell the lobbyists who think their money and their influence speak louder than our voices that they don't own this government, we do; and we are here to take it back.

The time has come for a president who will be honest about the choices and the challenges we face; who will listen to you and learn from you even when we disagree; who won't just tell you what you want to hear, but what you need to know. And in New Hampshire, if you give me the same chance that Iowa did tonight, I will be that president for America.

Thank you.

I'll be a president who finally makes health care affordable and available to every single American the same way I expanded health care in Illinois— by bringing Democrats and Republicans together to get the job done.

I'll be a president who ends the tax breaks for companies that ship our jobs overseas and put a middle-class tax cut into the pockets of the working Americans who deserve it.

I'll be a president who harnesses the ingenuity of farmers and scientists and entrepreneurs to free this nation from the tyranny of oil once and for all.

And I'll be a president who ends this war in Iraq and finally brings our troops home, who restores our moral standing, who understands that 9/11 is not a way to scare up votes, but a challenge that should unite America and the world against the common threats of the twenty-first century, common threats of terrorism and nuclear weapons, climate change and poverty, genocide and disease.

Tonight, we are one step closer to that vision of America because of what you did here in Iowa. And so I'd especially like to thank the organizers and the precinct captains, the volunteers and the staff, who made this all possible.

And while I'm at it, on "thank-yous," I think it makes sense for me to thank the love of my life, the rock of the Obama family, the closer on the campaign trail. Give it up for Michelle Obama.

I know you didn't do this for me. You did this because you believed so deeply in the most American of ideas—that in the face of impossible odds, people who love this country can change it.

I know this—I know this because while I may be standing here tonight, I'll never forget that my journey began on the streets of Chicago doing what so many of you have done for this campaign and all the campaigns here in Iowa—organizing, and working, and fighting to make people's lives just a little bit better.

I know how hard it is. It comes with little sleep, little pay, and a lot of sacrifice. There are days of disappointment, but sometimes, just sometimes, there are nights like this—a night, a night that, years from now, when we've made the changes we believe in; when more families can afford to see a doctor; when our children, when Malia and Sasha and your children, inherit a planet that's a little cleaner and safer; when the world sees America differently, and America sees itself as a nation less divided and more united; you'll be able to look back with pride and say that this was the moment when it all began.

This was the moment when the improbable beat what Washington always said was inevitable.

This was the moment when we tore down barriers that have divided us for too long—when we rallied people of all parties and ages to a common cause, when we finally gave Americans who'd never participated in politics a reason to stand up and to do so.

This was the moment when we finally beat back the politics of fear, and doubt, and cynicism, the politics where we tear each other down instead of lifting this country up. This was the moment.

Years from now, you'll look back and you'll say that this was the moment— this was the place—where America remembered what it means to hope.

For many months, we've been teased, even derided, for talking about hope.

But we always knew that hope is not blind optimism. It's not ignoring the enormity of the task ahead or the roadblocks that stand in our path. It's not sitting on the sidelines or shirking from a fight. Hope is that thing inside us that insists, despite all evidence to the contrary, that something better awaits us if we have the courage to reach for it, and to work for it, and to fight for it.

Hope is what I saw in the eyes of the young woman in Cedar Rapids who works the night shift after a full day of college and still can't afford health care for a sister who's ill; a young woman who still believes that this country will give her the chance to live out her dreams.

Hope is what I heard in the voice of the New Hampshire woman who told me that she hasn't been able to breathe since her nephew left for Iraq, who still goes to bed each night praying for his safe return.

Hope is what led a band of colonists to rise up against an empire; what led the greatest of generations to free a continent and heal a nation; what led young women and young men to sit at lunch counters and brave fire hoses and march through Selma and Montgomery for freedom's cause.

Hope—hope—is what led me here today—with a father from Kenya, a mother from Kansas, and a story that could only happen in the United States of America. Hope is the bedrock of this nation, the belief that our destiny will not be written for us, but by us, by all those men and women who are not content to settle for the world as it is, who have the courage to remake the world as it should be.

That is what we started here in Iowa, and that is the message we can now carry to New Hampshire and beyond, the same message we had when we were up and when we were down, the one that can change this country brick by brick, block by block, calloused hand by calloused hand—that together, ordinary people can do extraordinary things. Because we are not a collection of red states and blue states, we are the United States of America; and at this moment, in this election, we are ready to believe again. Thank you, Iowa.

11

NIGHT OF NEW HAMPSHIRE PRIMARY

January 8, 2008
Nashua South High School, Nashua, New Hampshire

For most of this campaign, we were far behind.
We always knew our climb would be steep.
But in record numbers, you came out and you spoke up for change.
And with your voices and your votes, you made it clear that at this moment,
in this election, there is something happening in America.

The *Obama Express* landed triumphantly at the Manchester, New Hampshire, airport at three in the morning on Wednesday, January 4, 2008. Obama and his team had just achieved one of the biggest upsets in modern political history: the night before, they had won the Iowa caucus and shaken the foundations of the Clinton dynasty. In their eyes, and in the view of their growing army of supporters, there was nothing they couldn't accomplish. Donations were pouring in faster than the campaign could spend the money. Within twenty-four hours of his Iowa victory, Obama had raised $750,000 online.[1]

The press shared the public's enthusiasm. The *New York Times* called Obama's win in Iowa a "startling setback" for Senator Hillary Clinton.[2] It certainly was. Clinton had spent an estimated $9.79 million dollars in Iowa, but her campaign was simply no match for the Obama organization and the millions he had spent on advertising. Commentators declared that there was something in the political air; some argued that Obama had launched a movement, not just a campaign.

Obama's first stop in New Hampshire, after a good night's sleep, was a midday rally in Concord, followed by a speech that evening at a New Hampshire Democratic Party dinner. With his Iowa victory fresh in the minds of voters, the Granite State appeared to be following suit. It looked like another Obama rout. Obama told supporters on January 4, "If you give me the same chance that Iowa gave me last night, I truly believe that I will be president of the United States."

Over the coming days, Obama picked up more key endorsements, including that of 2000 Democratic presidential candidate Bill Bradley. Polling numbers had now shifted dramatically in Obama's favor, and in New Hampshire, a state that had once been a lock for Clinton, Obama had a multipoint lead, nearing double digits in some polls (a USA Today/Gallup poll that had Obama and Clinton tied three weeks earlier now showed Obama with a thirteen-point lead).

Meanwhile, the Clinton camp was paralyzed, finding itself in a place it never could have anticipated. They knew that if Clinton didn't win New Hampshire, her hopes for the Democratic nomination were effectively over. Some in Clinton's inner circle had lost their confidence and had thrown in the towel. So, with only four days to go until the primary, Clinton jettisoned the naysayers and took the reins of her New Hampshire campaign.[3]

Obama's team, meanwhile, was riding high. The senator saw crowds of a magnitude that he never could have imagined. Lines to attend his events at high schools in Concord and Nashua stretched around the school gymnasiums and into the streets. Clinton, despite her falling poll numbers, still drew large crowds, as did her husband, the former president.

It was a grueling week. Both campaigns were taking nothing for granted. All the candidates—Bill Richardson, Dennis Kucinich, and John Edwards, as well as Obama and Clinton—crisscrossed the state, hopping from event to event, from one media interview to the next. The candidates, still recovering from Iowa, were exhausted by the time they got to the debate at St. Anselm College, in Manchester, on the evening of January 5.

Clinton came out of the gate swinging, playing up a theme she had been emphasizing on the stump all week—the idea that Obama delivered "great poetry" but lacked the experience and the "prose" to execute his visions. "You know," she said, "what we've got to do is translate talk into action and feeling into reality." Obama seemed miffed. When the debate moderator, Scott Spradling, asked Senator Clinton why she thought people found Barack Obama more likable than her, despite her experience, Clinton responded jocularly, "Well, that hurts my feelings." Obama retorted, in what was seen by the media and voters as a sarcastic snub, "You're likable enough, Hillary."[4]

Senator Obama left the debate without any idea that the media had taken his comments as a personal jab against Clinton; he knew he wasn't perfect that night, but no one in his camp realized that he had created a political firestorm. Support for Clinton swelled again. On Saturday, she held an event at Nashua High School that matched the size of Obama's the previous day. Then, on Monday, Clinton sat down for coffee at Cafe Espresso in Portsmouth with a group of sixteen voters, a majority of whom were women. She was asked by one woman how she soldiered on through the punishing primary season. With the unexpected Iowa loss still fresh in her memory, Clinton was overcome with emotion and replied, "It's not easy, and I couldn't do it if I didn't just passionately believe it was the right thing to do. . . . I have so many opportunities from this country. I just don't want to see us fall backwards."

With Clinton visibly stirred, tears in her eyes, her small audience broke into applause. Clinton continued, regaining her composure, "Some of us put ourselves out there and do this against some pretty difficult odds. And we do it, each one of us, because we care about our country."[5] The event lasted only a few minutes, but her comment—and the analysis of it—would dominate the cable news cycle the day before the vote.

Kathleen Strand, Clinton's New Hampshire press secretary, called the state's campaign manager, Nick Clemons, to let him know they had a new problem—Clinton had broken down in public. But Clemons wasn't so sure.[6] He saw it as a moment that showcased Clinton's raw humility and emotion; it had possibly given her an underdog image behind which voters could rally. Clemons had been on the phone with his new unofficial campaign adviser, Bill Clinton, all week. The two agreed that the incident could go either way. Women might respond favorably to Clinton; they had never seen her so vulnerable.

Obama made no public comment about the event. When John Edwards was asked for his opinion, however, he said, "Presidential campaigns are tough business, but being president of the United States is also very tough business."[7] Edwards would later backtrack, saying that he hadn't seen the clip at that time, but it was too late—his words only added to the perception that Clinton was being ganged up on. Even though Edwards and Bill

Richardson were still in the fight in the eyes of the media, it had come down to a mano a mano contest between Obama and Clinton. (Neither Richards nor Edwards had the financial means or organizational strength to stay in the race much longer. Richardson ultimately dropped out on January 10 and Edwards followed on January 30, after the South Carolina primary.)

Jon Favreau had left Iowa with Obama and the traveling campaign team, meeting up with another speechwriter, Ben Rhodes, once he arrived in New Hampshire. Like Adam Frankel in Iowa, Rhodes had been in New Hampshire for the last month preparing for the upcoming primary. Favreau spent the next few days traversing the state with Senator Obama, helping him tweak his stump speech. Then, as in Iowa, he went off the road two days before the contest to work with Rhodes on the election night speech.

Holed up in a hotel room in Concord, where Rhodes had been staying, Favreau and Rhodes spent more than a day writing a draft. At some point on primary eve, they both realized that it was getting late and they had no way of getting back to Nashua, where Obama would spend Election Day. Rhodes and Favreau didn't have a car, so they begged a volunteer to lend them his. Rhodes drove and Favreau continued to type on his laptop, as they made their way to Nashua. At around eleven Favreau's phone rang. It was Obama, wanting to download his thoughts on the primary speech.

The senator was confident he would win New Hampshire—he didn't even think it would be close. He also didn't think Clinton would drop out, even if she lost by ten points, as some in the media were predicting.

Primary day was a whirlwind of activity. Both the Obama and the Clinton teams were tense, for different reasons. Obama, holding on to his near double-digit lead in the polls, was preparing for what could be his ascension to frontrunner for the Democratic nomination (the CNN/WMUR, Rasmussen, and USA Today/Gallup polls had Obama ahead by nine, ten, and thirteen points, respectively). Clinton, on the other hand, hoped to keep the margin of defeat to within a few points to rationalize continuing the fight.

Obama's last event, at Concord High School, was packed; there was a current of electricity in the air. The crowd was particularly boisterous, as they were expecting Obama to sail to victory. People stamped their feet and cheered "Obama, Obama."

One of the campaign's pollsters, Joel Benenson, predicted to the senior staff that despite "tightening up" in the polls, Obama would still win by eight percentage points.[8] Reporters swarmed Obama's chief strategist, David Axelrod, hoping that he would make a prediction—would Clinton drop out if she suffered yet another defeat? What would her political obituary say?

Clinton was up at the crack of dawn on the day of the primary, handing out coffee at polling locations, shaking hands with volunteers, and making one last argument for her candidacy. Ever the fighter, she stopped by five voting precincts that morning and even staged a last-minute event in Manchester, when her campaign team saw an opportunity for one more press hit on WMUR-TV.[9] Bill Clinton began to do what he did better than any other politician—crunch the raw data and look for trends. He liked what he saw.

Obama and his team sat patiently in their suite at the Manchester Radisson, waiting for the results. Nearby, in the campaign boiler room, the state director, Matt Rodriguez, was shocked with early precinct results. Clinton was winning in places he had assumed Obama would win.[10]

The day before Obama had told Favreau, "Even though it looks good for us, I don't think we should take anything for granted. I think there should be a section of the speech that says, 'You know, we have to keep on fighting, it's going to be a long struggle.' Just don't make it like everything is perfect.'" Obama feared that his campaign was starting to resemble Icarus—overly confident and flying a bit too close to the sun. Even if they did win, he had to prepare his supporters for the reality that this was going to be a long fight. Winning wasn't going to be easy; it never was. The Clintons were not quitters and his campaign and his supporters couldn't get too confident. It turned out to be prescient advice.

As election night wore on, Clinton continued to fare better in the exit polling than could have been predicted. The Clinton team was shocked; after seeing the early polls, they couldn't believe they were even still in the game. The Obama squad was equally surprised.

By 10:00 p.m., it was clear to Axelrod, communications director Robert Gibbs, and campaign manager David Plouffe, that Clinton was going to take the night. The Clinton campaign hadn't declared victory yet, but the Associated Press was about to call it for Hillary; it seemed that nearly

every undecided woman had swung to Clinton (she ultimately won the women's vote by 12 percent). The Obama troika of Axelrod, Gibbs, and Plouffe went to see the boss and told him it looked as though he was going to fall a few points short of victory. The country's first primary—at least the popular vote—would go to Clinton. Obama told them, "We were a little too cocky, weren't we? This is going to go on for a while, isn't it?"[11] Obama's comment would frame the next months of his candidacy and his philosophy: bite your lip, note your mistakes, correct them, and, more importantly, prepare for the long haul.

Losing New Hampshire weakened Obama's momentum after Iowa, but he had to keep moving forward. Super Tuesday—twenty-two states' primaries—was less than a month away, on February 5. At this point, it didn't matter whether the reason for his loss was his misstep during the debate or the moment when Clinton's emotions opened her up to her New Hampshire constituency. The fact was, Obama was leaving New Hampshire without the victory his team so badly wanted.

Favreau, equally surprised by the loss, had little time to tinker with his boss's planned victory speech. As he had in Iowa, Favreau spent primary night surrounded by other senior staff in a hotel room at the Manchester Radisson adjacent to the candidate's room. As the evening progressed and the numbers continued to narrow, Gibbs pulled Favreau and Rhodes aside and suggested that they begin drafting another version of their victory speech. Pressed for time, Favreau and Rhodes looked over the speech they had crafted and decided that they only needed to make one major change to the speech: they added a congratulatory note at the top to Senator Clinton.

Favreau quickly briefed Obama on the minor change he had made. The senator had already made line edits to the draft earlier in the evening, so there wasn't much tinkering to do. They sent the speech to the Tele-Prompter; as in Iowa, Obama never had a chance to practice.

Later that evening, Obama would tell his staff and supporters, paraphrasing Frederick Douglass, "Power concedes nothing without a struggle." That was, in short, Obama's message that night—and it struck the perfect chord with his supporters. It also lifted the spirits of the entire staff who, understandably, were in a state of shock.

The remarks Favreau had written, expecting a win, made the point that victory would take a "struggle." But, as he put it, reviving an old Obama refrain, "There has never been anything false about hope. For when we have faced down impossible odds; when we've been told that we're not ready, or that we shouldn't try or that we can't, generations of Americans have responded with a simple creed that sums up the spirit of a people. Yes, we can."

According to Favreau, the line "there has never been anything false about hope" was a direct slap at a comment Clinton had made during the New Hampshire debate: "We don't need to be raising the false hopes of our country about what can be delivered."

Intentionally or not, the Obama camp turned defeat in New Hampshire into another turning point in the campaign; the speech became a rallying cry for the fifteen hundred supporters at Nashua High School South and the millions more in their living rooms. Winning wouldn't be easy, but they would eventually get there—yes, they could.

For Obama, "Yes, we can" dated back to his 2004 run for the U.S. Senate. But the origins of the slogan actually date back to 1972, when the United Farm Workers' cofounders, Cesar Chavez and Dolores Huerta, first used "*Sí, se puede*" during Chavez's twenty-four-day fast. Both in 1972 and again in 2008, "Yes, we can" caught on like wildfire.

Obama approached the podium at around eleven that night to deliver the thirteen-minute concession speech; like in Iowa, he was surrounded on the stage by a sea of supporters. Although hoarse, he looked triumphant. It worked.

The next day, instead of focusing on the loss, newspapers and columnist zeroed in on Obama's upbeat language and the meaning of the moment. The *Los Angeles Times* headline declared, "Obama Has New Rallying Cry: Yes, We Can!" Maria La Ganga wrote, "Senator Barack Obama . . . left [his staunch supporters] no less ready for a fight."[12] Political commentator E. J. Dionne compared Obama to Reagan, writing in his *Washington Post* column, "Obama gets his crowds swooning. So did Reagan."[13] Mark Warren of *Esquire* later wrote, "Had there ever been a more triumphal concession speech, ever? . . . Speeches claiming victory are never as interesting as those conceding defeat, because people are never more interesting than when they lose."[14] Essentially, the media downplayed Clinton's come-from-behind victory.

With this loss, Obama had told America something about himself and his view of the campaign, which would carry on for another five months. "For most of this campaign, we were far behind. We always knew our climb would be steep. But in record numbers, you came out and you spoke up for change. And with your voices and your votes you made it clear that at this moment, in this election, there is something happening in America." That something was a movement. It was no longer just about Obama; it was about a groundswell of people who wanted change. And, as Obama put, "No matter what obstacles stand in our way, nothing can stand in the way of the power of millions of voices calling for change."

REMARKS OF SENATOR BARACK OBAMA: NIGHT OF NEW HAMPSHIRE PRIMARY

I want to congratulate Senator Clinton on a hard-fought victory here in New Hampshire.

A few weeks ago, no one imagined that we'd have accomplished what we did here tonight. For most of this campaign, we were far behind, and we always knew our climb would be steep.

But in record numbers, you came out and spoke up for change. And with your voices and your votes, you made it clear that at this moment—in this election there is something happening in America.

There is something happening when men and women in Des Moines and Davenport, in Lebanon and Concord, come out in the snows of January to wait in lines that stretch block after block because they believe in what this country can be.

There is something happening when Americans who are young in age and in spirit—who have never before participated in politics—turn out in numbers we've never seen because they know in their hearts that this time must be different.

There is something happening when people vote not just for the party they belong to but the hopes they hold in common—that whether we are rich or poor, black or white, Latino or Asian; whether we hail from Iowa or New Hampshire, Nevada, or South Carolina, we are ready to take this country in a fundamentally new direction. That is what's happening in America right now. Change is what's happening in America.

You can be the new majority who can lead this nation out of a long political darkness—Democrats, independents, and Republicans who are tired of the division and distraction that has clouded Washington; who know that we can disagree without being disagreeable; who understand that if we mobilize our voices to challenge the money and influence that's stood in our way and challenge ourselves to reach for something better, there's no problem we can't solve—no destiny we cannot fulfill.

Our new American majority can end the outrage of unaffordable, unavailable health care in our time. We can bring doctors and patients, workers and businesses, Democrats and Republicans together; and we can tell the drug and insurance industry that while they'll get a seat at the table, they don't get to buy every chair. Not this time. Not now.

Our new majority can end the tax breaks for corporations that ship our jobs overseas and put a middle-class tax cut into the pockets of the working Americans who deserve it.

We can stop sending our children to schools with corridors of shame and start putting them on a pathway to success. We can stop talking about how great teachers are and start rewarding them for their greatness. We can do this with our new majority.

We can harness the ingenuity of farmers and scientists, citizens and entrepreneurs, to free this nation from the tyranny of oil and save our planet from a point of no return.

And when I am president, we will end this war in Iraq and bring our troops home; we will finish the job against al Qaeda in Afghanistan; we will care for our veterans; we will restore our moral standing in the world; and we will never use 9/11 as a way to scare up votes, because it is not a tactic to win an election, it is a challenge that should unite America and the world against the common threats of the twenty-first century: terrorism and nuclear weapons, climate change and poverty, genocide and disease.

All of the candidates in this race share these goals. All have good ideas. And all are patriots who serve this country honorably.

But the reason our campaign has always been different is because it's not just about what I will do as president, it's also about what you, the people who love this country, can do to change it.

That's why tonight belongs to you. It belongs to the organizers and the volunteers and the staff who believed in our improbable journey and rallied so many others to join.

We know the battle ahead will be long, but always remember that no matter what obstacles stand in our way, nothing can withstand the power of millions of voices calling for change.

We have been told we cannot do this by a chorus of cynics who will only grow louder and more dissonant in the weeks to come. We've been asked to pause for a reality check. We've been warned against offering the people of this nation false hope.

But in the unlikely story that is America, there has never been anything false about hope. For when we have faced down impossible odds; when we've been told that we're not ready, or that we shouldn't try, or that we can't, generations of Americans have responded with a simple creed that sums up the spirit of a people.

Yes, we can.

It was a creed written into the founding documents that declared the destiny of a nation.

Yes, we can.

It was whispered by slaves and abolitionists as they blazed a trail toward freedom through the darkest of nights.

Yes, we can.

It was sung by immigrants as they struck out from distant shores and pioneers who pushed westward against an unforgiving wilderness.

Yes, we can.

It was the call of workers who organized; women who reached for the ballot; a president who chose the moon as our new frontier; and a King who took us to the mountaintop and pointed the way to the Promised Land.

Yes, we can, to justice and equality. Yes, we can, to opportunity and prosperity. Yes we can heal this nation. Yes we can repair this world. Yes we can.

And so tomorrow, as we take this campaign south and west; as we learn that the struggles of the textile worker in Spartanburg are not so different than the plight of the dishwasher in Las Vegas; that the hopes of the little girl who goes to a crumbling school in Dillon are the same as the dreams of the boy who learns on the streets of L.A.; we will remember that there is something happening in America, that we are not as divided as our politics suggests, that we are one people; we are one nation; and together, we will begin the next great chapter in America's story with three words that will ring from coast to coast; from sea to shining sea: Yes. We. Can.

SOUTH CAROLINA PRIMARY
VICTORY SPEECH

January 26, 2008
Columbia Hotel, Columbia, South Carolina

This election is . . . about the past versus the future.
It's about whether we settle for the same divisions and distractions
and drama that passes for politics today, or whether we reach
for a politics of common sense and innovation —
a shared sacrifice and shared prosperity.

In the eyes of his senior staff, South Carolina marked a turning point in the Obama campaign. Not only had the Illinois senator overcome his chief opponent, Hillary Clinton, and John Edwards, who had won the state four years earlier, but his victory was so convincing that even Obama's naysayers were surprised.

Obama captured 55 percent of the Democratic vote. Clinton took 27 percent and Edwards, 18 percent. Turnout was a record 530,000 people—nearly 100,000 more voters than the Republican primary. As the *New York Times* trumpeted the next morning, "Obama Carries South Carolina by Wide Margin." But that alone wasn't what wowed the political commentators. Rather, it was how Obama bested Clinton's husband, the former president, who went all-out in the state on his wife's behalf, and how, despite predictions to the contrary, Obama won a significant portion of the white vote.

Senator Obama had worked his heart out in South Carolina. Leading up to the election, he had spent more than two weeks in the state, pounding the pavement, holding rallies and giving interviews. In fact, Obama had been visiting the state for months. As early as December 2007, he held a rally at Williams-Brice Stadium in Columbia—and more than 29,000 people showed up to hear Obama, his wife, and the headliner, Oprah Winfrey.

It is often forgotten that Obama entered primary day in South Carolina in a bit of a slump. He had pulled out an historic victory in Iowa, but that was nearly a month earlier. Since then, he had lost the New Hampshire primary and the Nevada caucus. South Carolina was hardly a guaranteed victory.

During this time, a narrative had developed among some journalists and the Democratic Party as to whether Obama had the broad national appeal to win in a general election. Could he attract the white vote? The electability question was particularly relevant in South Carolina where, in 2008, 45 percent of the Democratic primary voters were white. This skepticism wasn't entirely unfounded. Most of those who had shown up to see Obama and Winfrey in Columbia a month earlier were black. Winfrey's comments at the event accentuated the point: "Think about where you would be in your life if you waited when the people told you no. . . . The moment is now . . . Dr. King dreamed the dream. But we don't have to just dream the dream anymore. We get a chance to vote that dream into reality."[1]

In fact, many African Americans in South Carolina were hesitant to support Obama before he won Iowa; they were concerned that he simply couldn't win in November. And losing would be worse for the cause. A November 2007 USA Today/Gallup poll gave Clinton 57 percent of the black vote to Obama's 33. A local African American religious leader, the Reverend J. W. Sanders, called Clinton "the right choice . . . a lady who has proven herself to do exactly what should be done."[2]

In February 2007, a well-respected black state senator, Robert Ford, had announced that he was backing Clinton, saying, "Everybody else on the ballot is doomed." Asked about Obama, he said, "Every Democratic candidate running on the ticket would lose because he's black and he's at the top of the ticket—we'd lose the House, the Senate, and the governors and everything."[3] Some had darker fears: if Obama did win, he would be the victim of a certain assassination. This was especially true among black women, who had always supported the Clintons and were torn over the gender issue.

According to the Nation, Clinton did all the right things early on to garner the black vote in South Carolina—she won endorsements of key preachers, demanded the removal of the Confederate flag from the State-house, and spent many hours at black churches and colleges.[4]

But in the end, Obama quelled this issue and captured the black vote. He seized on comments like State Senator Ford's, declaring at rallies in African American communities, "I've been reading the papers in South Carolina. Can't have a black man at the top of the ticket. But I know this: that when folks were saying, 'We're going to march for our freedom,' they said, 'You can't do that.' When somebody said, 'You can't sit at the lunch counter. . . . You can't do that.' We did. And when somebody said, 'Women belong in the kitchen not in the board room. You can't do that.' Yes, we can."[5]

With his victory in Iowa, Obama proved that he could win—and after that, blacks left Clinton in droves. And, as in Iowa, Obama's campaign operation in South Carolina was second to none. Under the direction of Steve Hildebrand, the campaign amassed an army of more than thirteen thousand volunteers by primary day (in addition to forty paid staffers). It was an operation that Clinton simply couldn't match. The Obama camp also unleashed an initiative targeting more than nine hundred barber shops and beauty salons.

Obama's message in South Carolina wasn't tailored specifically to Af-rican Americans. It was the same rhetoric he had employed successfully elsewhere, striking the notes of change, unity, and responsibility. This isn't to say that he shunned policy issues that appealed to blacks, or that he eschewed Baptist churches and a preacher's tone if the moment called for it—he did both. But he learned early on in South Carolina and else-where—sometimes the hard way—that he had to be careful about being too colloquial with black audiences.

In April 2007, at a speech to the legislative black caucus in South Carolina, Obama joked, "A good economic development plan for our community would be if we make sure folks weren't throwing garbage out of their cars." He was quickly criticized in the black community for his comments, which, some said, embodied the "oldest racial stereotypes."[6] Obama didn't make that mistake again.

In the end, Obama's message transcended color lines, and he took 24 percent of the white vote among South Carolina's Democrats, a number that caught the Clinton campaign by surprise. He also grabbed 80 percent of black women Democrats—a group that had been hesitant to throw their lot in with him and his campaign. This quickly quelled any questions about his ability to capture a cross-section of the voters—one of the central electability issues.

The other surprise was the level of nastiness and invective—the bare knuckles and brass tactics—that entered the South Carolina race. This primary, in particular, marked the high point of the negative cross-fire between the Obama and Clinton campaigns.

First, there was Bill Clinton. He and Hillary had decided that Obama was vulnerable in South Carolina. It wasn't a caucus, where Obama's organization had proven its might. The Clintons decided to increase their spending in South Carolina in the weeks leading up to the election, despite the advice of many in the state, including Clinton's South Carolina campaign manager, Donnie Fowler. Fowler later told Dan Balz, skeptically, "I believe they felt that they could either win or come very close." The former president believed that his historical popularity with African Americans would help Senator Clinton siphon off some of the black vote from the black candidate. "Bill Clinton wanted to demonstrate that he still had political force and influence within the African American community," Fowler said.[7]

This thinking wasn't without merit. Throughout his tenure, President Clinton had seen by blacks as a champion for civil rights, equal opportunity, and economic empowerment. More than his predecessors, he had strong ties to the black community, dating back to his days as governor of Arkansas. If Senator Clinton could land most of the white vote, and 10 to 15 percent of the black vote, she could win South Carolina.

So, employing that strategy, Bill Clinton zigzagged the state on behalf of his wife, attending town halls and rallies in every city that would have him. One national paper declared in its headline, "In S. Carolina, It's Obama vs. Clinton. That's Bill Clinton."[8] In fact, in the days leading up to the election, Senator Clinton spent most days out of the state, looking toward Super Tuesday states. She campaigned in Arizona, California, New Jersey, and New Mexico. Her advisers claimed she was running a national campaign, which included, among others, South Carolina. It was up to the former president, joined regularly by their daughter, Chelsea, to court fellow Southerners and turn up the rhetoric. From the stump, President Clinton questioned Obama's record on Iraq, his position on choice, and the legitimacy of his economic plan.

It was clear that the former president was getting under Obama's skin. As Obama walked down a rope line in South Carolina, Jeff Zeleny, a reporter from the *New York Times,* needled him on Clinton's claims, asking, "Are you letting Bill Clinton get inside your head?" Obama snapped at him, "Don't try cheap stunts like that, Jeff. Come on, you're better than that." He did follow up with, "My suspicion is that the other side must be rattled if they're continuing saying false things about us."[9]

The Bill Clinton-Barack Obama matchup had been brewing for some time. Many of Obama's staffers were still annoyed by Bill Clinton's "fairy tale" comments a few weeks earlier on the eve of the New Hampshire primary. President Clinton maintained that he was speaking about Obama's stance on the Iraq War. Many in the Obama camp, however, including those in the mainstream media, believed he was referring to Obama's candidacy.

It didn't help Clinton's cause that a few days later, on January 13, Robert Johnson, the founder of Black Enterprise Television, and a Clinton supporter, made an off-hand comment to reporters about Obama's cocaine use during his youth, which he had admitted to in *Dreams from My Father.*[10] Johnson said, "As an African American, I am frankly insulted that the Obama campaign would imply that we are so stupid that we would think Hillary and Bill Clinton, who have been deeply and emotionally involved in black issues since Barack Obama was doing something in the neighborhood—and I won't say what he was doing, but he did say it in the book."[11]

This was a touchy issue that many believed was loaded with racial implications. Obama's team suspected that the Clinton campaign, including Bill Clinton, was behind Johnson's comments. A month earlier, Hillary Clinton's New Hampshire campaign co-chairman, Billy Shaheen—the husband of the former New Hampshire governor, Jeanne Shaheen—had made similar comments. The Clinton campaign denied any role in either Johnson's or Shaheen's statements, but Obama and the members of the media were suspicious. Others, such as Congressman Jim Clyburn of South Carolina, an African American and longtime friend of the Clintons, also questioned this series of coincidences. He also worried about a possible backlash, advising President Clinton that he "should watch what and how he says it because there are a lot of people who see Barack Obama as their hopes and dreams. And they're going to start to feel like you're throwing cold water on their dream."[12]

In the run-up to the Nevada caucus, Obama said in an interview with the *Reno Gazette*: "Ronald Reagan changed the trajectory of America in a way that . . . Richard Nixon did not and in a way that Bill Clinton did not. He put us on a fundamentally different path because the country was ready for it."[13] He later claimed that the "change in trajectory" he was referring to was President Reagan's ability to rally Democrats behind his agenda. Obama claimed that he was not attacking the Clinton years or endorsing Reagan's policies per se, but the latter's ability to unify the country.

Bill Clinton smelled an opportunity to attack; he immediately questioned Obama's statements. Clinton couldn't believe that Obama was praising Ronald Reagan, the archetype of the Republican evil he had run against in 1992. "Her principal opponent said that since 1992, the Republicans have had all the good ideas," Clinton said with a grin to a crowd of supporters in Nevada. He continued, "I can't imagine any Democrat seeking the presidency would say [that the GOP was] the party of new ideas for the last fifteen years."[14] Senator Clinton reiterated this point—with sharp elbows—in her debate with Obama a few days later.

Bill Clinton didn't let up; he saw a window of opportunity and wanted to drive a train right through it. By the time the South Carolina debate rolled around, Obama had had enough. At the debate he said to Hillary Clinton, in a somewhat annoyed tone, "Well, I can't tell who I'm running against sometimes."

After nineteen debates, this was the first time that Obama and Clinton were slinging mud at each other directly. Both sides unloaded all of the opposition research they had been compiling—and hoarding—for months. The tension between the two campaigns was at an all-time high.

Early in the debate, Clinton pressed Obama on the consistency of his position in Iraq: "You gave a great speech in 2002 opposing the war in Iraq. . . . By the next year, the speech was off your Web site. By the next year, you were telling reporters that you agreed with President Bush in his conduct of the war. . . . It was more about the distinction between words and actions." She then piled on about Obama's comments on Reagan: "The facts are that he has said in the last week that he really liked the ideas of the Republicans over the last ten to fifteen years." You could cut the tension in the room with a knife.

Obama also lashed out, disputing the Reagan attack and questioning Clinton's record and her commitment to hard-pressed Americans. "What I said is that Ronald Reagan was a transformative political figure because he was able to get Democrats to vote against their economic interests. . . . While I was working on those streets watching those folks see their jobs shift overseas, you were a corporate lawyer sitting on the board at Walmart."

Clinton shot back, "I was fighting against those [Republican] ideas when you were practicing law and representing your contributor, Rezco, in his slum landlord business in inner-city Chicago."

Both the Clinton and Obama campaigns were shocked. BlackBerries were buzzing as both sides tried to figure out how to handle the post-debate spin contest. Even the reporters covering the debate were surprised. For more than a year they had waited for the moment when the candidates would finally take off their gloves. This was finally it.

And the attacks didn't let up until primary day. In fact, they crept into Obama's seventeen-minute victory speech at the Columbia Hotel in the South Carolina capital. Obama had wanted to put aside partisanship completely and reach across party lines—it was one of his key campaign themes. But the Reagan exchange proved just how difficult it would be to put aside, as he put it, "politics that uses religion as a wedge and patriotism as a bludgeon, a politics that tells us that we have to think, act, and even vote within the confines of the categories that supposedly define us." Obama wanted to move past the same old partisan campaign attacks, but South Carolina made that an impossible task.

When he called his chief speechwriter on the eve of the primary, Obama seemed frustrated with where the campaign had veered. It had fallen into the traps that he wanted to avoid, yet he knew that he had to fight back. According to Favreau, "In South Carolina, there was a threat to the whole idea that Obama had been putting forth for the entire campaign, that we could come together, that we could heal some of the divisions in the country."

As he prepared his remarks, Obama told Favreau on a phone call from the campaign plane, "I know we are all focused on the Clintons, but I don't blame them personally. It's like what we're up against, not just the Clintons themselves as people, but an entire notion of politics that says this country has to be divided. That says that there are special categories we all have to be in, black, white, North, South. Even if we win South Carolina, it doesn't end it. This is what we're going to be up against now until we win this election and this is what people need to realize what we're fighting against. That kind of change we seek will not come easy."

He then dictated a core paragraph of his speech to Favreau: "But there are real differences between the candidates. We are looking for more than just a change of party in the White House. We're looking to fundamentally change the status quo in Washington. It's a status quo that extends beyond any particular party. And right now that status quo is fighting back with everything it's got, with the same old tactics that divide and distract us from solving the problems people face, whether those problems are health care that folks can't afford or a mortgage they cannot pay."

Still, despite his lofty intentions, Obama knew that he couldn't stand back and take punches without defending himself. This was going to be a long, drawn-out battle with Clinton; he had to draw clear distinctions between himself and his opponent. In his remarks, he ticked off a series of "differences." First, he said, "We're up against the belief that it's okay for lobbyists to dominate our government—that they are just part of the system in Washington." Second, in a clear attack on Clinton, he said, "We are up against the conventional thinking that says your ability to lead as president comes from longevity in Washington or proximity to the White House." Third, in a reference to the deeply partisan Clinton administration years, he added, "We are up against decades of bitter partisanship that cause politicians to demonize their opponents instead of coming together to make college affordable or energy cleaner." Finally, Favreau crafted searing language aimed at both Clintons: "This election is . . . about the past versus the future. It's about whether we settle for the same divisions and distractions and drama that passes for politics today or whether we reach for a politics of common sense and innovation—a shared sacrifice and shared prosperity." Those lines were a clear attack on the Clinton administration and the bitter partisanship and scandals of the 1990s. The "past-versus-future" refrain would become an Obama favorite on the stump.

Favreau, along with speechwriters Ben Rhodes and Adam Frankel, had to settle the score after the brutal battle with the Clinton camp. It was evident in what they wrote that they were angry. They wanted to show that they had shut down the Clinton machine; the choice between the candidates couldn't be clearer. "I remember we watched that speech that Saturday night at headquarters and we were more excited than we were when we had won the Iowa caucus," Favreau said.

Interestingly, Obama also took on the subject of race, one of his first times publicly, questioning a politics premised on the idea that "African Americans can't support the white candidate, whites can't support the African American candidate, black and Latinos can't come together. . . . When I hear the cynical talk that blacks and whites and Latinos can't join together and work together, I'm reminded of the Latino brothers and sisters I organized with and stood with and fought with side by side for jobs and justice on the streets of Chicago."

"Up until then," says Favreau, "we had always blurred race—it had never been that much of an issue before." But it was in South Carolina and race had been a significant issue—so they addressed it. "We proved the naysayers wrong, so we had to mention it and put it to rest," he added.

Favreau sent a draft of the speech to the traveling party on Saturday as Obama snaked his way through the state. The candidate didn't make any edits. He seemed pleased with the draft, particularly the ending, where the speechwriters had captured two stories Obama had told them the day before. One was about a former Strom Thurmond Republican who "went out onto the streets of South Carolina and knocked on doors for [the Obama] campaign." The other was about an elderly woman who sent the campaign an envelope with $3.01, along "with a verse of the Scripture tucked inside." Favreau worked them into the address, along with the sentences, "So don't tell us change isn't possible. That woman knows change is possible."

South Carolina was a devastating loss for Clinton. MSNBC released a poll two days before the primary showing Obama leading by eight points, so everyone expected Obama to win, but no one had expected the blowout that occurred—55 percent to Obama, 27 percent to Clinton, and 17 percent to

Edwards. The win reversed the momentum Clinton had picked up in New Hampshire and Nevada and strengthened Obama's electability argument. Clinton's campaign had also spent millions in South Carolina, although they desperately needed the funds for the dozens of Super Tuesday races ahead.

For the first time in Democratic primary history, South Carolina's primary was in January—the fourth primary contest. The Democratic National Committee had done this to give African Americans a stronger voice in the early stages of the nomination process. Ironically, although black voters voted overwhelmingly for Obama and carried him to victory, what sealed his decisive win was securing an unexpected 24 percent of the white Democratic vote.

Favreau summarized the win: "It was pivotal. The New Hampshire loss speech gave us a morale boost; the South Carolina win didn't put aside the race issue, but we at least answered the initial doubt that a black man could get white votes. We took the biggest barrage of attacks from the Clintons that almost anyone had taken at that point. But we beat them back and won." It was understandable that he concluded his boss's speech that night with, "Don't tell me we can't change. Yes, we can change. . . . Yes. We. Can."

REMARKS BY SENATOR BARACK OBAMA: SOUTH CAROLINA PRIMARY VICTORY SPEECH

Over two weeks ago, we saw the people of Iowa proclaim that our time for change has come. But there were those who doubted this country's desire for something new—who said Iowa was a fluke not to be repeated again.

Well, tonight, the cynics who believed that what began in the snows of Iowa was just an illusion were told a different story by the good people of South Carolina.

After four great contests in every corner of this country, we have the most votes, the most delegates, and the most diverse coalition of Americans we've seen in a long, long time.

They are young and old, rich and poor. They are black and white, Latino and Asian. They are Democrats from Des Moines and independents from Concord, Republicans from rural Nevada, and young people across this country who've never had a reason to participate until now. And in nine days, nearly half the nation will have the chance to join us in saying that we are tired of business-as-usual in Washington, we are hungry for change, and we are ready to believe again.

But if there's anything we've been reminded of since Iowa, it's that the kind of change we seek will not come easy. Partly because we have fine candidates in the field—fierce competitors, worthy of respect. And as contentious as this campaign may get, we have to remember that this is a contest for the Democratic nomination, and that all of us share an abiding desire to end the disastrous policies of the current administration.

But there are real differences between the candidates. We are looking for more than just a change of party in the White House. We're looking to fundamentally change the status quo in Washington—a status quo that extends beyond any particular party. And right now, that status quo is fighting back with everything it's got; with the same old tactics that divide and distract us from solving the problems people face, whether those problems are health care they can't afford or a mortgage they cannot pay.

So this will not be easy. Make no mistake about what we're up against.

We are up against the belief that it's okay for lobbyists to dominate our government—that they are just part of the system in Washington. But we know that the undue influence of lobbyists is part of the problem, and this election is our chance to say that we're not going to let them stand in our way anymore.

We are up against the conventional thinking that says your ability to lead as president comes from longevity in Washington or proximity to the White House. But we know that real leadership is about candor, and judgment, and the ability to rally Americans from all walks of life around a common purpose—a higher purpose.

We are up against decades of bitter partisanship that cause politicians to demonize their opponents instead of coming together to make college affordable or energy cleaner; it's the kind of partisanship where you're not even allowed to say that a Republican had an idea—even if it's one you never agreed with. That kind of politics is bad for our party, it's bad for our country, and this is our chance to end it once and for all.

We are up against the idea that it's acceptable to say anything and do anything to win an election. We know that this is exactly what's wrong with our politics; this is why people don't believe what their leaders say anymore; this is why they tune out. And this election is our chance to give the American people a reason to believe again.

And what we've seen in these last weeks is that we're also up against forces that are not the fault of any one campaign, but feed the habits that prevent us from being who we want to be as a nation. It's the politics that uses religion as a wedge, and patriotism as a bludgeon. A politics that tells us that we have to think, act, and even vote within the confines of the categories that supposedly define us. The assumption that young people are apathetic. The assumption that Republicans won't cross over. The assumption that the wealthy care nothing for the poor, and that the poor don't vote. The assumption that African Americans can't support the white candidate; whites can't support the African American candidate; blacks and Latinos can't come together.

But we are here tonight to say that this is not the America we believe in. I did not travel around this state over the last year and see a white South Carolina or a black South Carolina. I saw South Carolina. I saw crumbling schools that are stealing the future of black children and white children. I saw shuttered mills and homes for sale that once belonged to Americans from all walks of life, and men and women of every color and creed who serve together, and fight together, and bleed together under the same proud flag. I saw what America is, and I believe in what this country can be.

That is the country I see. That is the country you see. But now it is up to us to help the entire nation embrace this vision. Because in the end, we are not just up against the ingrained and destructive habits of Washington, we are also struggling against our own doubts, our own fears, and our own cynicism. The change we seek has always required great struggle and sacrifice. And so this is a battle in our own hearts and minds about what kind of country we want and how hard we're willing to work for it.

So let me remind you tonight that change will not be easy. That change will take time. There will be setbacks, and false starts, and sometimes we will make mistakes. But as hard as it may seem, we cannot lose hope. Because there are people all across this country who are counting on us; who can't afford another four years without health care or good schools or decent wages because our leaders couldn't come together and get it done.

Theirs are the stories and voices we carry on from South Carolina.

The mother who can't get Medicaid to cover all the needs of her sick child—she needs us to pass a health care plan that cuts costs and makes health care available and affordable for every single American.

The teacher who works another shift at Dunkin' Donuts after school just to make ends meet—she needs us to reform our education system so that she gets better pay, and more support, and her students get the resources they need to achieve their dreams.

The Maytag worker who is now competing with his own teenager for a seven-dollar-an-hour job at Walmart because the factory he gave his life to shut its doors—he needs us to stop giving tax breaks to companies that ship our jobs overseas and start putting them in the pockets of working Americans who deserve it. And struggling homeowners. And seniors who should retire with dignity and respect.

The woman who told me that she hasn't been able to breathe since the day her nephew left for Iraq, or the soldier who doesn't know his child because he's on his third or fourth tour of duty—they need us to come together and put an end to a war that should've never been authorized and never been waged.

The choice in this election is not between regions or religions or genders. It's not about rich versus poor, young versus old, and it is not about black versus white.

It's about the past versus the future.

It's about whether we settle for the same divisions and distractions and drama that passes for politics today, or whether we reach for a politics of common sense and innovation—a shared sacrifice and shared prosperity.

There are those who will continue to tell us we cannot do this. That we cannot have what we long for. That we are peddling false hopes.

But here's what I know. I know that when people say we can't overcome all the big money and influence in Washington, I think of the elderly woman who sent me a contribution the other day—an envelope that had a money order for three dollars and one cent along with a verse of Scripture tucked inside. So don't tell us change isn't possible.

When I hear the cynical talk that blacks and whites and Latinos can't join together and work together, I'm reminded of the Latino brothers and sisters I organized with, and stood with, and fought with side by side for jobs and justice on the streets of Chicago. So don't tell us change can't happen.

When I hear that we'll never overcome the racial divide in our politics, I think about that Republican woman who used to work for Strom Thurmond, who's now devoted to educating inner-city children and who went out onto the streets of South Carolina and knocked on doors for this campaign. Don't tell me we can't change.

Yes, we can change.

Yes, we can heal this nation.

Yes, we can seize our future.

And as we leave this state with a new wind at our backs, and take this journey across the country we love with the message we've carried from the plains of Iowa to the hills of New Hampshire, from the Nevada desert to the South Carolina coast, the same message we had when we were up and when we were down—that out of many, we are one, that while we breathe we hope, and where we are met with cynicism, and doubt, and those who tell us that we can't, we will respond with that timeless creed that sums up the spirit of a people in three simple words:

Yes. We. Can.

13

NIGHT OF SUPER TUESDAY PRIMARIES

February 5, 2008 · *Hyatt Regency Hotel, Chicago, Illinois*

We are the ones we've been waiting for.
We are the change that we seek.

In practical terms, the Super Tuesday primary results were a draw between
the two frontrunners for the Democratic nomination, Hillary Clinton
and Barack Obama. After twenty-three contests (twenty-two states and
American Samoa), Senator Clinton added 834 to her delegate count and
Obama added 847 to his. The magical number to capture the nomination was 2,025. Obama carried fourteen states, six more than Clinton. In
total more than 15,417,521 people had voted for one of the Democrats.
Patrick Healy of the *New York Times* put it best, saying, "Mrs. Clinton and
Mr. Obama smiled broadly [on election night] but were relatively low
key. . . . They knew that their state-by-state successes did not add up to
the grand prize of Democratic standard-bearer."[1]

Super Tuesday had its name for a reason: in 2008, thanks to changes in
party rules, more states held primaries that day than ever before. In one day,
more than 1,681 of the 3,253 of the pledged delegates were up for grabs.

Clinton won the "big states," including New York, New Jersey, Arizona, California, and Massachusetts. Her victory in Massachusetts was
a major upset and a blow to the two sitting senators, Ted Kennedy and
John Kerry, and Governor Deval Patrick, all of whom had endorsed
Obama earlier in the week. Senator Kennedy had compared Obama to his
brother, President John F. Kennedy. Winning the larger, more delegate-
rich states was part of Clinton's campaign strategy of showing her prow-
ess and electability in the traditional blue states. Ultimately, however, she
lost the Super Tuesday war to Obama by thirteen delegates.

The Obama campaign adopted a far different Super Tuesday strategy

—one that his campaign manager, David Plouffe, had been cooking up for more than a year. Early on, Plouffe had figured that, because of her national name recognition, Clinton would win the big blue primary states. So, Obama would need another way to capture delegates.

First, even if Obama didn't win a single state outright, Plouffe understood that he still could capture a significant number of delegates. Unlike the general election's winner-take-all system, the Democratic primary had proportional voting. So even if he didn't win New York or New Jersey, Obama could still have a strong showing and pick up a significant number of delegates in those states.[2]

Second, Plouffe believed that he could out-organize and outperform the Clinton organization in the caucus states. These states were small, and turnout was traditionally low, but their delegates added up. To succeed, he would use one of his campaign's greatest strengths to turn out the vote—its deep bench of volunteers, its active, high-tech online community, its use of social marketing, its sophisticated ground operation, and its well-oiled campaign structure. If Obama won by large enough margins in these smaller states, he could neutralize Clinton's gains in the larger, traditional blue states.

Beginning in the fall of 2007, Plouffe began opening offices and dispatching volunteers to all Super Tuesday states. While the Clinton team was busy focusing on the first four states—Iowa, New Hampshire, Nevada, and South Carolina—the Obama campaign took the long view. In September, they sent nine staffers to Minnesota, eight to Colorado, two to Idaho, and five to Kansas. They also began organizing in Alaska and North Dakota. By the late fall they had paid staff in sixteen of the twenty-two Super Tuesday states, far more than Clinton.[3]

Clinton's people had always believed that they'd lock up the nomination early, but Obama's team had always known that it would take a prolonged battle for them to win. So they hung up their shingle in places where no Democratic campaign, including Clinton, had ever paid much attention.

Caucuses rely heavily on organization and an understanding of the rules, so the Obama campaign dug in early, tapping their volunteers, developing manuals on the rules, and identifying the key Democrats in these states—even if the number of Democrats was relatively small. It is true that the relatively few Democrats in states such as Idaho and Alaska skewed toward Obama's core demographic—younger, better educated, African American, and wealthier. But Clinton's people never even planted a flag in most of those states before it was too late, so it was difficult to know whether her prime supporters—women, older, Hispanic, working-class—would have surfaced.

Plouffe's strategy paid off. In New Jersey, Clinton won the popular vote by ten percentage points, gaining 54 percent of the vote to Obama's 44—but she won only eleven more pledged delegates than Obama (of 107 total). On the other hand, in Idaho, Obama overwhelmed Clinton, with 79 percent to Clinton's 17, and gained twelve more delegates than the New York senator.[4] These kinds of results explain why the *Washington Post* led its election coverage on February 6 with the headline, "For Clinton, a Lively Dead Heat."

Both sides offered their own spin on the results; the Obama camp called it a "split decision" and downplayed expectations. Some of Clinton's surrogates went the other way, particularly after the victories in Massachusetts and New Jersey were announced, declaring that it was "a big, big night for Hillary." Pundits gave the "edge" in the spin war to Clinton.[5]

In reality, however, Clinton needed a major victory that night to overcome a tsunami of momentum building on the other side. As Roger Cohen wrote in the *New York Times,* Clinton didn't get the bounce she needed—"the defining day defined nothing"—from Super Tuesday.[6] And the longer the battle went on, the more established and credentialed Obama became. Obama was out–fund-raising Clinton's organization significantly (he raised $32 million in January, more than twice what Clinton raised) and extending his grassroots effort into almost every state. After spending nearly every nickel she raised in Iowa and New Hampshire, Clinton had to lend her campaign $5 million just to get through Super Tuesday. And the map of upcoming contests wasn't favorable to her: there were caucuses in Nebraska (February 9), Washington (February 9), and Maine (February 10). Clinton's caucus track record was far from stellar. These contests would be followed by primary contests in Maryland, Washington, D.C., and Virginia, on February 12—all places that leaned toward Obama and had far stronger organizations on the ground. One reporter even asked Obama whether he would consider adding Clinton to his ticket. He politely demurred.

Obama didn't want to take any chances. He campaigned his heart out leading into Super Tuesday, landing his plane in places that Plouffe had mapped out a year earlier. He began election day with a rally in Boise at the Taco Bell Arena; more than fourteen thousand supporters showed up—three times the number who caucused in Idaho in 2004. He then flew to Minnesota, where he was greeted by eighteen thousand people in the Target Center basketball arena in Minneapolis, and then to St. Louis, where twenty thousand people exploded in applause when he arrived at the Edward Jones Dome, home to the St. Louis Rams. Similar turnouts greeted him at rallies in Delaware and Connecticut.[7]

Super Tuesday ran late into the night. As polls across the country closed, neither candidate had a decisive edge, and the lead was traded back and forth. Clinton scored big victories early in the evening, capturing New York and New Jersey, and the media portrayed her win in Massachusetts as a major upset. She was also winning in Arizona, where Latinos played a key role (many had questioned Obama's ability to secure the critical Latino vote in a general election). But as the night wore on, the wisdom of Plouffe's strategy was borne out. Obama routed Clinton in five of six caucus states and accumulated a large portion of the delegates even in the big blue states that Clinton had won.

Jon Favreau, Obama's chief speechwriter, was now used to the speedy nature of primary politics. As he had done in Iowa, New Hampshire, and South Carolina, he first started typing Obama's remarks just a day before the vote.

Favreau had spoken with Axelrod a couple of days before Super Tuesday, and Axelrod had largely given Favreau and his team a free hand with the speech's first draft. Axelrod did have one comment: it was time to begin to transition to a general election message—to start to take the attack to Senator John McCain, the likely Republican nominee.

That said, the primary contest was far from over. The three speechwriters, Favreau, Ben Rhodes, and Adam Frankel, together crafted a speech that accomplished three objectives: First, it illustrated why Obama was the best candidate, not only to win the Democratic nomination but also to carry the party's banner in the general election. Second, it painted the stark differences between him and his opponent. Finally, it offered Obama's vision for the country.

The speechwriters were still putting the finishing touches on the speech on the morning of Super Tuesday. After some last-minute edits, Favreau sent it to Axelrod and Gibbs, who were on the road, and they made a few additional tweaks before printing it out for Obama.

The outcome was still uncertain when Obama delivered his remarks to a room full of supporters in a ballroom of the Hyatt Regency. It was only 10:45 p.m. Central time in Chicago when he faced the TelePrompTer—the polls in California hadn't even closed and the final votes were still being tallied in several other states. His aides were confident of the outcome, but Obama knew that even if the night ultimately broke his way, the aggregate delegate count would be close. Senator Clinton wasn't exiting the stage anytime soon. Everyone knew that the Clintons weren't quitters.

The speech celebrated Obama's victories in Georgia (where turnout was at its highest since 1992), Illinois, and Missouri, and drew a clear contrast between him and his opponent. Like a careful lawyer, Obama meticulously presented the "real choice," step by step—"change versus more of the same . . . the future versus the past."

This theme had worked for Obama since his presidential announcement speech. Clinton was the Washington establishment; her husband had been impeached, she took money from lobbyists, and she was on the receiving end of and a participant in deeply partisan attacks. He called it "running on the politics of yesterday" instead of "be[ing] the party of tomorrow."

Obama, on the other hand, styled himself a "post-partisan" politician, who could cobble together a new national electoral map in the general election, instead of the deeply fractured one likely facing his opponent. He asserted that "it's a choice between going into this election with Republicans and independents already united against us, or going against their nominee with a campaign that has united Americans of all parties around a common purpose." As Axelrod had requested, Favreau crafted a speech that told the nation why Obama was the best candidate to beat John McCain and the Republicans.

To further support that point, Obama ticked through his major policy differences with Clinton—her vote authorizing military action against Iraq, her hawkish posture on Iran, and her failure to protest the use of torture—and in other policy areas, such as health care, where he had strong differences with the Republicans.

Obama ended his speech with a take on his by-now familiar "Yes, we can" refrain, but he added another line that was widely praised in the media: "We are the ones we've been waiting for. We are the change that we seek."

Some commentators attributed the line to the late black feminist poet June Jordan. Favreau, however, said that he borrowed the line from Maria Shriver, a member of the Kennedy clan who had endorsed Obama a week earlier. (Shriver's endorsement had been a major blow to the Clintons, who had been close to Jackie Kennedy and Senator Ted Kennedy. It was yet another sign that America was shifting toward Obama and away from the Clinton machine.)

Whatever the intention, the press ate it up. Henry Allen, a staff writer with the *Washington Post,* called the line "poetry."[8] Poetry or not, no Democratic voter could miss Obama's message that night.

REMARKS BY SENATOR BARACK OBAMA: NIGHT OF SUPER TUESDAY PRIMARIES

Before I begin, I just want to send my condolences to the victims of the storms that hit Tennessee and Arkansas. They are in our thoughts and in our prayers.

Well, the polls are just closing in California and the votes are still being counted in cities and towns across the country. But there is one thing on this February night that we do not need the final results to know—our time has come, our movement is real, and change is coming to America.

Only a few hundred miles from here, almost one year ago to the day, we stood on the steps of the Old State Capitol to reaffirm a truth that was spoken there so many generations ago—that a house divided cannot stand; that we are more than a collection of red states and blue states. We are, and always will be, the United States of America.

What began as a whisper in Springfield soon carried across the corn fields of Iowa, where farmers and factory workers, students and seniors stood up in numbers we've never seen. They stood up to say that maybe this year, we don't have to settle for a politics where scoring points is more important than solving problems. This time we can finally do something about health care we can't afford or mortgages we can't pay. This time can be different.

Their voices echoed from the hills of New Hampshire to the deserts of Nevada, where teachers and cooks and kitchen workers stood up to say that maybe Washington doesn't have to be run by lobbyists anymore. They reached the coast of South Carolina when people said that maybe we don't have to be divided by race and region and gender, that crumbling schools are stealing the future of black children and white children, that we can come together and build an America that gives every child, everywhere, the opportunity to live their dreams. This time can be different.

And today, on this Tuesday in February, in states north and south, east and west, what began as a whisper in Springfield has swelled to a chorus of millions calling for change. A chorus that cannot be ignored. That cannot be deterred. This time can be different because this campaign for the presidency is different.

It's different not because of me, but because of you. Because you are tired of being disappointed and tired of being let down. You're tired of hearing promises made and plans proposed in the heat of a campaign only to have nothing change when everyone goes back to Washington. Because the lobbyists just write another check. Or because politicians start worrying about how they'll win the next election instead of why they should. Or because they focus on who's up and who's down instead of who matters.

And while Washington is consumed with the same drama and division and distraction, another family puts up a "for sale" sign in the front yard. Another factory shuts its doors. Another soldier waves goodbye as he leaves on another tour of duty in a war that should've never been authorized and never been waged. It goes on and on and on.

But in this election—at this moment—you are standing up all across this country to say, not this time. Not this year. The stakes are too high and the challenges too great to play the same Washington game with the same Washington players and expect a different result. This time must be different.

Now, this isn't about me and it's not about Senator Clinton. As I've said before, she was a friend before this campaign and she'll be a friend after it's over. I respect her as a colleague, and I congratulate her on her victories tonight.

But this fall we owe the American people a real choice. It's change versus more of the same. It's the future versus the past.

It's a choice between going into this election with Republicans and independents already united against us, or going against their nominee with a campaign that has united Americans of all parties around a common purpose.

It's a choice between having a debate with the other party about who has the most experience in Washington, or having one about who's most likely to change Washington. Because that's a debate we can win.

It's a choice between a candidate who's taken more money from Washington lobbyists than either Republican in this race, and a campaign that hasn't taken a dime of their money because we've been funded by you.

And if I am your nominee, my opponent will not be able to say that I voted for the war in Iraq; or that I gave George Bush the benefit of the doubt on Iran; or that I support the Bush-Cheney policy of not talking to leaders we don't like. And he will not be able to say that I wavered on something as fundamental as whether or not it's ok for America to use torture—because it is never ok. That is the choice in this election.

The Republicans running for president have already tied themselves to the past. They speak of a hundred year war in Iraq and billions more on tax breaks for the wealthiest few who don't need them and didn't ask for them—tax breaks that mortgage our children's future on a mountain of debt at a time when there are families who can't pay their medical bills and students who can't pay their tuition.

They are running on the politics of yesterday, and that is why our party must be the party of tomorrow. And that is the party I will lead as president.

I'll be the president who ends the tax breaks to companies that ship our jobs overseas and start putting them in the pockets of working Americans who deserve it. And struggling homeowners. And seniors who should retire with dignity and respect.

I'll be the president who finally brings Democrats and Republicans together to make health care affordable and available for every single American. We will put a college education within reach of anyone who wants to go, and instead of just talking about how great our teachers are, we will reward them for their greatness, with more pay and better support. And we will harnesses the ingenuity of farmers and scientists and entrepreneurs to free this nation from the tyranny of oil once and for all.

And when I am president, we will put an end to a politics that uses 9/11 as a way to scare up votes, and start seeing it as a challenge that should unite America and the world against the common threats of the twenty-first century: terrorism and nuclear weapons, climate change and poverty, genocide and disease.

We can do this. It will not be easy. It will require struggle and sacrifice. There will setbacks and we will make mistakes. And that is why we need all the help we can get. So tonight I want to speak directly to all those Americans who have yet to join this movement but still hunger for change—we need you. We need you to stand with us, and work with us, and help us prove that together, ordinary people can still do extraordinary things.

I am blessed to be standing in the city where my own extraordinary journey began. A few miles from here, in the shadow of a shuttered steel plant, is where I learned what it takes to make change happen.

I was a young organizer then, intent on fighting joblessness and poverty on the South Side, and I still remember one of the very first meetings I put together. We had worked on it for days, but no one showed up. Our volunteers felt so defeated, they wanted to quit. And to be honest, so did I.

But at that moment, I looked outside and saw some young boys tossing stones at a boarded-up apartment building across the street. They were like boys in so many cities across the country—boys without prospects, without guidance, without hope. And I turned to the volunteers, and I asked them, "Before you quit, I want you to answer one question. What will happen to those boys?" And the volunteers looked out that window, and they decided that night to keep going—to keep organizing, keep fighting for better schools, and better jobs, and better health care. And so did I. And slowly, but surely, in the weeks and months to come, the community began to change.

You see, the challenges we face will not be solved with one meeting in one night. Change will not come if we wait for some other person or some other time.

We are the ones we've been waiting for. We are the change that we seek.

We are the hope of those boys who have little; who've been told that they cannot have what they dream; that they cannot be what they imagine.

Yes, they can.

We are the hope of the father who goes to work before dawn and lies awake with doubts that tell him he cannot give his children the same opportunities that someone gave him.

Yes, he can.

We are the hope of the woman who hears that her city will not be rebuilt, that she cannot reclaim the life that was swept away in a terrible storm.

Yes, she can.

We are the hope of the future, the answer to the cynics who tell us our house must stand divided, that we cannot come together, that we cannot remake this world as it should be.

Because we know what we have seen and what we believe—that what began as a whisper has now swelled to a chorus that cannot be ignored; that will not be deterred; that will ring out across this land as a hymn that will heal this nation, repair this world, and make this time different than all the rest. Yes. We. Can.

14

"A MORE PERFECT UNION"

March 18, 2008

National Constitution Center, Philadelphia, Pennsylvania

I can no more disown him than I can disown the black community.
I can no more disown him than I can my white grandmother . . .
a woman who loves me as much as she loves anything in this world,
but a woman who once confessed her fear of black men
who passed by her on the street.

If you had asked any campaign commentator, March 18 was a make-or-break moment for candidate Barack Obama. Earlier that month, his long-time pastor from Chicago, the Reverend Jeremiah Wright, had ignited a political firestorm when a series of his racially charged sermons appeared online and threatened Obama's presidential bid. Obama's race had always been a latent issue; the Wright crisis put it front and center.

Among other controversial statements relating to the treatment of African Americans, Wright had preached: "The government gives [blacks] the drugs, builds bigger prisons, passes a three-strike law and then wants us to sing 'God Bless America.' No, no, no, God damn America, that's in the Bible for killing innocent people." Another video on YouTube captured Wright on the Sunday after September 11, 2001, saying, "We have supported state terrorism against the Palestinians and the black South Africans. . . . America's chickens are coming home to roost."[1]

Not surprisingly, conservatives smelled blood. Kathryn Jean Lopez, an editor at the conservative magazine *National Review,* wrote: "At the moment, we know [Obama's] contributed money to, voluntarily listened to, and publicly defended a cleric who peddles racial warfare."[2] The conservative African American columnist Erik Rush called Wright's church "quite cultish, quite separatist."[3] The right saw this as the moment to capitalize on latent fears about Obama's race and to peg him as a lefty-radical with skeletons in his closet and a hidden agenda. Did Obama agree with Wright's views? Was Obama going to be a champion for African Americans or for *all* Americans?

Wright wasn't a tangential figure in Obama's life. As Obama described in his book, *Dreams from My Father*, Wright played an important role in his spiritual journey: "It became clear in that very first meeting that, despite the reverend's frequent disclaimers, it was this capacious talent of his—this ability to hold together, if not reconcile, the conflicting strains of the black experience—upon which Trinity's [his church] success had ultimately been built."

Over time, after many Sunday sermons, Obama concluded, "To be right with yourself, to do right by others, to lend meaning to a community's suffering and take part in the healing—that required something more . . . It required faith."

Wright was, Obama later said, "like family to me." He had officiated at Obama's wedding, baptized his children, and led Sunday services at the eight-thousand-member Trinity United Church of Christ that Obama attended, which counted Oprah Winfrey and other prominent black professionals among its parishioners. Obama also credited Wright as the source for the title of his best-selling book *The Audacity of Hope.*

Still, aware that he had detractors, Obama had begun distancing himself from Wright a year earlier. He called Wright the night before his announcement speech in Springfield and asked him not to deliver the invocation as planned, although he still invited him to attend and prayed with him beforehand. Wright was also named to the campaign's African American Religious Leadership Committee. The campaign had praised Wright at the time of the appointment, noting, "Senator Obama is proud of his pastor and his church."[4]

Obama's position changed markedly in March, after the controversial videos were played and replayed and he saw the tenor of Wright's statements. Obama quickly denied ever hearing the incendiary remarks from the pulpit of Trinity Church, but still "condemned" the "objectionable things . . . outright." His campaign aide Bill Burton noted that Obama "said repeatedly that personal attacks such as this have no place in this campaign or our politics . . . . There are things he says with which Senator Obama deeply disagrees."[5]

But Burton's statement didn't satisfy the press or the public. There were those who didn't think Obama went far enough in denouncing Wright. On March 25, in Pittsburgh, Clinton took on the issue and told the press, "He would not have been my pastor. You don't choose your family, but you choose what church you want to attend. . . . Hate speech [is] unacceptable in any setting. . . . I just think you have to speak out against that."[6]

Watching the Wright story consume one media cycle after another, Obama and his aides realized that Wright was overwhelming the campaign. Obama himself had to go out. He made the rounds on the cable news channels Friday evening, but it still wasn't enough to stem the growing criticism. If the campaign failed to quell the public's fears about Obama's relationship with his minister, or if it missed this opportunity to address underlying tensions about the candidate's race, the election could slip from its grasp.

It was clear to Obama that he needed to play offense; he couldn't let his opponents continue to frame the narrative. On their weekly Saturday-morning strategy conference call, the leadership team—strategist David Axelrod, campaign manager David Plouffe, and communications director Robert Gibbs—told Obama's speechwriter, Jon Favreau, that Obama had decided to deliver a major speech on race in Philadelphia that coming Tuesday. They urged him to start writing immediately, but Favreau insisted on speaking to Obama first. He didn't feel that he could capture Obama's voice on such a deeply personal topic without hearing from him directly. This was simply too important a speech; in many ways, his candidacy hung in the balance. They all agreed. Obama was out campaigning all day, but he would call Favreau later that night.

Favreau went to his Chicago office later that afternoon, discussed the speech with Axelrod, and then stared at the keyboard for a number of hours. Anxious and unproductive, he decided to head home and wait by the phone until Obama called. Favreau had just moved into a new group house downtown with friends from the campaign; they didn't even have their Internet access set up yet. And he was home alone. It was St. Patrick's Day, so everyone was out at the local bars celebrating.

Obama finally called at ten. He wasn't in the best of spirits—not surprising, as he had had a long and emotional day dealing with the Wright controversy. But, he told Favreau, this was just another obstacle in a long series of many to come: "I'm running for president and I have to explain this to people. This is a test, and I owe people an explanation."

Obama opened up. He spent more than an hour detailing what he hoped to see in the speech. Favreau typed as fast he possibly could. Obama asked Favreau to please send him a first draft by Sunday night—less than twenty-four hours later. Favreau quickly reread his notes and realized that instead of a stream of consciousness, Obama had actually given him a thorough outline of everything he wanted to say. With a framework in hand, Favreau did what anyone under that level of pressure would do—he joined his friends for a St. Patrick's Day drink.

The next morning Favreau woke up at the crack of dawn, made his way to the Piper's Alley Starbucks, and began writing. At six that evening, Obama called to let him know that he was "putting his girls to bed," so he didn't need to see a draft until eight thirty. Favreau used every last minute his boss gave him before sending him the draft. Obama stayed up until 3:00 a.m. editing it.

Obama spent all of Monday campaigning, continuing to edit the draft in between events. He didn't send his version back to Favreau, Axelrod, and Plouffe until 2:00 a.m. Tuesday morning. When Favreau opened up the document, all he could see was a tangle of red lines; Obama had made extensive revisions and additions. "The personal stuff he added about race, his upbringing, and his relationship with Wright," Favreau said. "I could have never written that."

In some ways, it was a speech that had been in the making Obama's entire life; it detailed the influence of his childhood in Hawaii, his time in college and law school, his time as a community organizer and civil rights attorney in Chicago, and as a state senator in Springfield.

Obama planned to deliver his speech at the National Constitution Center in Philadelphia, just steps away from Independence Hall, where our Founding Fathers signed both the Declaration of Independence and the Constitution. All eyes—and television cameras—were on Obama as he approached the podium shortly before eleven that morning. The title of his speech, and Obama's opening words, "A More Perfect Union," were taken from the preamble of the Constitution, which starts: "We the people, in order to form a more perfect union." This phrase also foreshadowed his thesis, that we have come a long way in our struggle to achieve racial equality in America, but we still have work to do to address black anger, white resentment, and a myriad of larger social ills.

Obama's broad objective was to broach these themes openly, but he also used the speech to knock back criticism over Wright and, indirectly, to demonstrate that he could overcome even the fiercest of crises. In fact, the chain of events, and how Obama handled this controversy, actually belied his perceived inexperience with the most difficult situations—a true test for any presidential candidate.

His remarks began with his acknowledgment that for him as the "son of a black man from Kenya and a white woman from Kansas," race had always been in the shadows of the campaign. It had been part of the press coverage and the public conversation, including discussion as to whether he was "too black" or "not black enough."

Obama addressed the issue of Pastor Wright candidly and shrewdly. He acknowledged his strong ties to Wright and embraced him as the man "who helped introduce me to my Christian faith" and stated that, "as imperfect as he may be, he has been like family to me." That said, he strongly criticized his pastor's remarks as "incendiary language" that had the potential to "widen the racial divide" and "rightly offend white and black alike." He also acknowledged that he had heard Reverend Wright "make remarks that could be considered controversial while [he] sat in church." And that some of his pastor's comments were "not only divisive, [but] divisive at a time when we need unity." But, he noted, many Americans "have heard remarks from your pastors, priests or rabbis with which you strongly disagree"—and it was clear that Obama disagreed.

Obama then went a step further. He explained that, like many Americans, black and white, Wright was filled with contradictions. "I can no more disown him than I can disown the black community. I can no more disown him than I can my white grandmother—a woman who helped raised me . . . a woman who once confessed her fear of black men who passed by her on the street, and who on more than one occasion has uttered racial or ethnic stereotypes that made me cringe." This was a bold but effective stroke. He refused to completely jettison Wright.

Obama then commented on the clear generational divide between Americans who had lived through the years of segregation and legalized discrimination—when it was nearly impossible to overcome the system

—and those who came of age in the forty years since, when opportunity was more plentiful.

He noted that a "similar anger exists within segments of the white community," where "most working- and middle-class white Americans don't feel that they have been particularly privileged by their race. Their experience is the immigrant experience." They've had to overcome their own odds in employment, education, housing, and the like; as such, Obama offered, many are angry over "welfare and affirmative action."

Obama didn't dismiss those Americans or the feelings they held. Rather, he embraced them, artfully using the point to transition to his broader message about race and, in a nutshell, his campaign—the idea that "America can change." We can overcome the legacy of discrimination and we can benefit from the opportunities our country has to offer, he said: "Your dreams do not have to come at the expense of my dreams." He deftly coupled that point with his policy agenda, stating plainly, and in detail, that opportunity would only be accomplished with "deeds," not just "words"—"by investing in our schools and our communities; by enforcing our civil rights laws and ensuring fairness in our criminal justice system; by providing this generation with ladders of opportunity that were unavailable for previous generations."

Beyond that, Obama communicated another critical point: he would be a president for all Americans. His race helped shape him. It didn't define him.

It's fair to say that this speech helped rescue Obama's candidacy from the brink of failure. It was almost universally praised by liberals and conservatives alike—many of whom actually became supporters after hearing him speak.

Peggy Noonan, the conservative columnist and former Reagan speechwriter, made two keen observations in the *Wall Street Journal.* First, she said, "It was a speech to think to, not clap to." Second, "The speech will be labeled by history as the speech that saved a candidacy."[7] Republican presidential hopeful Mike Huckabee similarly praised Obama's speech, saying that he "handled this about as well as anybody could."[8] The liberal *New York Times* columnist Frank Rich wrote, "Mr. Obama's speech is the most remarkable utterance on the subject by a public figure in modern memory."[9] James Fallows of *The Atlantic* agreed: "It was a moment that

Obama made great through the seriousness, intelligence, eloquence, and courage of what he said."[10]

Bob Herbert, an op-ed columnist for the New York Times, said the speech "should be required reading in classrooms across the country" and that in embracing "both justice and healing, Senator Obama is better on these [racial] issues than any American leader since King."[11] Atlantic writer and blogger Andrew Sullivan called it "searing, nuanced, gut-wrenching . . . a speech we have all been waiting for for a generation."[12] Perhaps Hendrik Hertzberg, writing in the first post-election issue of New Yorker summarized it best: "The speech helped elect Obama as the President of the United States."[13]

A former Clinton presidential speechwriter, Jeff Shesol, called the speech "brave, thoughtful, honest—how often are any of these adjectives applied to a speech by a politician, let alone in the heat of a campaign? Barack Obama's speech on race was all of these things. Though it was born of political necessity, it went far beyond what was required, and marked what might well be a turning point in the way that most Americans think and talk about race."

There were also a few critics, of course, mainly from the right. Sean Hannity of Fox News said, "If you can't disown Reverend Wright, you're not qualified to be the president of the United States."[14]

But for the most part, Obama's speech was viewed as an unqualified success, and his poll numbers clearly reinforced this view. A CBS News poll taken two nights after the speech showed that 71 percent of Americans felt that Obama had effectively explained his relationship with the controversial reverend. A Fox News poll indicated that 57 percent of respondents were convinced that Obama and Wright did not share the same views. Given that by the end of May, 4.5 million people had viewed the speech on YouTube, it was fair at that point to say, as CNN's Candy Crowley put it, "I've heard him. Let's move on."[15] And America did.

REMARKS BY SENATOR BARACK OBAMA:
"A MORE PERFECT UNION"

"We the people, in order to form a more perfect union."

Two hundred and twenty-one years ago, in a hall that still stands across the street, a group of men gathered and, with these simple words, launched America's improbable experiment in democracy. Farmers and scholars, statesmen and patriots who had traveled across an ocean to escape tyranny and persecution finally made real their declaration of independence at a Philadelphia convention that lasted through the spring of 1787.

The document they produced was eventually signed but ultimately unfinished. It was stained by this nation's original sin of slavery, a question that divided the colonies and brought the convention to a stalemate until the founders chose to allow the slave trade to continue for at least twenty more years, and to leave any final resolution to future generations.

Of course, the answer to the slavery question was already embedded within our Constitution—a Constitution that had at its very core the ideal of equal citizenship under the law; a Constitution that promised its people liberty, and justice, and a union that could be and should be perfected over time.

And yet words on a parchment would not be enough to deliver slaves from bondage, or provide men and women of every color and creed their full rights and obligations as citizens of the United States. What would be needed were Americans in successive generations who were willing to do their part—through protests and struggle, on the streets and in the courts, through a civil war and civil disobedience and always at great risk—to narrow that gap between the promise of our ideals and the reality of their time.

This was one of the tasks we set forth at the beginning of this campaign—to continue the long march of those who came before us, a march for a more just, more equal, more free, more caring, and more prosperous America. I chose to run for the presidency at this moment in history because I believe deeply that we cannot solve the challenges of our time

unless we solve them together—unless we perfect our union by understanding that we may have different stories, but we hold common hopes,
that we may not look the same and we may not have come from the same
place, but we all want to move in the same direction—towards a better
future for our children and our grandchildren.

This belief comes from my unyielding faith in the decency and generosity of the American people. But it also comes from my own American story.

I am the son of a black man from Kenya and a white woman from
Kansas. I was raised with the help of a white grandfather who survived
a Depression to serve in Patton's army during World War II and a white
grandmother who worked on a bomber assembly line at Fort Leavenworth
while he was overseas. I've gone to some of the best schools in America
and lived in one of the world's poorest nations. I am married to a black
American who carries within her the blood of slaves and slave owners—an
inheritance we pass on to our two precious daughters. I have brothers,
sisters, nieces, nephews, uncles, and cousins, of every race and every hue,
scattered across three continents, and for as long as I live, I will never forget that in no other country on earth is my story even possible.

It's a story that hasn't made me the most conventional candidate. But it
is a story that has seared into my genetic makeup the idea that this nation
is more than the sum of its parts—that out of many, we are truly one.

Throughout the first year of this campaign, against all predictions to
the contrary, we saw how hungry the American people were for this message of unity. Despite the temptation to view my candidacy through a
purely racial lens, we won commanding victories in states with some of
the whitest populations in the country. In South Carolina, where the Confederate flag still flies, we built a powerful coalition of African Americans
and white Americans.

This is not to say that race has not been an issue in the campaign. At
various stages in the campaign, some commentators have deemed me
either "too black" or "not black enough." We saw racial tensions bubble to
the surface during the week before the South Carolina primary. The press
has scoured every exit poll for the latest evidence of racial polarization, not
just in terms of white and black, but black and brown as well.

And yet, it has only been in the last couple of weeks that the discussion
of race in this campaign has taken a particularly divisive turn.

On one end of the spectrum, we've heard the implication that my candidacy is somehow an exercise in affirmative action; that it's based solely on the desire of wide-eyed liberals to purchase racial reconciliation on the cheap. On the other end, we've heard my former pastor, Reverend Jeremiah Wright, use incendiary language to express views that have the potential not only to widen the racial divide, but views that denigrate both the greatness and the goodness of our nation, that rightly offend white and black alike.

I have already condemned, in unequivocal terms, the statements of Reverend Wright that have caused such controversy. For some, nagging questions remain. Did I know him to be an occasionally fierce critic of American domestic and foreign policy? Of course. Did I ever hear him make remarks that could be considered controversial while I sat in church? Yes. Did I strongly disagree with many of his political views? Absolutely—just as I'm sure many of you have heard remarks from your pastors, priests, or rabbis with which you strongly disagreed.

But the remarks that have caused this recent firestorm weren't simply controversial. They weren't simply a religious leader's effort to speak out against perceived injustice. Instead, they expressed a profoundly distorted view of this country—a view that sees white racism as endemic, and that elevates what is wrong with America above all that we know is right with America; a view that sees the conflicts in the Middle East as rooted primarily in the actions of stalwart allies like Israel, instead of emanating from the perverse and hateful ideologies of radical Islam.

As such, Reverend Wright's comments were not only wrong but divisive, divisive at a time when we need unity; racially charged at a time when we need to come together to solve a set of monumental problems—two wars, a terrorist threat, a falling economy, a chronic health care crisis and potentially devastating climate change; problems that are neither black or white or Latino or Asian, but rather problems that confront us all.

Given my background, my politics, and my professed values and ideals, there will no doubt be those for whom my statements of condemnation are not enough. Why associate myself with Reverend Wright in the first place, they may ask? Why not join another church? And I confess that if all that I knew of Reverend Wright were the snippets of those sermons that have run in an endless loop on the television and YouTube, or if Trinity United Church of Christ conformed to the caricatures being peddled by some commentators, there is no doubt that I would react in much the same way.

But the truth is, that isn't all that I know of the man. The man I met more than twenty years ago is a man who helped introduce me to my Christian faith, a man who spoke to me about our obligations to love one another, to care for the sick and lift up the poor. He is a man who served his country as a U.S. Marine, who has studied and lectured at some of the finest universities and seminaries in the country, and who for over thirty years led a church that serves the community by doing God's work here on earth—by housing the homeless, ministering to the needy, providing day care services and scholarships and prison ministries, and reaching out to those suffering from HIV/AIDS.

In my first book, *Dreams from My Father*, I described the experience of my first service at Trinity: "People began to shout, to rise from their seats and clap and cry out, a forceful wind carrying the reverend's voice up into the rafters. . . . And in that single note—hope!—I heard something else; at the foot of that cross, inside the thousands of churches across the city, I imagined the stories of ordinary black people merging with the stories of David and Goliath, Moses and Pharaoh, the Christians in the lion's den, Ezekiel's field of dry bones. Those stories—of survival, and freedom, and hope—became our story, my story; the blood that had spilled was our blood, the tears our tears; until this black church, on this bright day, seemed once more a vessel carrying the story of a people into future generations and into a larger world. Our trials and triumphs became at once unique and universal, black and more than black; in chronicling our journey, the stories and songs gave us a means to reclaim memories that we didn't need to feel shame about . . . memories that all people might study and cherish—and with which we could start to rebuild."

That has been my experience at Trinity. Like other predominantly black churches across the country, Trinity embodies the black community in its entirety—the doctor and the welfare mom, the model student and the former gang-banger. Like other black churches, Trinity's services are full of raucous laughter and sometimes bawdy humor. They are full of dancing, clapping, screaming and shouting that may seem jarring to the untrained ear. The church contains in full the kindness and cruelty, the fierce intelligence and the shocking ignorance, the struggles and successes, the love and, yes, the bitterness and bias that make up the black experience in America.

And this helps explain, perhaps, my relationship with Reverend Wright.

As imperfect as he may be, he has been like family to me. He strengthened my faith, officiated my wedding, and baptized my children. Not once in my conversations with him have I heard him talk about any ethnic group in derogatory terms, or treat whites with whom he interacted with anything but courtesy and respect. He contains within him the contradictions—the good and the bad—of the community that he has served diligently for so many years.

I can no more disown him than I can disown the black community. I can no more disown him than I can my white grandmother—a woman who helped raise me, a woman who sacrificed again and again for me, a woman who loves me as much as she loves anything in this world, but a woman who once confessed her fear of black men who passed by her on the street, and who on more than one occasion has uttered racial or ethnic stereotypes that made me cringe.

These people are a part of me. And they are a part of America, this country that I love.

Some will see this as an attempt to justify or excuse comments that are simply inexcusable. I can assure you it is not. I suppose the politically safe thing would be to move on from this episode and just hope that it fades into the woodwork. We can dismiss Reverend Wright as a crank or a dema-gogue, just as some have dismissed Geraldine Ferraro, in the aftermath of her recent statements, as harboring some deep-seated racial bias.

But race is an issue that I believe this nation cannot afford to ignore right now. We would be making the same mistake that Reverend Wright made in his offending sermons about America—to simplify and stereotype and amplify the negative to the point that it distorts reality.

The fact is that the comments that have been made and the issues that have surfaced over the last few weeks reflect the complexities of race in this country that we've never really worked through—a part of our union that we have yet to perfect. And if we walk away now, if we simply retreat into our respective corners, we will never be able to come together and solve challenges like health care, or education, or the need to find good jobs for every American.

Understanding this reality requires a reminder of how we arrived at this point. As William Faulkner once wrote, "The past isn't dead and buried. In fact, it isn't even past." We do not need to recite here the history of racial

injustice in this country. But we do need to remind ourselves that so many of the disparities that exist in the African American community today can be directly traced to inequalities passed on from an earlier generation that suffered under the brutal legacy of slavery and Jim Crow.

Segregated schools were, and are, inferior schools; we still haven't fixed them, fifty years after *Brown v. Board of Education*, and the inferior education they provided, then and now, helps explain the pervasive achievement gap between today's black and white students.

Legalized discrimination—where blacks were prevented, often through violence, from owning property, or loans were not granted to African American business owners, or black homeowners could not access FHA mortgages, or blacks were excluded from unions, or the police force, or fire departments—meant that black families could not amass any meaningful wealth to bequeath to future generations. That history helps explain the wealth and income gap between black and white, and the concentrated pockets of poverty that persists in so many of today's urban and rural communities.

A lack of economic opportunity among black men, and the shame and frustration that came from not being able to provide for one's family, contributed to the erosion of black families—a problem that welfare policies for many years may have worsened. And the lack of basic services in so many urban black neighborhoods—parks for kids to play in, police walking the beat, regular garbage pick-up and building code enforcement—all helped create a cycle of violence, blight, and neglect that continue to haunt us.

This is the reality in which Reverend Wright and other African Americans of his generation grew up. They came of age in the late fifties and early sixties, a time when segregation was still the law of the land and opportunity was systematically constricted. What's remarkable is not how many failed in the face of discrimination, but rather how many men and women overcame the odds; how many were able to make a way out of no way for those like me who would come after them.

But for all those who scratched and clawed their way to get a piece of the American Dream, there were many who didn't make it—those who were ultimately defeated, in one way or another, by discrimination. That legacy of defeat was passed on to future generations—those young men and, increasingly, young women who we see standing on street corners or languishing in our prisons, without hope or prospects for the future. Even for those blacks who did make it, questions of race, and racism, continue to define their worldview in fundamental ways. For the men and women of Reverend Wright's generation, the memories of humiliation and doubt and fear have not gone away; nor has the anger and the bitterness of those years. That anger may not get expressed in public, in front of white cowork- ers or white friends. But it does find voice in the barbershop or around the kitchen table. At times, that anger is exploited by politicians, to gin up votes along racial lines, or to make up for a politician's own failings.

And occasionally it finds voice in the church on Sunday morning, in the pulpit and in the pews. The fact that so many people are surprised to hear that anger in some of Reverend Wright's sermons simply reminds us of the old truism that the most segregated hour in American life occurs on Sunday morning. That anger is not always productive. Indeed, all too often it distracts attention from solving real problems; it keeps us from squarely facing our own complicity in our condition, and prevents the Af- rican American community from forging the alliances it needs to bring about real change. But the anger is real, it is powerful, and to simply wish it away, to condemn it without understanding its roots, only serves to widen the chasm of misunderstanding that exists between the races.

In fact, a similar anger exists within segments of the white community. Most working- and middle-class white Americans don't feel that they have been particularly privileged by their race. Their experience is the immigrant experience—as far as they're concerned, no one's handed them anything, they've built it from scratch. They've worked hard all their lives, many times only to see their jobs shipped overseas or their pension dumped after a lifetime of labor. They are anxious about their futures, and feel their dreams slipping away. In an era of stagnant wages and global competi- tion, opportunity comes to be seen as a zero-sum game, in which your dreams come at my expense. So when they are told to bus their children to a school across town; when they hear that an African American is getting an advantage in landing a good job or a spot in a good college because of an injustice that they themselves never committed; when they're told that their fears about crime in urban neighborhoods are somehow prejudiced, resentment builds over time.

Like the anger within the black community, these resentments aren't always expressed in polite company. But they have helped shape the political landscape for at least a generation. Anger over welfare and affirmative action helped forge the Reagan Coalition. Politicians routinely exploited fears of crime for their own electoral ends. Talk show hosts and conservative commentators built entire careers unmasking bogus claims of racism while dismissing legitimate discussions of racial injustice and inequality as mere political correctness or reverse racism.

Just as black anger often proved counterproductive, so have these white resentments distracted attention from the real culprits of the middle-class squeeze—a corporate culture rife with inside dealing, questionable accounting practices, and short-term greed; a Washington dominated by lobbyists and special interests; economic policies that favor the few over the many. And yet, to wish away the resentments of white Americans, to label them as misguided or even racist, without recognizing they are grounded in legitimate concerns—this too widens the racial divide, and blocks the path to understanding.

This is where we are right now. It's a racial stalemate we've been stuck in for years. Contrary to the claims of some of my critics, black and white, I have never been so naïve as to believe that we can get beyond our racial divisions in a single election cycle, or with a single candidacy—particularly a candidacy as imperfect as my own.

But I have asserted a firm conviction—a conviction rooted in my faith in God and my faith in the American people—that working together we can move beyond some of our old racial wounds, and that in fact we have no choice if we are to continue on the path of a more perfect union.

For the African American community, that path means embracing the burdens of our past without becoming victims of our past. It means continuing to insist on a full measure of justice in every aspect of American life. But it also means binding our particular grievances—for better health care, and better schools, and better jobs—to the larger aspirations of all Americans—the white woman struggling to break the glass ceiling, the white man who's been laid off, the immigrant trying to feed his family. And it means taking full responsibility for own lives—by demanding more from our fathers, and spending more time with our children, and reading to

them, and teaching them that while they may face challenges and discrimination in their own lives, they must never succumb to despair or cynicism;
they must always believe that they can write their own destiny.

Ironically, this quintessentially American—and, yes, conservative—notion of self-help found frequent expression in Reverend Wright's sermons.
But what my former pastor too often failed to understand is that embarking
on a program of self-help also requires a belief that society can change.

The profound mistake of Reverend Wright's sermons is not that he spoke
about racism in our society. It's that he spoke as if our society was static; as
if no progress has been made; as if this country—a country that has made
it possible for one of his own members to run for the highest office in the
land and build a coalition of white and black, Latino and Asian, rich and
poor, young and old—is still irrevocably bound to a tragic past. But what we
know—what we have seen—is that America can change. That is [the] true
genius of this nation. What we have already achieved gives us hope—the
audacity to hope—for what we can and must achieve tomorrow.

In the white community, the path to a more perfect union means acknowledging that what ails the African American community does not just
exist in the minds of black people; that the legacy of discrimination—and
current incidents of discrimination, while less overt than in the past—are
real and must be addressed. Not just with words, but with deeds—by investing in our schools and our communities, by enforcing our civil rights
laws and ensuring fairness in our criminal justice system, by providing
this generation with ladders of opportunity that were unavailable for previous generations. It requires all Americans to realize that your dreams do
not have to come at the expense of my dreams, that investing in the health,
welfare, and education of black and brown and white children will ultimately help all of America prosper.

In the end, then, what is called for is nothing more, and nothing less,
than what all the world's great religions demand—that we do unto others
as we would have them do unto us. Let us be our brother's keeper, Scripture tells us. Let us be our sister's keeper. Let us find that common stake
we all have in one another, and let our politics reflect that spirit as well.

For we have a choice in this country. We can accept a politics that breeds
division, and conflict, and cynicism. We can tackle race only as spectacle—
as we did in the O.J. trial—or in the wake of tragedy, as we did in the after-

math of Katrina—or as fodder for the nightly news. We can play Reverend Wright's sermons on every channel, every day, and talk about them from now until the election, and make the only question in this campaign whether or not the American people think that I somehow believe or sympathize with his most offensive words. We can pounce on some gaffe by a Hillary supporter as evidence that she's playing the race card, or we can speculate on whether white men will all flock to John McCain in the general election, regardless of his policies.

We can do that.

But if we do, I can tell you that in the next election, we'll be talking about some other distraction. And then another one. And then another one. And nothing will change.

That is one option. Or, at this moment, in this election, we can come together and say, "Not this time." This time we want to talk about the crumbling schools that are stealing the future of black children and white children and Asian children and Hispanic children and Native American children. This time we want to reject the cynicism that tells us that these kids can't learn; that those kids who don't look like us are somebody else's problem. The children of America are not those kids, they are our kids, and we will not let them fall behind in a 21st century economy. Not this time.

This time we want to talk about how the lines in the emergency room are filled with whites and blacks and Hispanics who do not have health care, who don't have the power on their own to overcome the special interests in Washington, but who can take them on if we do it together.

This time we want to talk about the shuttered mills that once provided a decent life for men and women of every race, and the homes for sale that once belonged to Americans from every religion, every region, every walk of life. This time we want to talk about the fact that the real problem is not that someone who doesn't look like you might take your job; it's that the corporation you work for will ship it overseas for nothing more than a profit.

This time we want to talk about the men and women of every color and creed who serve together, and fight together, and bleed together under the same proud flag. We want to talk about how to bring them home from a war that never should've been authorized and never should've been waged, and we want to talk about how we'll show our patriotism by caring for them, and their families, and giving them the benefits they have earned.

I would not be running for president if I didn't believe with all my heart that this is what the vast majority of Americans want for this country. This union may never be perfect, but generation after generation has shown that it can always be perfected. And today, whenever I find myself feeling doubtful or cynical about this possibility, what gives me the most hope is the next generation—the young people whose attitudes and beliefs and openness to change have already made history in this election.

There is one story in particularly that I'd like to leave you with today—a story I told when I had the great honor of speaking on Dr. King's birthday at his home church, Ebenezer Baptist, in Atlanta.

There is a young, twenty-three-year-old white woman named Ashley Baia who organized for our campaign in Florence, South Carolina. She had been working to organize a mostly African American community since the beginning of this campaign, and one day she was at a roundtable discussion where everyone went around telling their story and why they were there.

And Ashley said that when she was nine years old, her mother got cancer. And because she had to miss days of work, she was let go and lost her health care. They had to file for bankruptcy, and that's when Ashley decided that she had to do something to help her mom.

She knew that food was one of their most expensive costs, and so Ashley convinced her mother that what she really liked and really wanted to eat more than anything else was mustard and relish sandwiches. Because that was the cheapest way to eat.

She did this for a year until her mom got better, and she told everyone at the roundtable that the reason she joined our campaign was so that she could help the millions of other children in the country who want and need to help their parents too.

Now Ashley might have made a different choice. Perhaps somebody told her along the way that the source of her mother's problems were blacks who were on welfare and too lazy to work, or Hispanics who were coming into the country illegally. But she didn't. She sought out allies in her fight against injustice.

Anyway, Ashley finishes her story and then goes around the room and asks everyone else why they're supporting the campaign. They all have different stories and reasons. Many bring up a specific issue. And finally they come to this elderly black man who's been sitting there quietly the entire time. And Ashley asks him why he's there. And he does not bring up a specific issue. He does not say health care or the economy. He does not say education or the war. He does not say that he was there because of Barack Obama. He simply says to everyone in the room, "I am here because of Ashley."

"I'm here because of Ashley." By itself, that single moment of recognition between that young white girl and that old black man is not enough. It is not enough to give health care to the sick, or jobs to the jobless, or education to our children.

But it is where we start. It is where our union grows stronger. And as so many generations have come to realize over the course of the two hundred and twenty-one years since a band of patriots signed that document in Philadelphia, that is where the perfection begins.

NIGHT OF NORTH CAROLINA
AND INDIANA PRIMARIES

May 6, 2008 • RBC Center, Raleigh, North Carolina

Tonight, many of the pundits have suggested
that this party is inalterably divided—
that Senator Clinton's supporters will not support me,
and that my supporters will not support her.
Well, I'm here tonight to tell you that I don't believe that.

Some commentators at the time dubbed May 6, 2008, "Super Tuesday II." After months of battling it out, after forty-three primaries and caucuses, Senators Obama and Clinton faced off in Indiana and North Carolina. The night carried greater significance than just the 217 delegates up for grabs. After a string of losses in Ohio, Pennsylvania, and Texas, and another Reverend Wright flare-up, the real question was whether Obama could get back on track and score a big victory in North Carolina. Or, would Clinton produce two strong showings and get the "game-changing" evening her campaign had been hoping for?

The weeks leading up to primary night were, communications director Robert Gibbs said, "a pretty tough two or three weeks for the Obama campaign." First, Obama had lost what the Clinton camp called the "big states" on Super Tuesday—New Jersey, New York, Ohio, and California. No Democratic candidate had ever captured the nomination without those delegates.

Second, after his defeat in Pennsylvania and Ohio, some naysayers wondered whether Obama could win enough working-class white voters in a general election. To date, Clinton had consistently won a majority of working-class whites; Obama's core voters remained African Americans and up-scale whites. Indiana and North Carolina brought this issue to the forefront.

Indiana's primary voters were predominantly white, rural, and culturally conservative; North Carolina's voters were largely African American.

CNN's Wolf Blitzer had asked Obama's campaign strategist, David Axelrod, "Here are some numbers that a lot of Democrats look at . . . in Indiana and North Carolina. And they're very worried when they see among Clinton supporters, when . . . asked if Obama is the nominee, who would you vote for? In Indiana . . . thirty-one percent . . . actually say they would vote for McCain, forty-nine percent say they'd vote for Obama. . . . That's a big chunk of Clinton supporters who aren't ready to commit for Obama right now. . . . [And there are] similar numbers in . . . North Carolina."[1] This concern about the general election was compounded by Obama's comments a few weeks earlier at a fund-raiser in liberal San Francisco. While trying to explain his trouble winning over white working-class voters (the traditional "Reagan Democrats"), Obama had said, "You go into these small towns in Pennsylvania and, like a lot of small towns in the Midwest, the jobs have been gone now for twenty-five years and nothing's replaced them. And it's not surprising, then, they get bitter, they cling to guns or religion or antipathy to people who aren't like them."[2]

The Clinton campaign immediately smelled blood—and so did a growing chorus of Clinton voters, who claimed they would vote for McCain if Obama won the nomination. The elite and erudite Obama wasn't their type of Democrat. Senator Clinton quickly fired a shot: "The people of faith I know don't 'cling' to religion because they're bitter," she said. "People don't need a president who looks down on them. They need a president who stands up for them."[3]

Finally, after these missteps, Reverend Jeremiah Wright, Obama's controversial pastor from Chicago, resurfaced. At a breakfast at the National Press Club, Wright praised the Reverend Louis Farrakhan, refused to take back his incendiary comments about how the United States had invited the 9/11 attacks and called Obama a run-of-the-mill politician. "Politicians say what they say and do what they do because of electability, based on sound bites, based on polls. . . . Whether he gets elected or not, I'm still going to have to be answerable to God November 5 and January 21."

Obama dismissed these comments outright, stating publicly, "He does not speak for me." Still, the comments were not helpful to his campaign, although it was clear to most people that Wright was unstable and no longer an Obama ally. Obama's polling numbers took a serious hit in Indiana, particularly concerning his "values" and "patriotism."[4] Obama told his senior staff that he didn't want to "win the nomination by limping across the finish line"; Indiana and North Carolina were critical.

Clinton, of course, had her own challenges. For one thing, after forty-two primaries and caucuses, Obama was dangerously close to having the 2,025 delegates he needed to lock up the nomination. Also, Clinton was burning through cash fast. She had already lent her cash-strapped campaign $5 million dollars and new donations weren't coming in quickly enough. At every opportunity, she asked her supporters to log onto "HillaryClinton.com" and make a donation. The good news was that it was working; she raised $10 million in the twenty-four hours following her win in Pennsylvania. Her supporters knew she was slipping further behind and they wanted to help Clinton—the clear underdog—stay in the race. Still, their small donations were no match for the Obama fund-raising juggernaut.

The primary fight had just entered its fifth month, not counting the months of campaigning in Iowa before the caucus. Leaders in the Democratic Party were increasingly restless; they were concerned that Democrats were spending too much time attacking each other instead of focusing on the real prize—John McCain and the Republicans.

This was the reason Joe Andrew, a former Indiana politician and Democratic Party heavyweight, offered for withdrawing his support of Hillary Clinton and endorsing Obama—a real boon to Obama's Indiana campaign. Andrew was a former head of Indiana's Democratic Party and, ironically, had been the chairman of the Democratic National Committee under Bill Clinton. He explained that his defection was an attempt to end the protracted primary fight, saying that Democrats were "doing [McCain's] work for him."[5] One Obama aide noted that Clinton "was helping do the work of the Republicans by just beating up on [Obama] in a pretty significant way."[6]

One issue where Clinton tried to best Obama was the gas tax. In a campaign speech, Clinton called for a summer holiday from the tax, given that prices had reached more than four dollars per gallon in many places. Obama cleverly turned the issue against her by using it as another example of Clinton's old-style, short-sighted gimmickry and pandering on populist issues—and it worked. The news coverage shifted off of Wright and onto the gasoline issue. It drew the narrative back to what Obama framed as the key difference between the two opponents: change versus more of the same.

On the eve of the primaries, Obama held a rally in downtown Indianapolis and drew a shocking 21,000 people; no one in Indiana politics could remember a crowd quite like it before. Polls showed that Clinton's double-digit lead was beginning to shrink. Meanwhile, it was evident that Clinton didn't have the same time or resources as Obama to pour into Indiana. She had to focus on North Carolina, which was still an uphill battle. With a significant African American population, Clinton had her work cut out for her in North Carolina. At the state's Jefferson-Jackson dinner, held at the state fair ground in Raleigh only days before the election, the room erupted when Obama walked onto the stage. Senator Clinton, on the other hand, received a far more tepid welcome.

Still, Clinton knew that North Carolina was make or break for her. She needed to deliver a solid showing. For days now, from early morning to late at night, she had crisscrossed the state, hopping from one speech to the next. She held late-night rallies and town hall meetings; she conducted interview after interview. North Carolina Governor Mike Easley said she was "as tough as a lighter knot."[7] Even her aides were in awe of her energy. Clinton barely slept.

Obama, on the other hand, could afford to cover both states with more paid media; his campaign was receiving record amounts of donations every day. Even so, despite blanketing the airwaves with ads, he was working harder and was more exhausted than aides could remember. He traveled by bus across northern Indiana, from Columbia City to South Bend and North Liberty to Union Mills; he stressed his biography, the economy, values, and patriotism. Avoiding what Jeff Zeleny of the *New York Times* called "super-size rallies that . . . defined his presidential bid, with their lofty oratory,"[8] he opted instead for smaller conversations without loud music and fanfare, where he could listen and not just talk—at the Oake Pointe retirement center, at the Dairy Beef Building at the county fairgrounds, and, over beers, at the VFW club.

Obama spent primary morning in Indiana and then flew to Raleigh,

North Carolina, to await the election results. Primary night did not deliver the "game-changer" that Clinton needed. Obama won big in North Carolina, taking 56 percent of the votes to Clinton's 42, and, surprisingly, only lost by two percentage points in Indiana. His tracking polls the night before had shown him down by twelve points.[9] It was his first victory in almost two months—and it was a huge one.

Obama opened his speech that night at North Carolina University's RBC Center in Raleigh with a sarcastic comment aimed at Senator Clinton that David Plouffe had crafted just moments earlier: "You know, some were saying that North Carolina would be a game-changer in this election. But today, what North Carolina decided is that the only game that needs changing is the one in Washington, D.C."

With his win that night, Obama was now only 279.5 delegates short of the 2,025 needed to lock down the nomination. Obama had won about 90 percent of North Carolina's African American Democratic voters, in a state where blacks were more than a third of the electorate.

Beyond that, the Obama campaign had won the perception war. Since North Carolina is in the Eastern time zone and Indiana in the Central, the networks called the state early in the evening, before Indiana, meaning that all of the prime-time programming led with Obama's massive victory. ABC's political analyst, George Stephanopoulos, a former aide to Bill Clinton, declared the Democratic race "over." Tim Russert, then the moderator of NBC's *Meet the Press,* added, "We now know who the Democratic nominee will be." Russert's analysis was devastating and the Clinton campaign knew it.

Senator Claire McCaskill of Missouri, a major Obama supporter, said the results meant "a big, big night" for Obama and demonstrated that Obama had overcome the Wright issue. "This shows he can take major blows and kind of rise above it. I think there was a sense that [Clinton] has some momentum, and I think it has just ground to a screeching halt tonight."[10]

Because of the late tally in Indiana, the Clinton campaign had to wait until 10:30 p.m. Eastern time to send her out to address her supporters, well after Obama had appeared and put his "stamp of victory" on the night. At a post-election rally in Indianapolis, Clinton tried to spin the outcome in the most favorable light: "Not long ago, my opponent made a prediction. He said I would probably win Pennsylvania. He would win North Carolina, and Indiana would be the tie-breaker. Well, tonight we've come from behind, we've broken the tie, and thanks to you, it's full speed on to the White House." The truth was anything but momentum for Clinton.

In reality, May 6 exposed the growing movement in the Democratic Party for unity, a feeling that was also surfacing in the media. A number of the party's senior officials—or "super delegates"—wanted Clinton to step aside. Both Bill and Hillary Clinton worked the phones to keep the defections to a minimum, but Indiana and North Carolina opened the floodgates. Beyond the public pressure, the bigger problem was that these super delegates all carried a vote independent of their state delegations and primary results; already behind 137.5 delegates, and nearly 350,000 popular votes, Clinton couldn't afford to lose anyone.

The Obama campaign was in a tricky position. They couldn't look like they were forcing Clinton, the "underdog," out of the race, but they had to send a signal to the party and to the press that the primary season was over. It was time to unite behind a candidate and focus their attacks on John McCain.

Jon Favreau drafted a speech for Obama that looked to the general election, instead of directing his words at Clinton. Number one on his list of issues was the worsening economy. Clinton had been the "economy candidate"; if Obama wanted to own it in the general election, he had to act fast. Both Axelrod and Plouffe wanted Obama to use his own life story to frame the campaign's approach to the economy and preempt John McCain, who they knew would struggle with the issue. McCain was a foreign policy expert; he was not known for his strength on the domestic front.

Despite the election results, Favreau made sure he continued to frame his candidate as the underdog, fighting against the odds in a political culture uncomfortable with too much change. The Obama team had seen firsthand what happened to Clinton in her role as the front-runner; they didn't want their candidate to be burdened with that mantle in the race against McCain.

Obama also used the speech to reiterate the core Obama principle of individual and collective responsibility. This was a theme that he had

first raised publicly before a national audience in his 2004 Democratic Convention keynote address. As Favreau put it, "This is a value that
[Obama's] believed in forever—[his governing philosophy] is all rooted
in responsibility."

Working from his office in Chicago, Favreau wrote a draft and sent it
to Obama, who was on the road campaigning. He had a sense of what his
boss wanted to say—the themes and the language had remained consistent throughout the primary. Axelrod helped fill in any blanks.

Favreau crafted a speech that acknowledged all that Clinton had accomplished, but gently nudged her supporters to join Obama in his fight
against McCain.

"This has been one of the longest, most closely fought contests in
history. And that's partly because we have such a formidable opponent
in Hillary Clinton," Obama said. "Tonight, many of the pundits have
suggested that this party is inalterably divided—that Senator Clinton's
supporters will not support me, and that my supporters will not support
her. Well, I'm here tonight to tell you that I don't believe that. Yes, there
have been bruised feelings on both sides. Yes, each side desperately wants
their candidate to win. But ultimately . . . this election is about you." He
continued, "This primary season may not be over, but when it is, we will
have to remember who we are as Democrats . . . This fall, we intend to
march forward as one Democratic Party."

Obama characterized his win in North Carolina as "a victory in a big
state, a swing state." The newspapers agreed and recognized that Clinton
failed to land a decisive victory in Indiana. The *New York Times* headline
read, "Obama Wins North Carolina Decisively; Clinton Takes Indiana by
Slim Margin." The *Washington Post* joined in with its headline, "Obama
Is Decisive Winner in NC; Clinton Ekes Out Victory in Indiana." In
their story in the *Post*, Dan Balz and Shailagh Murray wrote, "Although
she managed to squeeze out a victory in Indiana, the night produced a
far different outcome than the Clinton campaign had hoped for. Obama
won North Carolina . . . and his popular-margin there—about 230,000
votes—wiped out the gains Clinton had made . . . in Pennsylvania."[11]

In her election night remarks, Clinton pledged to fight on to West
Virginia, Kentucky, and the other remaining states, but, all in all, it
seemed that Obama had already moved on.

Remarks of Senator Barack Obama:
Night of North Carolina and Indiana Primaries

You know, some were saying that North Carolina would be a game-changer in this election. But today, what North Carolina decided is that the only game that needs changing is the one in Washington, D.C.

I want to start by congratulating Senator Clinton on her victory in the state of Indiana. And I want to thank the people of North Carolina for giving us a victory in a big state, a swing state, and a state where we will compete to win if I am the Democratic nominee for president of the United States.

When this campaign began, Washington didn't give us much of a chance. But because you came out in the bitter cold, and knocked on doors, and enlisted your friends and neighbors in this cause; because you stood up to the cynics, and the doubters, and the naysayers when we were up and when we were down; because you still believe that this is our moment, and our time, for change—tonight we stand less than two hundred delegates away from securing the Democratic nomination for president of the United States.

More importantly, because of you, we have seen that it's possible to overcome the politics of division and distraction; that it's possible to overcome the same old negative attacks that are always about scoring points and never about solving our problems. We've seen that the American people aren't looking for more spin or more gimmicks, but honest answers about the challenges we face. That's what you've accomplished in this campaign, and that's how we'll change this country together.

This has been one of the longest, most closely fought contests in history. And that's partly because we have such a formidable opponent in Senator Hillary Clinton. Tonight, many of the pundits have suggested that this party is inalterably divided—that Senator Clinton's supporters will not support me, and that my supporters will not support her.

Well, I'm here tonight to tell you that I don't believe it. Yes, there have been bruised feelings on both sides. Yes, each side desperately wants their candidate to win. But ultimately, this race is not about Hillary Clinton or Barack Obama or John McCain. This election is about you—the American people—and whether we will have a president and a party that can lead us toward a brighter future.

This primary season may not be over, but when it is, we will have to remember who we are as Democrats—that we are the party of Jefferson and Jackson; of Roosevelt and Kennedy; and that we are at our best when we lead with principle; when we lead with conviction; when we summon an entire nation around a common purpose—a higher purpose. This fall, we intend to march forward as one Democratic Party, united by a common vision for this country. Because we all agree that at this defining moment in history—a moment when we're facing two wars, an economy in turmoil, a planet in peril—we can't afford to give John McCain the chance to serve out George Bush's third term. We need change in America.

The woman I met in Indiana who just lost her job, and her pension, and her insurance when the plant where she worked at her entire life closed down—she can't afford four more years of tax breaks for corporations like the one that shipped her job overseas. She needs us to give tax breaks to companies that create good jobs here in America. She can't afford four more years of tax breaks for CEOs like the one who walked away from her company with a multi-million dollar bonus. She needs middle-class tax relief that will help her pay the skyrocketing price of groceries, and gas, and college tuition. That's why I'm running for president.

The college student I met in Iowa who works the night shift after a full day of class and still can't pay the medical bills for a sister who's ill—she can't afford four more years of a health care plan that only takes care of the healthy and the wealthy; that allows insurance companies to discriminate and deny coverage to those Americans who need it most. She needs us to stand up to those insurance companies and pass a plan that lowers every family's premiums and gives every uninsured American the same kind of coverage that Members of Congress give themselves. That's why I'm running for president.

The mother in Wisconsin who gave me a bracelet inscribed with the name of the son she lost in Iraq; the families who pray for their loved ones to come home; the heroes on their third and fourth and fifth tour of duty—

they can't afford four more years of a war that should've never been autho-rized and never been waged. They can't afford four more years of our vet-erans returning to broken-down barracks and substandard care. They need us to end a war that isn't making us safer. They need us to treat them with the care and respect they deserve. That's why I'm running for president.

The man I met in Pennsylvania who lost his job but can't even afford the gas to drive around and look for a new one—he can't afford four more years of an energy policy written by the oil companies and for the oil com-panies; a policy that's not only keeping gas at record prices, but funding both sides of the war on terror and destroying our planet in the process. He doesn't need four more years of Washington policies that sound good, but don't solve the problem. He needs us to take a permanent holiday from our oil addiction by making the automakers raise their fuel standards, corporations pay for their pollution, and oil companies invest their record profits in a clean energy future. That's the change we need. And that's why I'm running for president.

The people I've met in small towns and big cities across this country understand that government can't solve all our problems—and we don't expect it to. We believe in hard work. We believe in personal responsibility and self-reliance.

But we also believe that we have a larger responsibility to one another as Americans—that America is a place—that America is the place—where you can make it if you try. That no matter how much money you start with or where you come from or who your parents are, opportunity is yours if you're willing to reach for it and work for it. It's the idea that while there are few guarantees in life, you should be able to count on a job that pays the bills; health care for when you need it; a pension for when you retire; an education for your children that will allow them to fulfill their God-given potential. That's the America we believe in. That's the America I know.

This is the country that gave my grandfather a chance to go to college on the GI Bill when he came home from World War II; a country that gave him and my grandmother the chance to buy their first home with a loan from the government.

This is the country that made it possible for my mother—a single par-ent who had to go on food stamps at one point—to send my sister and me to the best schools in the country on scholarships.

This is the country that allowed my father-in-law—a city worker at a South Side water filtration plant—to provide for his wife and two children on a single salary. This is a man who was diagnosed at age thirty with multiple sclerosis—who relied on a walker to get himself to work. And yet, every day he went, and he labored, and he sent my wife and her brother to one of the best colleges in the nation. It was a job that didn't just give him a paycheck, but a sense of dignity and self-worth. It was an America that didn't just reward wealth, but the work and the workers who created it.

Somewhere along the way, between all the bickering and the influence-peddling and the game-playing of the last few decades, Washington and Wall Street have lost touch with these values. And while I honor John McCain's service to his country, his ideas for America are out of touch with these values. His plans for the future are nothing more than the failed policies of the past. And his plan to win in November appears to come from the very same playbook that his side has used time after time in election after election.

Yes, we know what's coming. We've seen it already. The same names and labels they always pin on everyone who doesn't agree with all their ideas. The same efforts to distract us from the issues that affect our lives by pouncing on every gaffe and association and fake controversy in the hope that the media will play along. The attempts to play on our fears and exploit our differences to turn us against each other for pure political gain—to slice and dice this country into red states and blue states; blue-collar and white-collar; white and black and brown.

This is what they will do—no matter which one of us is the nominee. The question, then, is not what kind of campaign they'll run; it's what kind of campaign we will run. It's what we will do to make this year different. I didn't get into race thinking that I could avoid this kind of politics, but I am running for president because this is the time to end it.

We will end it this time not because I'm perfect—I think by now this campaign has reminded all of us of that. We will end it not by duplicating the same tactics and the same strategies as the other side, because that will just lead us down the same path of polarization and gridlock.

We will end it by telling the truth—forcefully, repeatedly, confidently—and by trusting that the American people will embrace the need for change.

Because that's how we've always changed this country—not from the top-down, but from the bottom-up; when you—the American people—decide that the stakes are too high and the challenges are too great.

The other side can label and name-call all they want, but I trust the American people to recognize that it's not surrender to end the war in Iraq so that we can rebuild our military and go after al Qaeda's leaders. I trust the American people to understand that it's not weakness but wisdom to talk not just to our friends, but our enemies—like Roosevelt did, and Kennedy did, and Truman did.

I trust the American people to realize that while we don't need big government, we do need a government that stands up for families who are being tricked out of their homes by Wall Street predators; a government that stands up for the middle-class by giving them a tax break; a government that ensures that no American will ever lose their life savings just because their child gets sick. Security and opportunity, compassion and prosperity, aren't liberal values or conservative values—they're American values.

Most of all, I trust the American people's desire to no longer be defined by our differences. Because no matter where I've been in this country—whether it was the corn fields of Iowa or the textile mills of the Carolinas; the streets of San Antonio or the foothills of Georgia—I've found that while we may have different stories, we hold common hopes. We may not look the same or come from the same place, but we want to move in the same direction—towards a better future for our children and our grandchildren.

That's why I'm in this race. I love this country too much to see it divided and distracted at this moment in history. I believe in our ability to perfect this union because it's the only reason I'm standing here today. And I know the promise of America because I have lived it.

It is the light of opportunity that led my father across an ocean.

It is the founding ideals that the flag draped over my grandfather's coffin stands for—it is life, and liberty, and the pursuit of happiness.

It's the simple truth I learned all those years ago when I worked in the shadows of a shuttered steel mill on the South Side of Chicago—that in this country, justice can be won against the greatest of odds; hope can find its way back to the darkest of corners; and when we are told that we cannot bring about the change that we seek, we answer with one voice—yes, we can.

So don't ever forget that this election is not about me, or any candidate. Don't ever forget that this campaign is about you—about your hopes, about your dreams, about your struggles, about securing your portion of the American Dream.

Don't ever forget that we have a choice in this country—that we can choose not to be divided; that we can choose not to be afraid; that we can still choose this moment to finally come together and solve the problems we've talked about all those other years in all those other elections.

This time can be different than all the rest. This time we can face down those who say our road is too long; that our climb is too steep; that we can no longer achieve the change that we seek. This is our time to answer the call that so many generations of Americans have answered before—by insisting that by hard work, and by sacrifice, the American Dream will endure. Thank you, and may God bless the United States of America.

16

"A World That Stands as One"

July 24, 2008

Victory Column, Tiergarten, Berlin, Germany

I know my country has not perfected itself.
We've made our share of mistakes, and there are times when
our actions around the world have not lived up to our best intentions.
But I also know how much I love America.

By the time Barack Obama landed the Democratic nomination in May 2009, millions of voters saw him as an agent of change and hope. They knew he was a champion of health care reform, economic recovery, and post-partisan unity. Moreover, as he had stated in his presidential announcement speech, he wanted to repair America's tattered reputation in the world.

Like many Democrats, Obama believed that George W. Bush's approach to foreign policy, including the wars in Iraq and Afghanistan and his go-it-alone line of attack, had taken its toll on the country's standing. But, unlike his general election opponent, Senator John McCain, after a long primary process Obama still had one clear weakness: his foreign policy credentials.

During the primary season, in debates, press conferences and political advertisements, Senator Clinton had questioned Obama's foreign policy experience and judgment. In one of the first presidential debates, for instance, Obama stated that as president he would meet with the nation's more publicized "enemies," including Iran's Mahmoud Ahmadinejad, North Korea's Kim Jong Il, Venezuela's Hugo Chávez, and Cuba's Raúl Castro. Clinton quickly criticized him for taking a weak line and naively telegraphing his agenda. On the experience front, after less than one term in the United States Senate and seven years in the Illinois State

Legislature, Obama simply hadn't garnered extensive national security credentials.

In fact, Obama had only traveled abroad three times as a senator, when he went to Asia in 2005 and to Africa and the Middle East in 2006. Although he had visited Iraq once, he had never been to Afghanistan. Still, as a child, Obama had lived in Indonesia for four years while in elementary school. And though his mother was from Kansas, his father and many family members were Kenyan, enriching his perspective on the world.

It wasn't only Clinton who questioned his credentials. Left-leaning columnists such as Lionel Beehner of the Huffington Post, a former senior writer for the Council on Foreign Relations, took issue: "On foreign policy, Obama appears to have no new ideas. . . . After all, he still hammers us with his shrewd foresight on the Iraq War. But that was a decision he made over six years ago."[1] It is fair to say that in the eyes of the media and even some in his own party, Obama had much to prove.

By the general election, Obama was also running against one of the most seasoned foreign policy experts in the United States Senate, John McCain. McCain was a Vietnam veteran; he had spent five and a half years as a prisoner of war in the infamous Hanoi Hilton. For his more than twenty years in the Senate, his had been a hawkish yet reasoned voice for American foreign policy and a tireless champion of the military. McCain planned to use his national security experience to draw a stark distinction between himself and Obama, with hopes that in a time of war, it would help lead him to the White House.

The good news for Obama was that as the general election took shape, it was clear that the domestic economy, not national security, was going to be the primary issue. McCain himself admitted that he lacked strong economic experience; this afforded Obama a significant leg up over his opponent.

The other thing Obama had going for him was eight years of George W. Bush. Despite the outpouring of goodwill after the 9/11 attacks, it was commonly accepted that President Bush had rushed to war in Iraq without a plan to instill peace and that, time and again, the United States had acted unilaterally, shunting aside global diplomacy. McCain's problem was that he had too often toed the Bush company line. Obama could easily portray him as a mouthpiece of the Bush-era war rhetoric.

Since 2007, Obama's senior campaign team had been working to counter this vulnerability. They were planning an international trip of a kind that no presidential candidate had ever attempted, in terms of both its scope and importance. According to Dan Balz and Haynes Johnson, "What Obama's advisers had concluded was that as long as he cleared a minimum threshold in this area [foreign policy], he could be elected." This trip was their chance to cross the threshold. The stakes were high; one mistake or misstatement on the global stage would be exaggerated tenfold, but they couldn't afford to let McCain frame the narrative on Obama's foreign policy qualifications.[2]

During the primaries, Obama delivered several foreign policy speeches. On April 23, 2007, he addressed the Chicago Council on Global Affairs. From the podium, he promised to "ensure that every child, everywhere, is taught to build and not to destroy" and stated that America "must lead the world in battling immediate evils and promoting the ultimate social good." Later, he took his message about America's relationship with the world on the campaign trail to Clinton, Iowa, and Fayetteville, North Carolina.

Then, on June 28, 2008, while speaking with wounded veterans at Walter Reed Army Medical Center, just as the general election was ramping up, Obama announced he would take a whirlwind trip overseas, visiting eight countries in ten days. For the first leg, he would go to Kuwait, Afghanistan, and Iraq as part of an official Senate delegation. The itinerary for the second half of his trip would be as a candidate and include Jordan, Israel, Germany, France, and Great Britain. The Defense Department organized the visit to the war zones, but Obama's other stops were not official diplomatic events—they were political. Since he wasn't president yet, his staff wouldn't have the support of the local U.S. embassy and State Department staff. The campaign's senior staff and advance teams would have to choreograph a multicountry, media-filled political tour on foreign soil without government assistance.

Obama's announcement was welcomed abroad. In the German magazine Der Spiegel, the headline read, "Heading across the Atlantic: Obama to Meet His Fans in Europe."[3] On July 19, the delegation, comprising Obama and Senators Jack Reed and Chuck Hagel, touched down in Kuwait; Obama was accompanied by his Secret Service detail and his Senate foreign policy adviser, Mark Lippert. After enjoying a pickup basketball game with U.S. troops, Obama and the delegation flew on to Afghanistan before going to Iraq, where he met with Prime Minister Nouri al-Maliki. Two days earlier, in a pleasant surprise for Obama's staff, and a bit of a shock for the Bush White House, Maliki told a reporter from *Der Spiegel* that Obama's proposed sixteen-month timetable for withdrawing U.S. forces from Iraq "would be the right timeframe for a withdrawal."[4] The Obama campaign couldn't have asked for a better endorsement of and introduction to his trip.

Later, in Iraq, Obama met at length with General David Petraeus, the commander of U.S. forces there. Obama was up-front with Petraeus about his opposition to the troop surge in Iraq and his commitment to a strict timetable for withdrawal, but both sides were careful not to let their differences color the meeting or the positive tone of their public events together. Obama's trip made newspaper headlines on front pages all around the world.

From Iraq, Obama began the political phase of his itinerary—first to Amman, then to Israel, and, finally, after an arduous trip in the Middle East, to Europe.

Obama's staff knew just how popular their candidate was in Europe, and many wanted to capitalize on this popularity with a massive, blockbuster event at the Brandenburg Gate in Berlin, where Presidents Kennedy and Reagan had made groundbreaking statements. It was there, before the Berlin Wall that divided East and West Berlin, that Kennedy in 1963 said, "Ich bin ein Berliner" and Reagan, in 1987, said, "Mr. Gorbachev, tear down this wall!" When word leaked that Obama would deliver a public speech at the Brandenburg Gate, German Chancellor Angela Merkel protested the planned location for political reasons. Obama had concerns too, but by the time he raised them, the Brandenburg Gate was no longer being considered.[5]

Instead, the campaign settled on a site in the large Tiergarten Park, in front of the Victory Column, a monument built in 1864 to commemorate Prussia's victory over Denmark. Interestingly, the monument was originally located near the Reichstag (now the Bundestag, the German Parliament) in what after World War II became East Berlin, on the other side of the Wall. But Hitler had it relocated to the part of the city that later was in the Western sector. Recognizing the gravity of the day, and the fact that this was Obama's only big public event of the week, the campaign advance team spent weeks preparing every detail of the event—from the crane positioned for photographers to snap the perfect picture, to the campaign volunteers who solicited passersby to "stop here, we're registering American citizens to vote!"

With the Brandenburg Gate now in the distant background, Obama ascended the stage and walked to the lectern along a long, blue walkway. He waved and smiled to a grand ovation, masking the jet lag that had kept him awake the previous night. Before him was a sea of nearly two hundred thousand people, packed together like sardines, many of them waving American flags the campaign had handed out earlier that summer day. The spectators had begun arriving early that morning, and by seven thirty in the evening, when the address began, they stretched from the base of the Victory Column through the sprawling park all the way to the shadows of the Brandenburg Gate. Thousands of people and members of the press from dozens of countries, including the United States, lined the streets to watch Obama's motorcade snake up to the city center park. Nearly seven hundred German police officers were deployed.

The title of Obama's remarks was "A World That Stands as One," and his message was clear: it was time to restore the world's faith in American leadership. According to his speechwriters, Ben Rhodes and Jon Favreau, his speech wasn't meant to be overtly political. In fact, there were no Obama signs, and no direct attacks or even mentions of his opponent or of the sitting president. Obama was mindful that there can only be one president at a time, so while he took a serious tone, he was careful to stay in his lane.

That said, he did inject his signature political frame—"This is our moment"—and he did level a few indirect criticisms at the Bush administration. To cheers, he offered, "I know my country has not perfected itself. We've made our share of mistakes, and there are times when our actions around the world have not lived up to our best intentions. But I also know how much I love America."

He went on in his thirty-minute address to advance his view of the global stage, stressing that in the twenty-first century, America, and all countries, simply couldn't afford to go it alone. Instead, they had to join together to confront the world's challenges—from terror and nuclear nonproliferation to global warming and genocide to trade and poverty. He also stressed the importance of sending additional NATO troops to Afghanistan, although the vast majority of Germans opposed that policy (a point Chancellor Merkel had made to him in a meeting earlier that day): "No one nation, no matter how large or powerful, can defeat such challenges alone."

To help advance his argument, Obama deftly drew on history, including the Berlin Airlift of 1948, which saved the cut-off city, and the Marshall Plan, which helped rebuild Europe. Like the message he delivered at home, he argued for global unity over division and isolationism—what he called "walls" between countries (a phrase he used sixteen times). He added, "Look at Berlin, where Germans and Americans learned to work together and trust each other less than three years after facing each other on the field of battle. . . . Sixty years after the airlift, we are called upon again. . . . The fall of the Berlin Wall brought new hope. But that very closeness has given rise to new dangers—dangers that cannot be contained within the borders of a country or by the distance of an ocean. . . . That is why we cannot afford to be divided. No one nation, no matter how large or powerful, can defeat such challenges alone."

His speech was a remarkable success, and it reflected a significant amount of hard work. Several weeks before Obama had left for Iraq, Favreau, Rhodes, and Axelrod had arranged a conference call with the senator to discuss the substance and themes of what he hoped to cover in the speech. Everyone, especially the candidate, understood the significance of his trip and the importance of striking, "just the right tone," as Favreau put it. They knew that Obama had to walk a fine line between respecting the sitting president and sending a strong signal to the world that America's approach to foreign policy would be different under his administration.

After speaking with the candidate, Favreau and Rhodes held a call with the campaign's foreign policy advisers; Susan Rice and Denis McDonough were particularly helpful. They also spoke to Senator John Kerry, Favreau's former boss, who offered sage counsel, and to Andrei Cherny, who had just published a book, *The Candy Bombers: The Untold Story of the Berlin Airlift and America's Finest Hour*. Obama was a student of postwar history and a sincere believer in global cooperation, so Favreau and Rhodes knew that including details on Berlin, NATO, and the Marshall Plan in the remarks would be important to him.

After weeks of discussion, the two speechwriters had just three days to actually write the draft; Obama wanted it before his plane headed overseas. Given the necessary extent of preparation for the trip, the campaign headquarters was particularly busy, so Rhodes and Favreau headed off to a conference room at a Chicago law firm, Perkins Coie. There, they cloistered themselves for a multiday writing marathon and didn't leave until they had cobbled together a draft worth circulating to others.

From there, Rhodes headed to the airport for a flight to Europe, where he would meet Obama and hold the pen for the final edits. Obama toiled away on the draft for a couple of days and made extensive line edits. Between his changes and what the speechwriters had written, the speech was running long. Plus, some of the foreign policy advisers added a few more lines on topics that Rhodes and Favreau had neglected to touch on.

Rhodes cut down the draft. He and Favreau were particularly pleased that the conclusion they had written stayed intact: "I know my country has not perfected itself. At times, we've struggled to keep the promise of liberty and equality for all of our people. We've made our share of mistakes, and there are times when our actions around the world have not lived up to our best intentions."

After Berlin, Obama concluded his trip with stops in France to meet with President Nicolas Sarkozy and in Great Britain to sit down with Prime Minister Gordon Brown. By all accounts the trip was a resounding success. Although, to the team's chagrin, Obama only got a minor bump in domestic polls from the trip, the campaign had successfully neutralized a major issue for their candidate. No one would any longer ask whether the Democratic nominee had the fortitude or gravitas to represent the country abroad.

At home, while Obama was traveling, the McCain campaign had worked overtime to diminish the trip's impact, but with little success. At events across the country, the Republican candidate focused on the domestic economy, even holding an event at a German restaurant in Columbus, Ohio—a cheeky dig at Obama's speech in Berlin. McCain declared, "I'd love to give a speech in Germany—a political speech—or a speech that maybe the German people would be interested in, but I'd

much prefer to do it as president of the United States."[6] Then, in a radio
address on July 19, he reiterated the inexperience point: "In a time of
war, the commander in chief's job doesn't get a learning curve." McCain's
campaign team also launched perhaps the most famous ad of the general
election, calling Obama the "biggest celebrity in the world,"comparing
him to Paris Hilton and Britney Spears. This was McCain's attempt to
show Obama as a candidate for Hollywood and the world, not for hard-
working, average Americans. Even President Bush entered the fray, delivering an address on America's role in the world within hours of Obama's.
Still, despite all of their efforts, every cable news network covered Obama
live; no one covered the president's speech in real time. In the end, for the
week of July 20 to 26, Obama dominated news coverage across the globe.
The *Sun,* the United Kingdom's largest newspaper headlined, "Obama
Speech Hailed a Success."[7]

REMARKS BY SENATOR BARACK OBAMA:
"A WORLD THAT STANDS AS ONE"

Thank you to the citizens of Berlin and to the people of Germany. Let me
thank Chancellor Merkel and Foreign Minister Frank-Walter Steinmeier for
welcoming me earlier today. Thank you, Mayor Wowereit, the Berlin Senate, the police, and most of all, thank you [to the crowd] for this welcome.

I come to Berlin as so many of my countrymen have come before.
Tonight, I speak to you not as a candidate for president, but as a citizen
—a proud citizen of the United States, and a fellow citizen of the world.

I know that I don't look like the Americans who've previously spoken
in this great city. The journey that led me here is improbable. My mother
was born in the heartland of America, but my father grew up herding goats
in Kenya. His father—my grandfather—was a cook, a domestic servant to
the British.

At the height of the Cold War, my father decided, like so many others in
the forgotten corners of the world, that his yearning—his dream—required

the freedom and opportunity promised by the West. And so he wrote letter after letter to universities all across America until somebody, somewhere answered his prayer for a better life.

That is why I'm here. And you are here because you too know that yearning. This city, of all cities, knows the dream of freedom. And you know that the only reason we stand here tonight is because men and women from both of our nations came together to work, and struggle, and sacrifice for that better life.

Ours is a partnership that truly began sixty years ago this summer, on the day when the first American plane touched down at Templehof.

On that day, much of this continent still lay in ruin. The rubble of this city had yet to be built into a wall. The Soviet shadow had swept across Eastern Europe, while in the West, America, Britain, and France took stock of their losses, and pondered how the world might be remade.

This is where the two sides met. And on the twenty-fourth of June, 1948, the Communists chose to blockade the western part of the city. They cut off food and supplies to more than two million Germans in an effort to extinguish the last flame of freedom in Berlin.

The size of our forces was no match for the much larger Soviet Army. And yet retreat would have allowed Communism to march across Europe. Where the last war had ended, another world war could have easily begun. All that stood in the way was Berlin.

And that's when the airlift began—when the largest and most unlikely rescue in history brought food and hope to the people of this city.

The odds were stacked against success. In the winter, a heavy fog filled the sky above, and many planes were forced to turn back without dropping off the needed supplies. The streets where we stand were filled with hungry families who had no comfort from the cold.

But in the darkest hours, the people of Berlin kept the flame of hope burning. The people of Berlin refused to give up. And on one fall day, hundreds of thousands of Berliners came here, to the Tiergarten, and heard the city's mayor implore the world not to give up on freedom. "There is only one possibility," he said. "For us to stand together united until this battle is won. . . . The people of Berlin have spoken. We have done our duty, and we will keep on doing our duty. People of the world: now do your duty . . . People of the world, look at Berlin!"

People of the world—look at Berlin!

Look at Berlin, where Germans and Americans learned to work together and trust each other less than three years after facing each other on the field of battle.

Look at Berlin, where the determination of a people met the generosity of the Marshall Plan and created a German miracle; where a victory over tyranny gave rise to NATO, the greatest alliance ever formed to defend our common security.

Look at Berlin, where the bullet holes in the buildings and the somber stones and pillars near the Brandenburg Gate insist that we never forget our common humanity.

People of the world—look at Berlin, where a Wall came down, a continent came together, and history proved that there is no challenge too great for a world that stands as one.

Sixty years after the airlift, we are called upon again. History has led us to a new crossroad, with new promise and new peril. When you, the German people, tore down that Wall—a Wall that divided East and West, freedom and tyranny, fear and hope—walls came tumbling down around the world. From Kiev to Cape Town, prison camps were closed, and the doors of democracy were opened. Markets opened too, and the spread of information and technology reduced barriers to opportunity and prosperity. While the twentieth century taught us that we share a common destiny, the twenty-first has revealed a world more intertwined than at any time in human history.

The fall of the Berlin Wall brought new hope. But that very closeness has given rise to new dangers—dangers that cannot be contained within the borders of a country or by the distance of an ocean.

The terrorists of September eleventh plotted in Hamburg and trained in Kandahar and Karachi before killing thousands from all over the globe on American soil.

As we speak, cars in Boston and factories in Beijing are melting the ice caps in the Arctic, shrinking coastlines in the Atlantic, and bringing drought to farms from Kansas to Kenya.

Poorly secured nuclear material in the former Soviet Union, or secrets from a scientist in Pakistan, could help build a bomb that detonates in Paris. The poppies in Afghanistan become the heroin in Berlin. The poverty and violence in Somalia breeds the terror of tomorrow. The genocide in Darfur shames the conscience of us all.

In this new world, such dangerous currents have swept along faster than our efforts to contain them. That is why we cannot afford to be divided. No one nation, no matter how large or powerful, can defeat such challenges alone. None of us can deny these threats, or escape responsibility in meeting them. Yet, in the absence of Soviet tanks and a terrible wall, it has become easy to forget this truth. And if we're honest with each other, we know that sometimes, on both sides of the Atlantic, we have drifted apart, and forgotten our shared destiny.

In Europe, the view that America is part of what has gone wrong in our world, rather than a force to help make it right, has become all too common. In America, there are voices that deride and deny the importance of Europe's role in our security and our future. Both views miss the truth—that Europeans today are bearing new burdens and taking more responsibility in critical parts of the world; and that just as American bases built in the last century still help to defend the security of this continent, so does our country still sacrifice greatly for freedom around the globe.

Yes, there have been differences between America and Europe. No doubt, there will be differences in the future. But the burdens of global citizenship continue to bind us together. A change of leadership in Washington will not lift this burden. In this new century, Americans and Europeans alike will be required to do more—not less. Partnership and cooperation among nations is not a choice; it is the one way, the only way, to protect our common security and advance our common humanity.

That is why the greatest danger of all is to allow new walls to divide us from one another.

The walls between old allies on either side of the Atlantic cannot stand. The walls between the countries with the most and those with the least cannot stand. The walls between races and tribes; natives and immigrants; Christian and Muslim and Jew cannot stand. These now are the walls we must tear down.

We know they have fallen before. After centuries of strife, the people of Europe have formed a Union of promise and prosperity. Here, at the base of a column built to mark victory in war, we meet in the center of a Europe at peace. Not only have walls come down in Berlin, but they have come down in Belfast, where Protestant and Catholic found a way to live together; in the Balkans, where our Atlantic alliance ended wars and brought savage war criminals to justice; and in South Africa, where the struggle of a courageous people defeated apartheid.

So history reminds us that walls can be torn down. But the task is never easy. True partnership and true progress requires constant work and sustained sacrifice. They require sharing the burdens of development and diplomacy; of progress and peace. They require allies who will listen to each other, learn from each other and, most of all, trust each other.

That is why America cannot turn inward. That is why Europe cannot turn inward. America has no better partner than Europe. Now is the time to build new bridges across the globe as strong as the one that bound us across the Atlantic. Now is the time to join together, through constant cooperation, strong institutions, shared sacrifice, and a global commitment to progress, to meet the challenges of the twenty-first century. It was this spirit that led airlift planes to appear in the sky above our heads, and people to assemble where we stand today. And this is the moment when our nations—and all nations—must summon that spirit anew.

This is the moment when we must defeat terror and dry up the well of extremism that supports it. This threat is real and we cannot shrink from our responsibility to combat it. If we could create NATO to face down the Soviet Union, we can join in a new and global partnership to dismantle the networks that have struck in Madrid and Amman, in London and Bali, in Washington and New York. If we could win a battle of ideas against the Communists, we can stand with the vast majority of Muslims who reject the extremism that leads to hate instead of hope.

This is the moment when we must renew our resolve to rout the terrorists who threaten our security in Afghanistan, and the traffickers who sell drugs on your streets. No one welcomes war. I recognize the enormous difficulties in Afghanistan. But my country and yours have a stake in seeing that NATO's first mission beyond Europe's borders is a success. For the people of Afghanistan, and for our shared security, the work must be done. America cannot do this alone. The Afghan people need our troops and your troops; our support and your support to defeat the Taliban and al Qaeda, to develop their economy, and to help them rebuild their nation. We have too much at stake to turn back now.

This is the moment when we must renew the goal of a world without nuclear weapons. The two superpowers that faced each other across the wall of this city came too close too often to destroying all we have built and all that we love. With that wall gone, we need not stand idly by and watch the further spread of the deadly atom. It is time to secure all loose nuclear materials; to stop the spread of nuclear weapons; and to reduce the arsenals from another era. This is the moment to begin the work of seeking the peace of a world without nuclear weapons.

This is the moment when every nation in Europe must have the chance to choose its own tomorrow free from the shadows of yesterday. In this century, we need a strong European Union that deepens the security and prosperity of this continent, while extending a hand abroad. In this century—in this city of all cities—we must reject the Cold War mind-set of the past, and resolve to work with Russia when we can, to stand up for our values when we must, and to seek a partnership that extends across this entire continent.

This is the moment when we must build on the wealth that open markets have created, and share its benefits more equitably. Trade has been a cornerstone of our growth and global development. But we will not be able to sustain this growth if it favors the few, and not the many. Together, we must forge trade that truly rewards the work that creates wealth, with meaningful protections for our people and our planet. This is the moment for trade that is free and fair for all.

This is the moment we must help answer the call for a new dawn in the Middle East. My country must stand with yours and with Europe in sending a direct message to Iran that it must abandon its nuclear ambitions. We must support the Lebanese who have marched and bled for democracy, and the Israelis and Palestinians who seek a secure and lasting peace. And despite past differences, this is the moment when the world should support the millions of Iraqis who seek to rebuild their lives, even as we pass responsibility to the Iraqi government and finally bring this war to a close.

This is the moment when we must come together to save this planet. Let us resolve that we will not leave our children a world where the oceans rise and famine spreads and terrible storms devastate our lands. Let us resolve that all nations—including my own—will act with the same seriousness of purpose as has your nation, and reduce the carbon we send into our atmosphere. This is the moment to give our children back their future. This is the moment to stand as one.

And this is the moment when we must give hope to those left behind in a globalized world. We must remember that the Cold War born in this city was not a battle for land or treasure. Sixty years ago, the planes that flew over Berlin did not drop bombs; instead they delivered food, and coal, and candy to grateful children. And in that show of solidarity, those pilots won more than a military victory. They won hearts and minds, love and loyalty and trust—not just from the people in this city, but from all those who heard the story of what they did here.

Now the world will watch and remember what we do here—what we do with this moment. Will we extend our hand to the people in the forgotten corners of this world who yearn for lives marked by dignity and opportunity; by security and justice? Will we lift the child in Bangladesh from poverty, shelter the refugee in Chad, and banish the scourge of AIDS in our time?

Will we stand for the human rights of the dissident in Burma, the blogger in Iran, or the voter in Zimbabwe? Will we give meaning to the words "never again" in Darfur?

Will we acknowledge that there is no more powerful example than the one each of our nations projects to the world? Will we reject torture and stand for the rule of law? Will we welcome immigrants from different lands, and shun discrimination against those who don't look like us or worship like we do, and keep the promise of equality and opportunity for all of our people?

People of Berlin—people of the world—this is our moment. This is our time.

I know my country has not perfected itself. At times, we've struggled to keep the promise of liberty and equality for all of our people. We've made our share of mistakes, and there are times when our actions around the world have not lived up to our best intentions.

But I also know how much I love America. I know that for more than two centuries, we have strived—at great cost and great sacrifice—to form a more perfect union; to seek, with other nations, a more hopeful world. Our allegiance has never been to any particular tribe or kingdom—indeed, every language is spoken in our country; every culture has left its imprint on ours; every point of view is expressed in our public squares. What has always united us—what has always driven our people; what drew my father to America's shores—is a set of ideals that speak to aspirations shared by all people: that we can live free from fear and free from want; that we can speak our minds and assemble with whomever we choose and worship as we please.

These are the aspirations that joined the fates of all nations in this city. These aspirations are bigger than anything that drives us apart. It is because of these aspirations that the airlift began. It is because of these aspirations that all free people—everywhere—became citizens of Berlin. It is in pursuit of these aspirations that a new generation—our generation—must make our mark on the world.

People of Berlin—and people of the world—the scale of our challenge is great. The road ahead will be long. But I come before you to say that we are heirs to a struggle for freedom. We are a people of improbable hope. With an eye toward the future, with resolve in our hearts, let us remember this history, and answer our destiny, and remake the world once again.

17

"THE AMERICAN PROMISE":
DEMOCRATIC NATIONAL CONVENTION

August 28, 2008 • Invesco Field, Denver, Colorado

> *The greatest risk we can take is to try the same old politics*
> *with the same old players and expect a different result. . . .*
> *Change happens because the American people demand it —*
> *because they rise up and insist on new ideas and new*
> *leadership, a new politics for a new time.*

By the time he officially accepted the Democratic Party's nod for the presidency, Barack Obama knew a thing or two about audacity. In 2002, on the heels of 9/11, he took the contrarian view and opposed legislation authorizing President Bush to invade Iraq. Then, in 2007, after only two years in the United States Senate, he threw his hat in the ring for president. He boldly challenged the institutional favorite, Hillary Clinton, and he did so knowing that should he prevail, he would be the first African American in United States history to win the White House.

So, in some ways, it was no surprise that Obama decided to buck tradition and move his Democratic Convention speech, in which he would accept the party's nomination, out of the Pepsi Center, the indoor space where the rest of the convention would be held, to Invesco Field, the stadium where the Denver Broncos played. He was only the second presidential nominee to make a move to an outdoor stadium. The most recent was John F. Kennedy, who in 1960 moved his speech from the Los Angeles Memorial Sports Arena to the Los Angeles Memorial Coliseum (half the seats were empty—the event was referred to in one newspaper as "fresh air vaudeville"[1]).

Obama and his team were setting the bar high—and they knew it. Not only did he have to fill eighty thousand seats, as opposed to twenty thousand at the Pepsi Center, but he was signaling to the country that he would deliver a seminal address that could make or break his candidacy. According to the *New York Times*'s Adam Nagourney and Jeff Zeleny, his aides "chose the stadium to signal a break from typical politics and to permit thousands of his supporters . . . to hear him speak."[2] Either way, he was providing endless fodder to his Republican opponent, John McCain, who for months had sewn a narrative that Obama was more of a Hollywood pop star than a presidential candidate.

Upping the ante, Obama made this gamble while in a dead heat with McCain; the August 24 Gallup poll, the week of Obama's speech, had both senators with 45 percent of the votes if the election were held that day. Another Gallup survey, released toward the end of the contentious primary battle, had 28 percent of Clinton supporters voting for McCain in an Obama vs. McCain presidential election. Put another way, Obama had yet to capture the Clinton voters—and nerves in the Clinton camp were still raw. Many of her supporters were not happy that Obama had selected Senator Joe Biden of Delaware over Clinton as his running mate; others thought Obama was unelectable or simply too liberal. Some groused that the time slot the Obama campaign gave former president Bill Clinton to address the convention at 9:00 p.m. on its third night was a snub.

The only people not nervous about the event were the party faithful in Denver. This was the city's first time hosting a convention since William Jennings Bryan and the Democrats had gathered at the Denver Auditorium Arena in the "Mile High City" in 1908, when party leaders boasted that the convention would funnel "millions and millions of dollars" into Denver.[3]

On the convention's opening night, the late Senator Ted Kennedy, then the only living brother of the former president and the last embodiment of Camelot, addressed the hall. Only a few months earlier, Kennedy had been diagnosed with terminal brain cancer. Some had urged him to give the cross-country trip a pass and send a video tribute to the convention instead. But Kennedy wouldn't have missed this opportunity for the world. This was his final hurrah, his chance to pass the torch to a new generation, in what he referred to as a "season of hope."[4]

Months earlier, in a controversial move, Kennedy had broken with the Clintons and endorsed Obama. So, despite the excruciating pain and exhaustion afflicting him, Senator Kennedy lifted himself from his hospital bed, rehearsed his speech one last time, and limped to the podium. As he closed with his signature phrase, "The dream lives on," the crowd embraced the "lion in winter" and his ringing endorsement of Obama.

On Tuesday, during prime time, Hillary Clinton entered the Pepsi Center to thunderous applause and the now-familiar chant of "Hillary . . . Hillary . . . Hillary." Blue placards printed with "Hillary" dotted the audience. One thing was immediately clear: Clinton's entrance and her welcoming fanfare were well orchestrated and carefully planned by the convention organizers. The last thing Obama's team wanted was even the remotest appearance that he was snubbing his fierce primary opponent— the woman who had received eighteen million votes.

Clinton returned the favor. Without an ounce of hesitation, she opened her speech with a ringing endorsement, "I'm here tonight as a proud mother, as a proud Democrat, as a proud senator from New York, a proud American, and a proud supporter of Barack Obama. . . . Whether you voted for me or voted for Barack, the time is now to unite as a single party with a single purpose. We are on the same team, and none of us can sit on the sidelines." Her supporters got the message that it was time to move on, put their anger and party rifts aside, and get behind Obama. When asked if she would now support Obama, one Clinton voter told the *New York Times,* "Absolutely. She just told us to, didn't she?"[5]

The next night, former president Clinton heaped on even more praise before an adoring crowd. It was widely known at the time that Bill Clinton was still smarting about his wife's defeat, and his apathy toward Obama was not helping. That is why his public endorsement at the convention was so important. It was a clear sign to the party faithful that he was ready to embrace Obama. Earlier that week, Obama had called both the former president and first lady to help repair the breach; campaign aides were quick to tell reporters that both conversations went very well.

After a three-minute ovation, Bill Clinton started to speak, and he left no question where he stood: "Last night, Hillary told us in no uncertain terms that she is going to do everything she can to elect Barack Obama. That makes two of us. . . . Like Hillary, I want all of you who supported her to vote for Barack Obama." Clinton was in his glory. After a bumpy few months in the spotlight and a few controversial statements, he was back in the statesman's driver's seat. "Everything I learned in my eight years as president, and in the work I've done since, in America and across the globe, has convinced me that Barack Obama is the man for this job." He then slapped the Republicans, saying, "They actually want us to reward them for the last eight years by giving them four more. Now let's send them a message that will echo from the Rockies all across America, a simple message: thanks, but no thanks. In this case, the third time is not the charm."

The next night, echoing a similar theme, Joe Biden accepted his party's vice presidential nomination. After a nearly flawless week and dozens of speeches, the foundation had been laid for Obama's address. As if to tease the audience, Obama joined Biden on stage after Biden finished his remarks to thank his running mate and greet the crowd.

Shockingly, when he walked onto stage that night, Obama's own speech wasn't finished—and his chief speechwriter, Jon Favreau, was in bed, asleep. It wasn't by choice. A few hours earlier, after a prep session with David Axelrod and the rest of the speechwriting team, Obama ordered Favreau to put down the pen and go to bed. Favreau was exhausted; he hadn't slept more than five hours in three nights and the candidate wanted him to be fresh for the final mile on Thursday.

Favreau said that, after two years of writing for Obama, this particular speech process was "the worst experience of my life." It had started nearly a month before, in early August, before the Obamas went to Hawaii for their summer vacation. At the candidate's request, Favreau organized a meeting with Obama, Axelrod, and campaign manager David Plouffe to discuss what Obama hoped to cover in his remarks, including his biography, the history of the moment, his policies, and his differences with John McCain. This was Obama's first and perhaps best opportunity to present his case to the American people. He asked Favreau to start writing a draft and he would do the same while he was away.

Favreau struggled with the first draft. He began with an outline, which was a rare step for him, and then, over weeks, churned out much of a first draft. The only piece of the speech he left unfinished was the concluding paragraphs. For that, his speech team assembled at the Chicago apartment of Cody Keenan, a junior member of the speechwriting team, for a group writing session. There, over dinner and a few beers, he,

Keenan, Ben Rhodes, Adam Frankel, and Sarah Hurwitz composed the last three pages. By three in the morning, they had a version worthy of being sent to Axelrod for review.

The tough part was keeping the speech under forty-five minutes, which was approximately the length of John Kerry's speech in 2004. Plouffe sat in his office with Favreau and read the draft; when he got to page six he looked up and said, "I like this. There's a lot of good stuff in here. I don't know if it all gels yet, but send it to Obama. Let's see what he thinks."

Obama had the same reaction. He liked it but still wanted to tweak it. So after he returned to Chicago from Hawaii, he escaped to a hotel room downtown to write. Obama knew, said Favreau, that if he slept at home with the kids, "he would never find the time to get away and jam on his computer." At 2:00 a.m. Monday morning, less than a week before he had to deliver the speech, Obama sent his redlined version to Favreau and Axelrod. It was way too long.

Favreau planned to edit it on the plane the next morning. Axelrod, Obama, and Favreau huddled in the front of the cabin of the campaign plane as it made its way across the country. Obama was beginning a four-day tour of swing states, beginning in Eau Claire, Wisconsin. Favreau joked with his boss, half seriously, "I think you added a lot of good stuff to the draft, but I just think we need to do a lot of cutting."

Obama pleaded, in a reversal of roles, "But come on, I spent all of this time on it." Favreau held the line—"We need to cut it down." They both started with the foreign policy section; it had grown too long.

All day Monday, between campaign events, Obama and his scribe sat in his cabin editing the draft. Favreau delivered a revised version that night, but he didn't get the chance to go over Obama's edits with him until Tuesday night, after Senator Clinton had finished her speech. (Obama was with a group of supporters in Montana at a "Hillary watch party.")

That night, Obama and Favreau continued editing in Axelrod's hotel room. Obama thought it was getting there, but that it was still "missing a core theme—it needed a spine." That is when he added the "promise of America" idea to the speech. "He wanted his philosophy of government presented in a more central way," said Favreau. By this time it was midnight and Obama wanted another version back by the morning. So

Favreau went back to his hotel room, cracked open a Red Bull, and pulled his "only legitimate all-nighter of the campaign."

The speech was still unfinished, so Favreau avoided Obama the next morning as the campaign plane coasted into Denver. Favreau still needed more time. And instead of writing, he spent most of that last leg from Montana talking with that state's U.S. senator Jon Tester. Deeply afraid of flying, Favreau was doing anything to keep his mind off of the flight as the strong winds buffeted the plane.

When they landed in Denver, Favreau regrouped with his writing team for one last editing session before sending the speech to Obama. Hurwitz, Frankel, and Rhodes had all arrived in Denver earlier in the week. That night the group huddled with Axelrod in a conference room near the candidate's hotel room in the Westin, waiting for Obama and making last-minute tweaks.

At ten, Obama finally arrived. He had just left the convention center, where he had appeared on stage with Biden. At this point Favreau was not in good shape. Despite being exhausted, he mentally prepared himself for another all-nighter. This was game time. But when Obama saw his chief writer, he insisted that Favreau go to bed. As for the speech, he told the group, "I think we're close." It was the night before the big event and Obama was still editing what arguably would be the most important speech of his career.

At 8:00 a.m. on Thursday, Favreau, Axelrod, and Gibbs met with Obama in his suite to make their final line edits. Favreau was pushing for as many cuts as Obama would allow; the candidate wasn't so eager to shorten the draft. But Favreau was on a mission.

At one in the afternoon, Obama ordered a break and the group disbanded until rehearsal began with the TelePrompTer and the campaign speech coach, Michael Sheehan. Just as Obama was about to begin, there was a knock on the door. It was a waiter with a chicken Caesar salad. Axelrod apologized and said it was for him. Obama carried the silver tray over to his strategist and served it to him. Everyone laughed; the tension in the room dissipated.

The first run-through was going well, until Obama reached the section of the speech where Favreau had inserted a quote from Dr. Martin Luther King Jr. It was then that the gravity of the moment hit Obama.

Visibly choked up, he excused himself for a moment and went to the bathroom to collect his thoughts. He came back, apologized, and finished the speech. It was the first time Favreau had seen his boss visibly overwhelmed by the historic significance of his candidacy.

After a second run-through, it was five thirty: time to get changed and head to the motorcade that would take them from the Westin to Invesco Field. Obama called Favreau one last time in his hotel room with an appeal to restore a line on science that had landed on the cutting-room floor. "Can we put it back in?" Favreau replied, "It's already in the Tele-Prompter. Let's not do this, sir." The line stayed out.

Obama's speech was the main event of the week and it was clear that the campaign had pulled out all the stops.

First, there were grand introductions: speeches by former vice president and Nobel Prize–winner Al Gore; a video tribute to Martin Luther King Jr.; and music by Sheryl Crow and Stevie Wonder, who sang "Signed, Sealed, Delivered (I'm Yours)." There was also a biographical documentary of Obama by Davis Guggenheim, the Academy Award–winning director of *An Inconvenient Truth.*

Second, there was the staging itself—a grand neoclassical set, described by McCain's campaign as the "Barackopolis." The *New York Post* called the faux-marble columns, painted in off-white, the "Temple of Obama."[6] Of the set, Dan Balz and Haynes Johnson wrote: "Hundreds of crew members had been working around the clock. On the fifty-yard line they built a stage resembling a miniature Greek temple. . . . Two hundred spotlights would bathe the scene in a sea of soft light."[7] It was no surprise that it was mocked, but it certainly added to the moment.

Third, there were the fireworks, and the red, white, and blue confetti that greeted Obama and his family after he delivered his final line, "Thank you, God bless you, and God bless the United States of America."

With a $6 million budget, the Obama operation spared no expense. The circular stage was inspired by the set at Kennedy's 1960 convention, Peter Gage, a member of Obama's advance team, told the *New York Times.*[8] There were also cameras at every angle, including one above the field to offer a bird's-eye view. Obama's family and a group of swing voters sat on the stage in front of the candidate.

Months earlier, the campaign had provided Obama with meteorological data showing that it only rained on August 28 once every twenty years. The weather held out that night—it was dry and hot—and Obama delivered his forty-two-minute speech to a packed stadium; every one of the eighty thousand seats was filled. The crowds began to amass before noon, and soon the line to get in and catch a glimpse of the nominee stretched more than two miles. Inside, volunteers registered voters, telephoned undecided voters, and text-messaged their friends and neighbors to support the campaign. Obama's team never missed an opportunity to spread the word; they never lost sight of the grassroots approach that had helped get them there.

Obama certainly didn't mince his words that night. His message was clear: eight years of failed Republican rule was enough. The country couldn't afford another four years under John McCain. It was time to come together, look beyond traditional political divisions, and vote for change and the Obama agenda.

The candidate opened his speech with the obligatory nods to his primary opponents, but then quickly pivoted into an attack on George Bush. He artfully utilized Bush's policies—on the deficit, on housing, on health care, on the war in Iraq—as a way to tie McCain to the deeply unpopular president. "We meet at one of those defining moments—a moment when our nation is at war, our economy is in turmoil, and the American promise has been threatened once more. . . . Tonight, I say to the American people . . . enough! . . . The record's clear: John McCain has voted with George Bush ninety percent of the time. . . . I don't know about you, but I'm not ready to take a ten percent chance on change."

That was the beginning of his aggressive attack on McCain—attacks that many Democrats had been pining for in the early months of the general election campaign. Many wondered if Obama had it in him to criticize his opponent head on. Obama didn't hesitate. He dismantled McCain's policy platform item by item, and particularly his comments on the primary issue at the time, the economy. "The truth is, on issue after issue that would make a difference in your lives—on health care and education and the economy—Senator McCain has been anything but independent. He said that our economy has made 'great progress' under this president. . . . He said that we were just suffering from a 'mental recession,' and that we've become . . . 'a nation of whiners.'" He capped that with, "It's not because John McCain doesn't care. It's because John McCain doesn't get it."

Harking back to his Knox College speech and to a point he had first delivered at an event on Social Security reform in 2005, Obama drew the distinction between his philosophy on government and McCain's: "For over two decades, [McCain has] subscribed to that old, discredited Republican philosophy—give more and more to those with the most and hope that prosperity trickles down to everyone else. In Washington, they call this the 'ownership society,' but what it really means is—you're on your own. Out of work? Tough luck. No health care? The market will fix it. Born into poverty? Pull yourself up by your own bootstraps—even if you don't have boots. . . . We Democrats have a very different measure of what constitutes progress in this country."

To buttress the distinction, Obama referenced the Clinton administration and the 1990s: "We measure progress in the twenty-three million new jobs that were created when Bill Clinton was president." This was ironic, because throughout the primary season, Obama had minimized the accomplishments of the Clinton years. But that was then and this was now; he was the nominee now. It was time to unite the party against the Republicans.

Obama's governing philosophy included several pillars that together added up to what he called the "promise of America." Everything from education and clean water to the tax code and energy were part of that promise. On the economy, he said, "The market should reward drive and innovation . . . [but] businesses should live up to their responsibilities to create American jobs, look out for American workers, and play by the rules of the road."

Obama then developed the "promise of America" concept further, saying: "Ours is [a] promise that says government cannot solve all our problems, but what it should do is that which we cannot do for ourselves. . . . Our government should work for us, not against us. It should help us, not hurt us. It should ensure opportunity not just for those with the most money and influence, but for every American who's willing to work. That's the promise of America—the idea that we are responsible for ourselves, but that we also rise or fall as one nation; the fundamental belief that I am my brother's keeper; I am my sister's keeper."

As he had done often in the past, Obama stressed the concept of personal and collective responsibility. Cynics could argue that this was nothing more than an appeal to the political right and to moderates; Bill Clinton too had used such language throughout his presidency. Either way, Obama's language was consistent with his message, going all the way back to his presidential announcement, and it would play a central role in his Inaugural Address, where he would call for a new "era of responsibility." Foreshadowing that notion, he said in Denver, "We must also admit that programs alone can't replace parents, that government can't turn off the television and make a child do her homework, that fathers must take more responsibility for providing the love and guidance their children need."

Although these were not new ideas for Obama to be expressing—he had touched on them at the 2004 Democratic Convention, at Knox College, and in his presidential announcement—this was certainly his most expansive commentary so far on the role of government. If you listened carefully, there was no question that he and John McCain had diametrically opposing views of government's role.

Obama reinforced his philosophy by discussing aspects of his own background, including the influence of his mother and grandmother, who struggled to provide for him the opportunities he had: "In the face of that young student who sleeps just three hours before working the night shift, I think about my mom, who raised my sister and me on her own while she worked and earned her degree, who once turned to food stamps but was still able to send us to the best schools in the country with the help of student loans and scholarships."

Beyond his governing ideology, Obama used the address to delve into the specifics of his agenda and to contrast his policies with McCain's. This was where he really stated the case for his election. Obama argued for an army of new teachers and for early childhood education; he wanted affordable, accessible health care for all Americans; and he insisted on fiscal responsibility and a more effective and efficient government. McCain, on the other hand, was still "grasping at the ideas of the past." He was out of touch on America's energy policy, on the economy, and on the wars in Iraq and Afghanistan. On the issue of Afghanistan, Obama asserted, "John McCain likes to say that he'll follow bin Laden to the gates of hell—but he won't even go to the cave where he lives."

Despite his sharp attacks on his opponent, Obama craftily managed to pivot to another common theme that predated his candidacy for president: the concept of political unity, or, as he put it in his remarks that night, "our sense of higher purpose." He did this after spending at least half of his speech slicing up McCain.

Yet, it was this theme that had long attracted supporters from both sides of the aisle because, like Obama, they sought to "cast off the worn-out ideas and politics of the past"—a system that used "stale tactics to scare the voters" and made "big election{s} about small things." Instead, they believed, as he did, in "the promise of a democracy where we can find the strength and grace to bridge divides and unite in common effort."

Obama argued that there was a common road beyond the traditional divisions; one that was open to change, to "new leadership" and "a new politics for a new time." He then cited specific opportunities where we could put aside the old politics "where Washington doesn't work" and bridge the divides. "We may not agree on abortion, but surely we can agree on reducing the number of unwanted pregnancies in this country. . . . I know there are differences on same-sex marriage, but surely we can agree that our gay and lesbian brothers and sisters deserve to visit the person they love in the hospital."

By now, Obama had the crowd in the palm of his hand. He was more Baptist minister with a Sunday morning cadence than a traditional politician standing behind a podium. He finished telling his audience that he was "not the likeliest candidate for this office" but that the "greatest risk" they could take was "to try the same old politics with the same old players."

Then, in a manner so subtle you could have easily missed the reference, Obama concluded his speech with a quote from "a young preacher from Georgia" who, forty years ago to the day, "spoke of his dream" to thousands of civil rights marchers in Washington, D.C. "We cannot walk alone," the preacher cried in the shadows of the Lincoln Memorial in August 1963. "And as we walk, we must make the pledge that we shall always march ahead. We cannot turn back." Obama had referenced the same line in a speech to mark Martin Luther King Day in January 2008 at Ebenezer Baptist Church, the church where Dr. King began his ministry and his campaign for social justice.

It was a masterful use of historical coincidence. Everyone was expecting Obama to infuse his acceptance speech with references to King, but Favreau instead went for the understated, yet extremely effective, approach: he didn't even mention King by name.

As his remarks ended, Michelle Obama and their two daughters, Malia and Sasha, rushed out onto the stage, along with the Bidens. It was hard to argue that the speech didn't achieve its mission. Despite the risks, Obama presented his philosophy, offered his agenda, and dissected his Republican opponent. And the polls—the ultimate arbiter—gave Obama an immediate six-point bump in the horse race.

Journalists weren't shy in expressing their affection. The *New York Times* declared, "Obama Takes the Fight to McCain," noting, "Obama looked completely at ease and unintimidated by his task or the huge crowd that surrounded him."[9] Likewise, the *Washington Post* headlined its August 28 edition, "Obama, Accepting Nomination, Draws Sharp Contrast with McCain." Jonathan Weisman and Shailagh Murray wrote, "Thursday's festivities were extraordinary. Not since John F. Kennedy accepted his party's nomination at Los Angeles's Memorial Coliseum in 1960 has a presidential contender thrown such a party."

Network and cable newscasters weren't coy either. Tom Brokaw of NBC News called the speech "a wonderfully crafted political speech" and ranked it "near the top in terms of what he needed to do." Andrea Mitchell of the same network later added, "I think, [he] went a long way toward persuading rank-and-file Democrats that he will fight for them and fight for change. . . . This will not be another John Kerry election, where he could be swift-boated or attacked by Republican attacks that he can't defend or won't defend against."[10]

After the speech was over, Favreau and the team of speechwriters joined other staffers and supporters at an A-list party not far from the stadium. They had earned a night of rest and relaxation. Favreau was in the back corner speaking with some friends when Barack and Michelle Obama arrived and went onstage to make a few remarks. As the senator wound up his remarks, he glanced over to the writers and told the boisterous crowd, "I want everyone to know that I have the best group of speechwriters in the country. Ben, Sarah, Adam—there is no one better." He then added, "There's one more person I'd like to recognize. He has been with me from the very beginning and he deserves a lot of credit for tonight. I just want to thank Jon Favreau." Obama then walked over and gave him a big hug.

Favreau told us, "It was the nicest thing he's ever done. It was over and above, especially on his big night." Moments later, with credentials in hand to every party in town, Favreau fell asleep on a chair in the back of the room. His colleagues carried him off to bed.

Early the next morning, as Favreau was just waking up, John McCain announced Sarah Palin as his running mate.

REMARKS BY SENATOR BARACK OBAMA:
"THE AMERICAN PROMISE"

To Chairman Dean and my great friend Dick Durbin, and to all my fellow citizens of this great nation, with profound gratitude and great humility, I accept your nomination for the presidency of the United States.

Let me express my thanks to the historic slate of candidates who accompanied me on this journey, and especially the one who traveled the farthest—a champion for working Americans and an inspiration to my daughters and to yours—Hillary Rodham Clinton. To President Clinton, who last night made the case for change as only he can make it; to Ted Kennedy, who embodies the spirit of service; and to the next vice president of the United States, Joe Biden, I thank you. I am grateful to finish this journey with one of the finest statesmen of our time, a man at ease with everyone from world leaders to the conductors on the Amtrak train he still takes home every night.

To the love of my life, our next first lady, Michelle Obama, and to Sasha and Malia—I love you so much, and I'm so proud of all of you.

Four years ago, I stood before you and told you my story—of the brief union between a young man from Kenya and a young woman from Kansas who weren't well-off or well known, but shared a belief that in America, their son could achieve whatever he put his mind to.

It is that promise that has always set this country apart—that through hard work and sacrifice, each of us can pursue our individual dreams but still come together as one American family, to ensure that the next generation can pursue their dreams as well.

That's why I stand here tonight. Because for two hundred and thirty-two years, at each moment when that promise was in jeopardy, ordinary men and women—students and soldiers, farmers and teachers, nurses and janitors—found the courage to keep it alive.

We meet at one of those defining moments—a moment when our nation is at war, our economy is in turmoil, and the American promise has been threatened once more.

Tonight, more Americans are out of work and more are working harder for less. More of you have lost your homes and even more are watching your home values plummet. More of you have cars you can't afford to drive, credit-card bills you can't afford to pay, and tuition that's beyond your reach.

These challenges are not all of government's making. But the failure to respond is a direct result of a broken politics in Washington and the failed policies of George W. Bush.

America, we are better than these last eight years. We are a better country than this.

This country is more decent than one where a woman in Ohio, on the brink of retirement, finds herself one illness away from disaster after a lifetime of hard work.

This country is more generous than one where a man in Indiana has to pack up the equipment he's worked on for twenty years and watch it shipped off to China, and then chokes up as he explains how he felt like a failure when he went home to tell his family the news.

We are more compassionate than a government that lets veterans sleep on our streets and families slide into poverty; that sits on its hands while a major American city drowns before our eyes.

Tonight, I say to the American people, to Democrats and Republicans and independents across this great land—enough! This moment—this election—is our chance to keep, in the twenty-first century, the American promise alive. Because next week, in Minnesota, the same party that brought you two terms of George Bush and Dick Cheney will ask this country for a third. And we are here because we love this country too much to let the next four years look like the last eight. On November fourth, we must stand up and say: "Eight is enough."

Now let there be no doubt. The Republican nominee, John McCain, has worn the uniform of our country with bravery and distinction, and for that we owe him our gratitude and respect. And next week, we'll also hear about those occasions when he's broken with his party as evidence that he can deliver the change that we need.

But the record's clear: John McCain has voted with George Bush ninety percent of the time. Senator McCain likes to talk about judgment, but really, what does it say about your judgment when you think George Bush has been right more than ninety percent of the time? I don't know about you, but I'm not ready to take a ten percent chance on change.

The truth is, on issue after issue that would make a difference in your lives—on health care and education and the economy—Senator McCain has been anything but independent. He said that our economy has made "great progress" under this president. He said that the fundamentals of the economy are strong. And when one of his chief advisers—the man who wrote his economic plan—was talking about the anxiety Americans are feeling, he said that we were just suffering from a "mental recession," and that we've become, and I quote, "a nation of whiners." A nation of whiners? Tell that to the proud auto workers at a Michigan plant who, after they found out it was closing, kept showing up every day and working as hard as ever, because they knew there were people who counted on the brakes that they made. Tell that to the military families who shoulder their burdens silently as they watch their loved ones leave for their third or fourth or fifth tour of duty. These are not whiners. They work hard and give back and keep going without complaint. These are the Americans that I know.

Now, I don't believe that Senator McCain doesn't care what's going on in the lives of Americans. I just think he doesn't know. Why else would he define middle-class as someone making under five million dollars a year? How else could he propose hundreds of billions in tax breaks for big corporations and oil companies but not one penny of tax relief to more than one hundred million Americans? How else could he offer a health care plan that would actually tax people's benefits, or an education plan that would do nothing to help families pay for college, or a plan that would privatize Social Security and gamble your retirement?

It's not because John McCain doesn't care. It's because John McCain doesn't get it.

For over two decades, he's subscribed to that old, discredited Republican philosophy—give more and more to those with the most and hope that prosperity trickles down to everyone else. In Washington, they call this the "ownership society," but what it really means is—you're on your own. Out of work? Tough luck. No health care? The market will fix it. Born into poverty? Pull yourself up by your own bootstraps—even if you don't have boots. You're on your own.

Well, it's time for them to own their failure. It's time for us to change America.

You see, we Democrats have a very different measure of what constitutes progress in this country.

We measure progress by how many people can find a job that pays the mortgage; whether you can put a little extra money away at the end of each month so you can someday watch your child receive her college diploma. We measure progress in the twenty-three million new jobs that were created when Bill Clinton was president—when the average American family saw its income go up seventy-five hundred dollars instead of down two thousand dollars, like it has under George Bush.

We measure the strength of our economy not by the number of billionaires we have or the profits of the Fortune 500, but by whether someone with a good idea can take a risk and start a new business, or whether the waitress who lives on tips can take a day off to look after a sick kid without losing her job—an economy that honors the dignity of work.

The fundamentals we use to measure economic strength are whether we are living up to that fundamental promise that has made this country great—a promise that is the only reason I am standing here tonight.

Because in the faces of those young veterans who come back from Iraq and Afghanistan, I see my grandfather, who signed up after Pearl Harbor, marched in Patton's army, and was rewarded by a grateful nation with the chance to go to college on the G.I. Bill.

In the face of that young student who sleeps just three hours before working the night shift, I think about my mom, who raised my sister and me on her own while she worked and earned her degree, who once turned to food stamps but was still able to send us to the best schools in the country with the help of student loans and scholarships.

When I listen to another worker tell me that his factory has shut down,

I remember all those men and women on the South Side of Chicago who I stood by and fought for two decades ago after the local steel plant closed.

And when I hear a woman talk about the difficulties of starting her own business, I think about my grandmother, who worked her way up from the secretarial pool to middle management, despite years of being passed over for promotions because she was a woman. She's the one who taught me about hard work. She's the one who put off buying a new car or a new dress for herself so that I could have a better life. She poured everything she had into me. And although she can no longer travel, I know that she's watching tonight, and that tonight is her night as well.

I don't know what kind of lives John McCain thinks that celebrities lead, but this has been mine. These are my heroes. Theirs are the stories that shaped me. And it is on their behalf that I intend to win this election and keep our promise alive as president of the United States.

What is that promise?

It's a promise that says each of us has the freedom to make of our own lives what we will, but that we also have the obligation to treat each other with dignity and respect.

It's a promise that says the market should reward drive and innovation and generate growth, but that businesses should live up to their responsibilities to create American jobs, look out for American workers, and play by the rules of the road.

Ours is a promise that says government cannot solve all our problems, but what it should do is that which we cannot do for ourselves—protect us from harm and provide every child a decent education, keep our water clean and our toys safe, invest in new schools and new roads and new science and technology.

Our government should work for us, not against us. It should help us, not hurt us. It should ensure opportunity not just for those with the most money and influence, but for every American who's willing to work.

That's the promise of America—the idea that we are responsible for ourselves, but that we also rise or fall as one nation; the fundamental belief that I am my brother's keeper. I am my sister's keeper.

That's the promise we need to keep. That's the change we need right now. So let me spell out exactly what that change would mean if I am president.

Change means a tax code that doesn't reward the lobbyists who wrote it, but the American workers and small businesses who deserve it.

Unlike John McCain, I will stop giving tax breaks to corporations that ship jobs overseas, and I will start giving them to companies that create good jobs right here in America.

I will eliminate capital gains taxes for the small businesses and the start-ups that will create the high-wage, high-tech jobs of tomorrow.

I will cut taxes—cut taxes—for ninety-five percent of all working families. Because in an economy like this, the last thing we should do is raise taxes on the middle-class.

And for the sake of our economy, our security, and the future of our planet, I will set a clear goal as president: in ten years, we will finally end our dependence on oil from the Middle East.

Washington's been talking about our oil addiction for the last thirty years, and John McCain has been there for twenty-six of them. In that time, he's said no to higher fuel-efficiency standards for cars, no to investments in renewable energy, no to renewable fuels. And today, we import triple the amount of oil as the day that Senator McCain took office.

Now is the time to end this addiction, and to understand that drilling is a stop-gap measure, not a long-term solution. Not even close.

As president, I will tap our natural gas reserves, invest in clean coal technology, and find ways to safely harness nuclear power. I'll help our auto companies retool, so that the fuel-efficient cars of the future are built right here in America. I'll make it easier for the American people to afford these new cars. And I'll invest one hundred fifty billion dollars over the next decade in affordable, renewable sources of energy—wind power and solar power and the next generation of biofuels, an investment that will lead to new industries and five million new jobs that pay well and can't ever be outsourced.

America, now is not the time for small plans.

Now is the time to finally meet our moral obligation to provide every child a world-class education, because it will take nothing less to compete in the global economy. Michelle and I are only here tonight because we were given a chance at an education. And I will not settle for an America where some kids don't have that chance. I'll invest in early childhood education. I'll recruit an army of new teachers, and pay them higher salaries and give them more support. And in exchange, I'll ask for higher standards and more accountability. And we will keep our promise to every young American—if you commit to serving your community or your country, we will make sure you can afford a college education.

Now is the time to finally keep the promise of affordable, accessible health care for every single American. If you have health care, my plan will lower your premiums. If you don't, you'll be able to get the same kind of coverage that members of Congress give themselves. And as someone who watched my mother argue with insurance companies while she lay in bed dying of cancer, I will make certain those companies stop discriminating against those who are sick and need care the most.

Now is the time to help families with paid sick days and better family leave, because nobody in America should have to choose between keeping their jobs and caring for a sick child or ailing parent.

Now is the time to change our bankruptcy laws, so that your pensions are protected ahead of CEO bonuses, and the time to protect Social Security for future generations.

And now is the time to keep the promise of equal pay for an equal day's work, because I want my daughters to have exactly the same opportunities as your sons.

Now, many of these plans will cost money, which is why I've laid out how I'll pay for every dime—by closing corporate loopholes and tax havens that don't help America grow. But I will also go through the federal budget, line by line, eliminating programs that no longer work and making the ones we do need work better and cost less—because we cannot meet twenty-first-century challenges with a twentieth-century bureaucracy.

And Democrats, we must also admit that fulfilling America's promise will require more than just money. It will require a renewed sense of responsibility from each of us to recover what John F. Kennedy called our "intellectual and moral strength." Yes, government must lead on energy independence, but each of us must do our part to make our homes and businesses more efficient. Yes, we must provide more ladders to success for young men who fall into lives of crime and despair. But we must also admit that programs alone can't replace parents, that government can't turn off the television and make a child do her homework, that fathers must take more responsibility for providing the love and guidance their children need.

Individual responsibility and mutual responsibility—that's the essence of America's promise.

And just as we keep our keep our promise to the next generation here at home, so must we keep America's promise abroad. If John McCain wants to have a debate about who has the temperament, and judgment, to serve as the next commander in chief, that's a debate I'm ready to have.

For while Senator McCain was turning his sights to Iraq just days after 9/11, I stood up and opposed this war, knowing that it would distract us from the real threats we face. When John McCain said we could just "muddle through" in Afghanistan, I argued for more resources and more troops to finish the fight against the terrorists who actually attacked us on 9/11, and made clear that we must take out Osama bin Laden and his lieutenants if we have them in our sights. John McCain likes to say that he'll follow bin Laden to the gates of hell—but he won't even go to the cave where he lives.

And today, as my call for a time frame to remove our troops from Iraq has been echoed by the Iraqi government and even the Bush Administration, even after we learned that Iraq has a $79 billion surplus while we're wallowing in deficits, John McCain stands alone in his stubborn refusal to end a misguided war.

That's not the judgment we need. That won't keep America safe. We need a president who can face the threats of the future, not keep grasping at the ideas of the past.

You don't defeat a terrorist network that operates in eighty countries by occupying Iraq. You don't protect Israel and deter Iran just by talking tough in Washington. You can't truly stand up for Georgia when you've strained our oldest alliances. If John McCain wants to follow George Bush with more tough talk and bad strategy, that is his choice—but it is not the change we need.

We are the party of Roosevelt. We are the party of Kennedy. So don't tell me that Democrats won't defend this country. Don't tell me that Democrats won't keep us safe. The Bush-McCain foreign policy has squandered the legacy that generations of Americans—Democrats and Republicans—have built, and we are here to restore that legacy.

As commander in chief, I will never hesitate to defend this nation, but I will only send our troops into harm's way with a clear mission and a sacred commitment to give them the equipment they need in battle and the care and benefits they deserve when they come home.

I will end this war in Iraq responsibly, and finish the fight against al Qaeda and the Taliban in Afghanistan. I will rebuild our military to meet future conflicts. But I will also renew the tough, direct diplomacy that can prevent Iran from obtaining nuclear weapons and curb Russian aggression. I will build new partnerships to defeat the threats of the twenty-first century: terrorism and nuclear proliferation; poverty and genocide; climate change and disease. And I will restore our moral standing, so that America is once again that last, best hope for all who are called to the cause of freedom, who long for lives of peace, and who yearn for a better future.

These are the policies I will pursue. And in the weeks ahead, I look forward to debating them with John McCain.

But what I will not do is suggest that the senator takes his positions for political purposes. Because one of the things that we have to change in our politics is the idea that people cannot disagree without challenging each other's character and patriotism.

The times are too serious, the stakes are too high for this same partisan playbook. So let us agree that patriotism has no party. I love this country, and so do you, and so does John McCain. The men and women who serve in our battlefields may be Democrats and Republicans and independents, but they have fought together and bled together and some died together under the same proud flag. They have not served a red America or a blue America—they have served the United States of America.

So I've got news for you, John McCain. We all put our country first.

America, our work will not be easy. The challenges we face require tough choices, and Democrats as well as Republicans will need to cast off the worn-out ideas and politics of the past. For part of what has been lost these past eight years can't just be measured by lost wages or bigger trade deficits. What has also been lost is our sense of common purpose—our sense of higher purpose. And that's what we have to restore.

We may not agree on abortion, but surely we can agree on reducing the number of unwanted pregnancies in this country. The reality of gun ownership may be different for hunters in rural Ohio than for those plagued by gang-violence in Cleveland, but don't tell me we can't uphold the Second Amendment while keeping AK-47s out of the hands of criminals. I know there are differences on same-sex marriage, but surely we can agree that our gay and lesbian brothers and sisters deserve to visit the person they love in the hospital and to live lives free of discrimination. Passions fly on immigration, but I don't know anyone who benefits when a mother is separated from her infant child or an employer undercuts American wages by hiring illegal workers. This too is part of America's promise—the promise of a democracy where we can find the strength and grace to bridge divides and unite in common effort.

I know there are those who dismiss such beliefs as happy talk. They claim that our insistence on something larger, something firmer and more honest in our public life is just a Trojan horse for higher taxes and the abandonment of traditional values. And that's to be expected. Because if you don't have any fresh ideas, then you use stale tactics to scare the voters. If you don't have a record to run on, then you paint your opponent as someone people should run from.

You make a big election about small things.

And you know what—it's worked before. Because it feeds into the cynicism we all have about government. When Washington doesn't work, all its promises seem empty. If your hopes have been dashed again and again, then it's best to stop hoping, and settle for what you already know.

I get it. I realize that I am not the likeliest candidate for this office. I don't fit the typical pedigree, and I haven't spent my career in the halls of Washington.

But I stand before you tonight because all across America something is stirring. What the naysayers don't understand is that this election has never been about me. It's been about you.

For eighteen long months, you have stood up, one by one, and said enough to the politics of the past. You understand that in this election, the greatest risk we can take is to try the same old politics with the same old players and expect a different result. You have shown what history teaches us—that at defining moments like this one, the change we need doesn't come from Washington. Change comes to Washington. Change happens because the American people demand it—because they rise up and insist on new ideas and new leadership, a new politics for a new time.

America, this is one of those moments.

I believe that as hard as it will be, the change we need is coming.

Because I've seen it. Because I've lived it. I've seen it in Illinois, when we provided health care to more children and moved more families from welfare to work. I've seen it in Washington, when we worked across party lines to open up government and hold lobbyists more accountable, to give better care for our veterans and keep nuclear weapons out of terrorist hands.

And I've seen it in this campaign. In the young people who voted for the first time, and in those who got involved again after a very long time. In the Republicans who never thought they'd pick up a Democratic ballot, but did. I've seen it in the workers who would rather cut their hours back a day than see their friends lose their jobs, in the soldiers who re-enlist after losing a limb, in the good neighbors who take a stranger in when a hurricane strikes and the floodwaters rise.

This country of ours has more wealth than any nation, but that's not what makes us rich. We have the most powerful military on earth, but that's not what makes us strong. Our universities and our culture are the envy of the world, but that's not what keeps the world coming to our shores.

Instead, it is that American spirit—that American promise—that pushes us forward even when the path is uncertain, that binds us together in spite of our differences, that makes us fix our eye not on what is seen, but what is unseen, that better place around the bend.

That promise is our greatest inheritance. It's a promise I make to my daughters when I tuck them in at night, and a promise that you make to yours—a promise that has led immigrants to cross oceans and pioneers to travel west; a promise that led workers to picket lines, and women to reach for the ballot.

And it is that promise that forty-five years ago today brought Americans from every corner of this land to stand together on a Mall in Washington, before Lincoln's Memorial, and hear a young preacher from Georgia speak of his dream.

The men and women who gathered there could've heard many things. They could've heard words of anger and discord. They could've been told to succumb to the fear and frustration of so many dreams deferred.

But what the people heard instead—people of every creed and color, from every walk of life—is that in America, our destiny is inextricably linked. That together, our dreams can be one.

"We cannot walk alone," the preacher cried. "And as we walk, we must make the pledge that we shall always march ahead. We cannot turn back."

America, we cannot turn back. Not with so much work to be done. Not with so many children to educate, and so many veterans to care for. Not with an economy to fix and cities to rebuild and farms to save. Not with so many families to protect and so many lives to mend. America, we cannot turn back. We cannot walk alone. At this moment, in this election, we must pledge once more to march into the future. Let us keep that promise—that American promise—and in the words of Scripture hold firmly, without wavering, to the hope that we confess.

Thank you, God bless you, and God bless the United States.

ELECTION NIGHT VICTORY SPEECH

November 4, 2008 · Grant Park, Chicago, Illinois

It's been a long time coming, but tonight,
because of what we did on this day, in this election,
at this defining moment, change has come to America.

In many ways, Barack Obama ended his presidential campaign the same way it all began—surrounded by a cadre of friends, family, and supporters in the state in which he had first been elected to public office. His message that November evening in Chicago was surprisingly similar to the one he had delivered in Springfield twenty-four months earlier: "It's been a long time coming, but tonight, because of what we did on this day, in this election, at this defining moment, change has come to America."

Obama addressed the "enormity" of the challenges facing America, including "two wars, a planet in peril, [and] the worst financial crisis in a century." He also touched on unity and the need to reach beyond the "pettiness" and "partisanship" that has "poisoned our politics for so long." He quoted Lincoln, as he had done when he launched his primary campaign: "We are not enemies, but friends . . . though passion may have strained it must not break our bonds of affection."

Despite the many parallels, there were striking differences between the two historical moments. In February 2007, Obama was a little-known, untested, first-term senator from Illinois. Back then, he was the inexperienced long-shot candidate up against the experienced operatives of the Clinton organization. True, his friends and family were with him back in Springfield, but the crowd was only fifteen thousand strong, and the press corps was hardly expansive.

Fast-forward to November 2008, when Obama approached the huge wooden podium flanked by a row of American flags, bullet-proof glass, and a crowd nearly a quarter-million strong. He was no longer the green junior U.S. senator; he was now the president-elect. Beyond that, he had routed his opponent, John McCain, in both the Electoral College and the popular vote, to become the first African American president of the United States.

To many onlookers, including those in Chicago and those watching at home, this was an improbable moment. After all, Obama was born into a world where schools, boardrooms, and buses were segregated and most African Americans were denied the basic right to vote. Now, the black vote and millions of others, had catapulted him into the presidency. In 1968, following Dr. Martin Luther King's assassination, Grant Park was the site of mass protests. Yet some forty years later, from the same field, Obama declared victory. He acknowledged, "I think about . . . the times we were told that we can't and the people who pressed on" to help make this election possible. Those who were "there for the buses in Montgomery, the hoses in Birmingham, [and] a bridge in Selma." Those like the "preacher from Atlanta who told a people that 'We Shall Overcome.'" Those who believed in the "American creed: yes, we can."

It was one of the few times during the campaign that Obama acknowledged his race and its historical meaning in the election—that "this election had many firsts." As he put it, "If there is anyone out there who still doubts that America is a place where all things are possible . . . tonight is your answer." He added, paraphrasing Dr. King and an abolitionist Unitarian minister, the Reverend Theodore Parker, "It's the answer that led those who have been told for so long by so many to be cynical . . . to put their hands on the arc of history and bend it once more toward the hope of a better day."

The Obama campaign hadn't taken a thing for granted during the final days of the campaign. His top aides, including his campaign manager, David Plouffe, and his chief strategist, David Axelrod, had packed those last hours with around-the-clock campaign events, as if Obama had been running ten points behind. For them, "Yes, we can" meant winning 270 electoral votes to take them over the top. They got there—and then some.

The candidate started his final full day of the campaign at one thirty in the morning in Jacksonville, Florida. He landed in the Sunshine State after a day spent in the rain in Cleveland, where eighty thousand people had welcomed him to the stage. Bruce Springsteen opened the event singing "This Land Is Your Land" to a crowd that was there to catch a last glimpse of candidate Obama. In Columbus, Ohio, Obama greeted sixty thousand supporters, and later pushed on to an event at the University of Cincinnati football stadium.[1]

After getting in a quick workout, Obama and his traveling party hop-scotched to rallies in Florida, North Carolina, and Virginia—all states that Bush had captured in 2000 and 2004, but that the Obama campaign saw as being within its reach.[2] McCain had been bleeding in Florida since the summer; his crowds and fund-raising there were anemic. The Obama machine had smelled an opportunity and they pounced.

The rain was coming down hard in Charlotte when Obama arrived, but that hadn't stopped crowds from waiting outdoors for him patiently for hours. From there, the motorcade drove back to the tarmac and the campaign plane took off for Dulles Airport, in Virginia, for his next event. When Obama pulled into Manassas—the location of the famous Civil War Battle of Bull Run—the crowd erupted. Obama was ninety minutes late, but the nearly ninety thousand jubilant supporters filled just about every inch of the park. No Democrat had won Virginia since Johnson in 1964, but Plouffe believed that Obama could sway the growing exurban Loudon and Prince William counties necessary to turn the state blue.

By midnight, Obama's plane was off for the nearly final leg of this last day's journey—this time back to Chicago. It was a teary eyed trip for a staff that had taken off and landed in that plane hundreds of times. It was a particularly emotional day for Obama, too; he had learned twenty-four hours earlier that his grandmother, Madelyn Dunham, who had raised him, had finally succumbed to a long illness. Her death weighed heavily on his heart as he pulled himself through the final moments of his campaign.

In his final late-night stroll down the aisle of the plane, Obama shook hands with staff and members of the media, and "offered a final, parting comment: 'It will be fun to see how the story ends.'"[3] The next morning, Obama made a quick, last-minute campaign stop in red state Indiana and then returned home to Chicago for his Election Day ritual—a basketball game with friends and staffers.

The story ended better than anyone could have imagined. Plouffe re-alized his dream to expand the electoral map beyond the traditional Democratic states. By 2:00 p.m. Eastern time, the exit polls were already breaking his candidate's way. Obama achieved milestone after milestone, including victories in Iowa, New Hampshire, Pennsylvania, New Mexico, Ohio, Florida, and Pennsylvania. He won in traditionally Republican states such as Nevada, North Carolina, Virginia, Colorado, and Indiana. He kept Wisconsin and Michigan in the Democratic column, as well as Minnesota, where the Republican National Convention had been held that year.

Obama's coattails were long; he helped his party secure significant gains in Congress, putting Democrats in control of the Senate, House, and White House for the first time since 1995. Obama was the first Democrat since Jimmy Carter in 1976 to receive more than 50 percent of the popular vote.

His near sweep of every demographic was equally impressive. He gained significant ground with Hispanic voters, taking seven in ten Hispanic votes). In 2008, black voters made up 13 percent of the electorate, compared to 11 percent in 2004, and 96 percent of them voted for Obama. About 10 percent of the voters had cast a ballot for the first time.

With the exception of seniors, Obama performed better with Democrats among all groups, including Jews, Protestants, Catholics, and women. He won 40 percent of the white male vote.

Shortly after the polls closed in California, the major networks and the Associated Press called the race for Obama. His wins in California and Washington State had put him over the top.

When CNN flashed the news over giant video screens in Grant Park, the crowd erupted in cheers. A television camera caught a glimpse of Oprah Winfrey and Jesse Jackson; both had tears running down their cheeks. Within minutes, at around eleven, Obama received congratulatory calls from Senator McCain and President George W. Bush. In the *New York Times,* Adam Nagourney wrote, "People rolled spontaneously into the streets to celebrate what many described as . . . a new era in a country where just 143 years ago, Mr. Obama, a black man, could have been owned as a slave." He called Obama a "phenomenon" and referred to his election as "a national catharsis."[4]

Obama's acceptance speech was a stem-winder. The Obama writers had outdone themselves—and they'd done it as a team. Favreau penned the first half, and the entire group, including Adam Frankel, Sarah Hurwitz, and Ben Rhodes, wrote the remainder together.

It was a sober statement. Given the grave economic crisis, Obama did not want pageantry and bombast. He didn't want to spend these sacred minutes crowing. So, despite the evening's $2 million price tag, there were no fireworks, as some had hoped for, and no recount of the landslide. Instead, Obama framed the moment and discussed its significance. He reached out to those who hadn't voted for him—and let them know that he would be their president, too. Obama knew that would be the key to his success as commander in chief; he was now the president of all Americans.

Obama declared, "It's been a long time coming, but . . . change has come to America"—an allusion to the Sam Cooke song "A Change Is Gonna Come." He spoke about Ann Nixon Cooper, a 106-year-old African American woman, who voted that day in Atlanta, as representative of that change. In her lifetime, Cooper had seen Pearl Harbor and Selma, but she never thought she'd see a black president. Just minutes before Obama declared victory, Favreau hid underneath his desk to find a quiet spot and called Cooper. She couldn't believe her ears when he told her that the president-elect would talk about her experience in his victory speech. Change had come.

Obama also spoke of the travails ahead, acknowledging the onerous challenges he was inheriting. Too many Americans had lost their jobs, their savings, and their homes; millions more were without health care. Brave soldiers were risking their lives in Iraq and Afghanistan. Obama knew that "our union [could] be perfected." But it wouldn't be easy. Echoing Martin Luther King's "I've Been to the Mountaintop" speech, Obama insisted, "The road ahead will be long, our climb will be steep. We may not get there in one year, or even in one term—but America, I have never been more hopeful than I am tonight that we will get there."

REMARKS BY PRESIDENT-ELECT BARACK OBAMA:
ELECTION NIGHT VICTORY SPEECH

If there is anyone out there who still doubts that America is a place where all things are possible; who still wonders if the dream of our founders is alive in our time; who still questions the power of our democracy, tonight is your answer.

It's the answer told by lines that stretched around schools and churches in numbers this nation has never seen; by people who waited three hours and four hours, many for the very first time in their lives, because they believed that this time must be different; that their voice could be that difference.

It's the answer spoken by young and old, rich and poor, Democrat and Republican, black, white, Latino, Asian, Native American, gay, straight, disabled, and not disabled—Americans who sent a message to the world that we have never been a collection of red states and blue states. We are, and always will be, the United States of America.

It's the answer that led those who have been told for so long by so many to be cynical, and fearful, and doubtful of what we can achieve to put their hands on the arc of history and bend it once more toward the hope of a better day.

It's been a long time coming, but tonight, because of what we did on this day, in this election, at this defining moment, change has come to America.

I just received a very gracious call from Senator McCain. He fought long and hard in this campaign, and he's fought even longer and harder for the country he loves. He has endured sacrifices for America that most of us cannot begin to imagine, and we are better off for the service rendered by this brave and selfless leader. I congratulate him and Governor Palin for all they have achieved, and I look forward to working with them to renew this nation's promise in the months ahead.

I want to thank my partner in this journey, a man who campaigned from his heart and spoke for the men and women he grew up with on the streets of Scranton and rode with on that train home to Delaware, the vice president–elect of the United States, Joe Biden.

I would not be standing here tonight without the unyielding support of my best friend for the last sixteen years, the rock of our family and the love of my life, our nation's next first lady, Michelle Obama. Sasha and Malia, I love you both so much, and you have earned the new puppy that's coming with us to the White House. And while she's no longer with us, I know my grandmother is watching, along with the family that made me who I am. I miss them tonight, and know that my debt to them is beyond measure.

To my campaign manager, David Plouffe, my chief strategist, David Axelrod, and the best campaign team ever assembled in the history of politics—you made this happen, and I am forever grateful for what you've sacrificed to get it done.

But above all, I will never forget who this victory truly belongs to—it belongs to you.

I was never the likeliest candidate for this office. We didn't start with much money or many endorsements. Our campaign was not hatched in the halls of Washington—it began in the backyards of Des Moines and the living rooms of Concord and the front porches of Charleston.

It was built by working men and women who dug into what little savings they had to give five dollars and ten dollars and twenty dollars to this cause. It grew strength from the young people who rejected the myth of their generation's apathy; who left their homes and their families for jobs that offered little pay and less sleep; from the not-so-young people who braved the bitter cold and scorching heat to knock on the doors of perfect strangers; from the millions of Americans who volunteered, and organized, and proved that more than two centuries later, a government of the people, by the people and for the people has not perished from this Earth. This is your victory.

I know you didn't do this just to win an election and I know you didn't do it for me. You did it because you understand the enormity of the task that lies ahead. For even as we celebrate tonight, we know the challenges that tomorrow will bring are the greatest of our lifetime—two wars, a planet in peril, the worst financial crisis in a century. Even as we stand here tonight, we know there are brave Americans waking up in the deserts of Iraq and the mountains of Afghanistan to risk their lives for us. There are mothers and fathers who will lie awake after their children fall asleep and wonder how they'll make the mortgage, or pay their doctor's bills, or save enough for college. There is new energy to harness and new jobs to be created; new schools to build and threats to meet and alliances to repair.

The road ahead will be long. Our climb will be steep. We may not get there in one year or even one term, but America—I have never been more hopeful than I am tonight that we will get there. I promise you—we as a people will get there.

There will be setbacks and false starts. There are many who won't agree with every decision or policy I make as president, and we know that government can't solve every problem. But I will always be honest with you about the challenges we face. I will listen to you, especially when we disagree. And above all, I will ask you join in the work of remaking this nation the only way it's been done in America for two hundred and twenty-one years—block by block, brick by brick, calloused hand by calloused hand.

What began twenty-one months ago in the depths of winter must not end on this autumn night. This victory alone is not the change we seek—it is only the chance for us to make that change. And that cannot happen if we go back to the way things were. It cannot happen without you.

So let us summon a new spirit of patriotism, of service and responsibility, where each of us resolves to pitch in and work harder and look after not only ourselves, but each other. Let us remember that if this financial crisis taught us anything, it's that we cannot have a thriving Wall Street while Main Street suffers—in this country, we rise or fall as one nation, as one people.

Let us resist the temptation to fall back on the same partisanship and pettiness and immaturity that has poisoned our politics for so long. Let us remember that it was a man from this state who first carried the banner of the Republican Party to the White House—a party founded on the values of self-reliance, individual liberty, and national unity. Those are values we all share, and while the Democratic Party has won a great victory tonight, we do so with a measure of humility and determination to heal the divides that have held back our progress. As Lincoln said to a nation far more divided than ours, "We are not enemies, but friends . . . though passion may have strained it must not break our bonds of affection." And to those Americans whose support I have yet to earn—I may not have won your vote, but I hear your voices, I need your help, and I will be your president too.

And to all those watching tonight from beyond our shores, from parliaments and palaces to those who are huddled around radios in the forgotten corners of our world—our stories are singular, but our destiny is shared, and a new dawn of American leadership is at hand. To those who would tear this world down—we will defeat you. To those who seek peace and security—we support you. And to all those who have wondered if America's beacon still burns as bright—tonight we proved once more that the true strength of our nation comes not from the might of our arms or the scale of our wealth, but from the enduring power of our ideals: democracy, liberty, opportunity, and unyielding hope.

For that is the true genius of America—that America can change. Our union can be perfected. And what we have already achieved gives us hope for what we can and must achieve tomorrow.

This election had many firsts and many stories that will be told for generations. But one that's on my mind tonight is about a woman who cast her ballot in Atlanta. She's a lot like the millions of others who stood in line to make their voice heard in this election except for one thing—Ann Nixon Cooper is one hundred six years old.

She was born just a generation past slavery, a time when there were no cars on the road or planes in the sky, when someone like her couldn't vote for two reasons—because she was a woman and because of the color of her skin.

And tonight, I think about all that she's seen throughout her century in America—the heartache and the hope; the struggle and the progress; the times we were told that we can't, and the people who pressed on with that American creed: Yes, we can.

At a time when women's voices were silenced and their hopes dismissed, she lived to see them stand up and speak out and reach for the ballot. Yes, we can.

When there was despair in the dust bowl and depression across the land, she saw a nation conquer fear itself with a New Deal, new jobs, and a new sense of common purpose. Yes, we can.

When the bombs fell on our harbor and tyranny threatened the world, she was there to witness a generation rise to greatness and a democracy was saved. Yes, we can.

She was there for the buses in Montgomery, the hoses in Birmingham, a bridge in Selma, and a preacher from Atlanta who told a people that "We Shall Overcome." Yes, we can.

A man touched down on the moon, a wall came down in Berlin, a world was connected by our own science and imagination. And this year, in this election, she touched her finger to a screen, and cast her vote, because after one hundred six years in America, through the best of times and the darkest of hours, she knows how America can change. Yes, we can.

America, we have come so far. We have seen so much. But there is so much more to do. So tonight, let us ask ourselves—if our children should live to see the next century; if my daughters should be so lucky to live as long as Ann Nixon Cooper, what change will they see? What progress will we have made?

This is our chance to answer that call. This is our moment. This is our time—to put our people back to work and open doors of opportunity for our kids; to restore prosperity and promote the cause of peace; to reclaim the American Dream and reaffirm that fundamental truth—that out of many, we are one; that while we breathe, we hope, and where we are met with cynicism, and doubt, and those who tell us that we can't, we will respond with that timeless creed that sums up the spirit of a people:

Yes, we can. Thank you, God bless you, and may God bless the United States of America.

ACKNOWLEDGMENTS

This book wouldn't have been possible without the cooperation and insights from President Obama's clan of speechwriters, especially their chief, Jon Favreau, and senior writers Adam Frankel and Sarah Hurwitz. Their willingness to share in the history they lived will benefit generations to come. They were unflaggingly humble throughout and abundantly generous with their limited time.

We would also like to thank the authors and journalists whose shoulders we stand on—those whose hard work provided endless insights. David Mendell, Dan Balz, Haynes Johnson, Jeff Zeleny, Mark Barabak, Rob Schlesinger, and a host of other writers' accounts added important facts and details to our narrative. We'd also like to thank those who offered their invaluable feedback, advice, and assistance on the book, including Don Baer, Jason Bordoff, Martha Minow, Jennifer Palmieri, Mark Penn, John Podesta, Steve Ricchetti, Jamie Rubin, Jeff Shesol, Marcy Simon, Bradley Tusk, and Michael Waldman.

We would also like to thank Ted Sorensen, not only for penning a thoughtful foreword to this book, but also for the inspiration he has given many of us to take up the craft of speechwriting—including many of the Obama speechwriters.

We wouldn't have a book if it weren't for the sustained commitment and enthusiasm of our editor, Gayatri Patnaik, and the entire staff at the Beacon Press, including Helene Atwan, Tom Hallock, and Pamela Mac-Coll. Gayatri has been a first-rate counselor from the beginning, and the book is stronger because of her additions and inquisitive nature. Obama's phrase "shining beacon on a hill" is apropos; Beacon Press is a special place for authors who are committed to building a stronger community.

Finally, we have both relied tremendously on our chief researcher, Kevin Almasy. Kevin is one of a kind. With quiet power, he toiled away at all hours of the night to meet our tight deadlines, without even a whisper of complaint. He not only found the best nuggets and offered smart edits, but also offered a keen perspective based on the volumes of material he read on President Obama. We can't thank him enough. We also relied on excellent assistance from Shelley Venus, Molly Masenga, and two bright University of Pennsylvania students, Danny Urgelles and Sarah Cockrum.

Even with all that help, writing any book puts a tremendous strain on the people you love the most. For Josh, Marla and their eight-month-old daughter, Ellie, were extremely patient, tolerating many weekends researching and writing at Bruegger's and scores of 2:00 a.m. nights spent typing away at the kitchen counter. Marla also played her usual role as consigliere, offering the best suggestions and professional-level edits, not to mention constant love and support. His parents, Donald, Gwenn, and Harry, in-laws Gabe and Nadine, sister Emily, and brother- and sister-in-law Brad and Harper were a source of love and encouragement. For Mary, Mindy handled this process with her usual equanimity, offering the best advice.

More than anything, this was a wonderful opportunity for the two of us to work and write together, to debate the issues, and enjoy the rhetoric of a remarkable orator.

NOTES

Authors' note: We were fortunate enough to have access to members of candidate Obama's speechwriting team. They are the source for much of the anecdotes and color in our analysis. Between the period from October 1 to October 29, 2009, we interviewed Senator Obama's—and now President Obama's—chief speechwriter, Jon Favreau, on several occasions, usually at the Starbucks a few hundred yards from the White House. We also spoke with Sarah Hurwitz and Adam Frankel, two of the campaign's and now White House speechwriters. They were all incredibly helpful and generous in their time, and they were never once anything but completely complimentary of the man they clearly respect unflaggingly. Quotes from these speechwriters are not attributed below.

INTRODUCTION

1. Peter Baker, "The President Whose Words Once Soared," *New York Times,* November 7, 2009.
2. Ronald C. White Jr., *Lincoln's Greatest Speech: The Second Inaugural* (New York: Simon & Schuster, 2002), p. 49.
3. Jeffrey K. Tulis, *The Rhetorical Presidency* (Princeton, NJ: Princeton University Press, 1987), p. 80.
4. Carol Gelderman, *All the Presidents' Words: The Bully Pulpit and the Creation of the Virtual Presidency* (New York: Walker, 1997), p. 4.
5. Ibid., p. 2.
6. Ibid., p. 5.
7. Robert Alexander Kraig, *Woodrow Wilson and the Lost World of the Oratorical Statesman* (College Station: Texas A&M University Press, 2004), p. 88.
8. Woodrow Wilson, *Constitutional Government in the United States* (Brookline, MA: Transaction Publishers, 2001; orig. 1917), pp. 70–71.
9. Michael Waldman, *POTUS Speaks: Finding the Words That Defined the Clinton Presidency* (New York: Simon & Schuster, 2000), p. 16. Obama statistic: Mark Knoller, "Obama's First Year: By the Numbers," CBS News, January 20, 2010.

10. Jon Ward, "Obama Emphasis on Words over Images Questioned by Former White House Communications Gurus," Daily Caller.com, March 8, 2010.

11. Transcript of Franklin Delano Roosevelt's Acceptance Speech, 1932 Democratic National Convention, July 2, 1932, Chicago.

12. Transcript of Lyndon Baines Johnson, "Great Society" speech, remarks at the University of Michigan, May 22, 1964, Ann Arbor, Michigan.

13. In Charles Pierce, "Just Words," *Boston Globe Sunday Magazine,* January 11, 2009.

14. Michael Eric Dyson, "His Way with Words Begins at the Pulpit," *Washington Post,* January 18, 2009.

15. Barack Obama, "Help Needed to Change Springfield," *Hyde Park Herald,* February 19, 1997.

16. Karen Shields, "Rush Re-elected; Obama Narrowly Carries Hyde Park," *Hyde Park Herald,* March 29, 2000.

17. Janny Scott, "In 2000, a Streetwise Veteran Schooled a Bold Young Obama," *New York Times,* September 9, 2007.

18. For Berenson, Hines, and Perrelli quotes: Michael Levenson and Jonathan Saltzman, "At Harvard Law, A Unifying Voice," *Boston Globe,* January 28, 2007.

19. Michael Heilemann, "When They Were Young," *New York,* October 14, 2007.

20. Mark Knoller, "Obama's First Year: By the Numbers," CBS News, January 20, 2010.

21. Richard Wolffe, "The Speech Lit a Fire. Meet Obama's Editor," *Newsweek,* January 6, 2008.

22. Jay Newton-Small, "How Obama Writes His Speeches," *Time,* August 28, 2008.

23. Gelderman, p. 13.

24. Wolffe, "The Speech Lit a Fire."

25. Larissa MacFarquhar, "The Conciliator," *New Yorker,* May 7, 2007.

26. Shomon and Mikva quotes from Scott, "In 2000, a Streetwise Veteran."

27. Levenson and Saltzman, "At Harvard Law."

28. Scott, "In 2000, a Streetwise Veteran."

29. Garrett M. Graff, "The Legend of Barack Obama," *Washingtonian,* November 2006.

30. MacFarquhar, "The Conciliator."

CHAPTER 1

1. Garrett M. Graff, "The Legend of Barack Obama," *Washingtonian,* November 2006.

2. Bill Glauber, "War Protesters Gentler, but Passion Still Burns," *Chicago Tribune,* February 3, 2002.

3. "Authorization for Use of Military Force against Iraq Resolution of 2002,"

Public Law 107–243, 107th Congress, Joint Resolution: To authorize the use of United States Armed Forces against Iraq, October 16, 2002 [H.J. Res. 114], http://frwebgate.access.gpo.gov/cgi-bin/getdoc.cgi?dbname =107_cong_public_laws&docid=f:publ243.107.

4. Patrick Healy, "Clinton Camp Challenges Obama on Iraq," *New York Times,* March 22, 2007.

5. Interview with Melissa Block, National Public Radio, July 24, 2004.

6. David Remnick, "Testing the Waters," *New Yorker* interview, November 6, 2006.

7. David Mendell, *Obama: From Promise to Power* (New York: HarperCollins/ Amistad, 2007), p. 174.

8. Ibid., p. 173.

9. Ibid., p. 174.

10. "Obama Still Stumps on 2002 Anti-War Declaration," National Public Radio, March 25, 2008.

11. Mendell, *Obama: From Promise to Power,* p. 177.

CHAPTER 2

1. Barack Obama, *The Audacity of Hope* (New York: Random House/Vintage, 2006), p. 418.

2. Dayo Olopade, "The Inside Story of How Obama Was Chosen for His Big Night at the 2004 Convention," *New Republic,* August 25, 2008.

3. Ibid.

4. David Bernstein, "The Speech," *Chicago,* June 2007.

5. Ibid.

6. Ibid.

7. David Mendell, *Obama: From Promise to Power* (New York: HarperCollins/ Amistad, 2007), p. 280.

8. Bernstein, "The Speech."

9. Larissa MacFarquhar, "The Conciliator," *New Yorker,* May 7, 2007.

10. Bernstein, "The Speech."

11. Ibid.

CHAPTER 3

1. David Mendell, *Obama: From Promise to Power* (New York: HarperCollins/ Amistad, 2007), p. 143.

2. Liza Mundy, "A Series of Fortunate Events," *Washington Post Magazine,* August 12, 2007.

3. Scott Helman, "Early Defeat Launched a Rapid Political Climb," *Boston Globe,* October 12, 2007.

4. Mendell, *Obama: From Promise to Power,* p. 141.

5. Ibid., p. 143.

6. Garrett M. Graff, "The Legend of Barack Obama," *Washingtonian,* November 2006.

7. Todd Spivak, "Bobby Rush Explains Endorsement of Hull," *Hyde Park Herald,* August 27, 2003.

8. Ted Kleine, "Is Bobby Rush in Trouble? Two Formidable Opponents in the Race for His Congressional Seat Are Banking on It," *Chicago Reader,* March 17, 2000.

9. Jim Geraghy, "Hothouse Flower: The Chicago Press Mostly Overlooked Obama's Worst Scandals, Instead Griping about the Trivial," *National Review* online, June 19, 2008.

10. Mendell, *Obama: From Promise to Power,* p. 213.

11. David Mendell, "Hull's Ex-Wife Called Him Violent Man in Divorce File," *Chicago Tribune,* February 28, 2004.

12. Mendell, *Obama: From Promise to Power,* p. 229.

13. Ibid., p. 263.

14. Graff, "The Legend of Barack Obama."

15. Liza Mundy, "A Series of Fortunate Events," *Washington Post,* August 12, 2007.

16. Jeremy Adragna, "Obama Hands Keyes Record-Breaking Defeat," *Hyde Park Herald,* November 10, 2004.

CHAPTER 4

1. Dan Balz and Haynes Johnson, *The Battle for America 2008: The Story of an Extraordinary Election* (New York: Penguin, 2008), p. 167.

2. Ibid., p. 168.

3. John Lewis and Michael D'Orso, *Walking with the Wind: A Memoir of the Movement* (Philadelphia: Harvest Books, 1999).

4. Balz and Johnson, *The Battle for America 2008,* p. 168.

5. Ibid.

6. Bob Kemper, "Lewis Says He's Supporting Obama," *Atlanta Journal Constitution,* February 27, 2008.

7. Jeff Zeleny, "John Lewis Changes Endorsement to Obama," *New York Times,* February 28, 2008.

8. Balz and Johnson, *The Battle for America 2008,* p. 168.

9. David Remnick, "The President's Hero," *New Yorker,* February 2, 2009.

CHAPTER 5

1. The Lincoln at Knox story can be found at http://www.knox.edu/oldmain .xml.

2. Kevin Sampier, "Providing Inspiration—Obama Urges Graduates to Accept Challenges of Future," *Peoria Journal Star,* June 5, 2005.

3. Kenneth Baer, "Hope is on the Way?" Talking Points Memo.com, June 10, 2005.

CHAPTER 6

1. Barack Obama, *The Audacity of Hope* (New York: Vintage Books (division of Random House, 2006), p. 238.
2. Michelle Goldberg, "What's the Matter with Barack Obama?" Huffington Post.com, June 30, 2006.
3. Obama, *Audacity of Hope,* p. 242.
4. Ibid., p. 247.
5. Ibid., p. 248.
6. Ibid., p. 251.
7. Ibid., p. 251.
8. Ibid., p. 251.
9. Ibid., p. 251.
10. Ibid., p. 252.
11. Ibid., pp. 257–58.
12. "Obama: Democrats Must Court Evangelicals," *Washington Post,* June 28, 2006.
13. Garrett M. Graff, "The Legend of Barack Obama," *Washingtonian,* November 2006.
14. "Obama Works to Win Evangelicals Back for Democrats," National Public Radio interview, July 14, 2006.
15. Andrew Sullivan, "Goodbye to All That: Why Obama Matters," *Atlantic,* December 2007.

CHAPTER 7

1. David Mendell, *Obama: From Promise to Power* (New York: Harper Collins/ Amistad, 2007), p. 326.
2. Ibid., p. 305.
3. Ibid., p. 322.
4. Ibid., pp. 324–25.
5. Ibid., p. 355.
6. Jeffrey Gettleman, "Obama Gets a Warm Welcome in Kenya," *New York Times,* August 26, 2006.
7. *Daily Nation* (Kenya), August 31, 2006.
8. Mendell, *Obama: From Promise to Power,* pp. 371, 370.
9. Gettleman, "Obama Gets a Warm Welcome in Kenya."

CHAPTER 8

1. Larissa MacFarquhar, "The Conciliator," *New Yorker,* May 2, 2007.
2. "Obama Declares His Candidacy—Invoking Lincoln, Illinois Senator Opens White House Bid," ABC News, February 10, 2007.

3. Ibid.

4. Jimmy Carter presidential announcement speech, National Press Club, Washington, D.C., December 12, 1974, www.4president.org/speeches/carter1976announcement.htm.

5. John Kerry presidential announcement speech, Patriot's Point, South Carolina, September 2, 2003, www.4president.org/speeches/johnkerry2004 announcement.htm.

6. Hillary Clinton presidential announcement speech, online at HillaryClinton .com, January 21, 2007, www.4president.org/speeches/2008/hillaryclinton 2008announcement.htm.

7. Bill Clinton presidential announcement speech, Old State House, Little Rock, Arkansas, October 3, 1991, www.4president.org/speeches/1992/bill clinton1992announcement.htm.

8. Rick Pearson and Ray Long, "Obama's Kickoff Is Steeped in Symbolism," *Chicago Tribune,* February 10, 2007.

CHAPTER 9

1. Chris Cillizza, "Does Obama Need to Win Iowa?" The Fix, WashingtonPost .com, October 2, 2007.

2. Dan Balz and Haynes Johnson, *The Battle for America 2008: The Story of an Extraordinary Election* (New York: Penguin, 2008), p. 117.

3. Ibid., p. 113.

4. John Dickerson, "The Philadelphia Pile-On: Hillary Clinton Debates Her Opponents and Herself," Slate.com, October 31, 2007.

5. Ruth Marcus, "Turning Up the Heat in Iowa," *Washington Post,* November 12, 2007.

6. Hillary Clinton remarks at the Iowa Jefferson-Jackson dinner, Des Moines, Iowa, American Presidency Project, November 10, 2007, www.presidency .ucsb.edu/ws/index.php?pid=77076.

7. Roger Simon, "Jefferson-Jackson a Warm-up for Iowa," Politico.com, November 11, 2007.

8. David Yepsen, "Obama's Superb Speech Could Catapult His Bid," *Des Moines Register,* November 12, 2007.

9. *Anderson Cooper 360,* CNN, November 12, 2007, http://transcripts.cnn.com/TRANSCRIPTS/0711/12/acd.01.html.

10. Walter Shapiro, "Obama Goes for the Capillaries," Salon.com, November 12, 2007.

11. Thomas Beaumont, "New Iowa Poll: Obama Widens Lead Over Clinton," *Des Moines Register,* December 31, 2007.

CHAPTER 10

1. Adam Nagourney, "Clinton Staff Memo Urged Skipping Iowa," *New York Times,* May 23, 2007.
2. Jeff Zeleny, "After Iowa, Challenges Lie Ahead for Obama," *New York Times,* January 4, 2008.
3. Dan Balz and Haynes Johnson, *The Battle for America 2008: The Story of an Extraordinary Election* (New York: Penguin, 2008), p. 290.
4. Thomas Beaumont, "New Iowa Poll: Obama Widens Lead Over Clinton," *Des Moines Register,* December 31, 2007.

CHAPTER 11

1. Michael Luo, "Small Online Contributions Add Up to Huge Fund-Raising Edge for Obama," *New York Times,* February 20, 2008.
2. Adam Nagourney, "Obama Takes Iowa in a Big Turnout as Clinton Falters," *New York Times,* January 4, 2008.
3. Dan Balz and Haynes Johnson, *The Battle for America 2008: The Story of an Extraordinary Election* (New York: Penguin, 2008), pp. 129–30.
4. Transcript: Democratic Debate in New Hampshire, published January 5, 2008, New York Times.com, http://www.nytimes.com/2008/01/05/us/politics/05text-ddebate.html?pagewanted=all.
5. Balz and Johnson, *The Battle for America 2008,* p. 137.
6. Ibid., p. 155. Also based on Gottheimer's insight.
7. Patrick Healy, "Clinton Tears Up," New York Times.com, The Caucus, January 7, 2008.
8. Balz and Johnson, *The Battle for America 2008,* pp. 139–40.
9. Ibid., p. 140.
10. Ibid., p. 141.
11. Ibid., p. 141.
12. Maria L. La Ganga, "Obama Has New Rallying Cry," *Los Angeles Times,* January 9, 2008.
13. E. J. Dionne, "The Last 'Yes, We Can' Candidate," *Washington Post,* February 29, 2008.
14. Mark Warren, "What Obama's 27-Year-Old Speechwriter Learned from George W. Bush," *Esquire,* December 3, 2008.

CHAPTER 12

1. Dan Balz and Haynes Johnson, *The Battle for America 2008: The Story of an Extraordinary Election* (New York: Penguin, 2008), p. 155.
2. Bob Moser, "South Carolina: Inside the 'Black Primary,'" *Nation,* December 20, 2007.
3. Ibid.
4. Ibid.

5. Balz and Johnson, *The Battle for America 2008,* p. 155

6. Moser, "South Carolina: Inside the 'Black Primary.'"

7. Balz and Johnson, *The Battle for America 2008,* p. 157.

8. Patrick Healy, "In S. Carolina, It's Obama vs. Clinton. That's Bill Clinton," *New York Times,* January 22, 2008.

9. Balz and Johnson, *The Battle for America 2008,* p. 164.

10. Garance Franke-Ruta, "Clinton Supporter Apologizes to Obama," *Washington Post,* January 17, 2008.

11. Katharine Q. Seelye, "BET Founder Slams Obama in South Carolina," *New York Times,* January 13, 2008, http://thecaucus.blogs.nytimes.com/2008/01/13/bet-chief-raps-obama-in-sc/.

12. Domenico Montanaro, "Clyburn on Clinton, Obama," MSNBC First Read, January 26, 2008, http://firstread.msnbc.msn.com/archive/2008/01/26/611355.aspx.

13. Obama interview with editorial board of the Reno (Nevada) *Gazette-Journal,* January 14, 2008.

14. Mike Memoli and Mark Murray, "Bill Also Hits Obama on GOP Ideas," First Read blog, MSNBC.com, January 18, 2008, http://firstread.msnbc.msn.com/archive/2008/01/18/589163.aspx.

CHAPTER 13

1. Patrick Healy, "Support Divided, Top Democrats Trade Victories," *New York Times,* February 6, 2008.

2. Dan Balz and Haynes Johnson, *The Battle for America 2008: The Story of an Extraordinary Election* (New York: Penguin, 2008), pp. 182 83.

3. Ibid., p. 186.

4. Ibid., p. 189.

5. Dana Milbank, "For Clinton, A Lively Dead Heat," *Washington Post,* February 6, 2008.

6. Roger Cohen, "Who Won Super Tuesday?" *New York Times,* February 6, 2008.

7. Balz and Johnson, *The Battle for America 2008,* p. 187.

8. Henry Allen, "His Way with Words: Cadence and Credibility," *Washington Post,* January 20, 2009.

CHAPTER 14

1. "Obama's Pastor: God Damn America, U.S. to Blame for 9/11," http://abcnews.go.com/Blotter/DemocraticDebate/story?id=4443788&page=1.

2. Kathryn Jean Lopez, "Wright and Wrong," *National Review* Online, March 14, 2008, http://article.nationalreview.com/351658/wright-and-wrong/kathryn-jean-lopez.

3. *Hannity and Colmes,* Fox News, February 28, 2008.

4. Jodi Kantor, "Disinvitation by Obama Is Criticized," *New York Times,* March 6, 2007.

5. Brian Ross and Rehab El-Buri, "Obama's Pastor: God Damn America, U.S. to Blame for 9/11," ABC News.com, March 13, 2008.

6. Mike Wereschagin et al., "Clinton: 'Wright Would Not Have Been My Pastor,'" *Pittsburgh Tribune-Review,* March 25, 2008.

7. Peggy Noonan, "A Thinking Man's Speech," *Wall Street Journal,* March 21, 2008.

8. "Huckabee Defends Obama . . . and the Rev. Wright," ABC News.com blog Political Punch, http://blogs.abcnews.com/politicalpunch/2008/03/huckabee-defend.html.

9. Frank Rich, "The Republican Resurrection," *New York Times,* March 23, 2008.

10. James Fallows, "Instant Reaction to Obama's Speech from Other Side of the World," *Atlantic* online, March 18, 2008, http://www.theatlantic.com/science/archive/2008/03/instant-reaction-to-obama-apos-s-speech-from-other-side-of-the-world/7973/.

11. Bob Herbert, "With a Powerful Speech, Obama Offers a Challenge," *New York Times,* March 25, 2008.

12. Andrew Sullivan, "The Speech," *Atlantic* online, Daily Dish blog, March 18, 2008, http://andrewsullivan.theatlantic.com/the_daily_dish/2008/03/the-speech.html.

13. Hendrik Hertzberg, "Obama Wins," *New Yorker,* November 17, 2008.

14. Hannity quoted in Howard Kurtz, "Media Notes: A Complex Speech, Boiled Down to Simple Politics," *Washington Post,* March 20, 2008.

15. CNN transcripts, CNN Election Center, "Obama Speaks Out against Reverend Wright; John McCain Stays Away from Wright-Obama Controversy," aired April 29, 2008, http://transcripts.cnn.com/TRANSCRIPTS/0804/29/ec.01.html.

CHAPTER 15

1. *The Situation Room,* CNN, May 7, 2008.

2. Transcript: San Francisco Fundraiser, April 11, 2008.

3. Perry Bacon Jr. and Shailagh Murray, "Opponents Paint Obama as an Elitist," *Washington Post,* April 12, 2008.

4. Dan Balz and Haynes Johnson, *The Battle for America 2008: The Story of an Extraordinary Election* (New York: Penguin, 2008), p. 211

5. Ibid., p. 211.

6. Ibid., p. 210.

7. Ibid., p. 212.

8. Jeff Zeleny, "Obama Leaves the Stage to Mix with His Skeptics," *New York Times,* May 2, 2008.

9. Balz and Johnson, *The Battle for America 2008,* p. 214.

10. Jeff Zeleny, "Obama Wins North Carolina Decisively, Clinton Takes Indiana by Slim Margin," *New York Times,* May 7, 2008.

11. Dan Balz and Shailagh Murray, "Obama is Decisive Winner in NC," *Washington Post,* May 7, 2008.

CHAPTER 16

1. Lionel Beehner, "Obama's Ideas on Foreign Policy Lack Luster," Huffington Post.com, September 30, 2008.

2. Dan Balz and Haynes Johnson, *The Battle for America 2008: The Story of an Extraordinary Election* (New York: Penguin, 2008), p. 300.

3. *Der Spiegel,* June 30, 2008.

4. "Iraq Leader Maliki Supports Obama's Withdrawal Plans," *Der Speigel,* July 19, 2008.

5. Balz and Johnson, *The Battle for America 2008,* p. 309.

6. Ibid., p. 312.

7. *The Sun* (UK), July 25, 2008.

CHAPTER 17

1. Adam Nagourney and Jeff Zeleny, "Obama Takes the Fight to McCain," *New York Times,* August 29, 2008.

2. Ibid.

3. Dan Balz and Haynes Johnson, *The Battle for America 2008: The Story of an Extraordinary Election* (New York: Penguin, 2008), p. 314.

4. Ibid., p. 317.

5. Patrick Healy, "Clinton Rallies Her Troops to Fight for Obama," *New York Times,* August 27, 2008.

6. Jeremy Olshan and Geoff Earles, "Temple of Dem on Mt. O-lympus," *New York Post,* August 28, 2008.

7. Balz and Johnson, *The Battle for America 2008,* p. 322.

8. Ibid., p. 322.

9. Nagourney and Zeleny, "Obama Takes the Fight to McCain."

10. Transcript: *Hardball with Chris Matthews,* "Special Coverage for the DNC," MSNBC.com, August 28, 2008.

CHAPTER 18

1. Dan Balz and Haynes Johnson, *The Battle for America 2008: The Story of an Extraordinary Election* (New York: Penguin, 2008), p. 368.

2. Ibid., pp. 368–71.

3. Ibid., p. 371.

4. Adam Nagourney, "Obama Elected President as Racial Barrier Falls," *New York Times,* November 4, 2008.